Throwed Away

Throwed Away

Failures of Progress in Eastern North Carolina

Linda Flowers

The University of Tennessee Press / *Knoxville*

 Manufactured in the United States of America.
First Edition.

Frontispiece: Tobacco barn abandoned. (Photo by Linda Flowers, 1989. Courtesy of Lula Shuff.)

Chapter 9 and the epilogue appeared previously, in slightly different form, in *The Coastal Plains: Writings on the Cultures of Eastern North Carolina,* ed. Leslie H. Garner, Jr., and Arthur Mann Kaye (Rocky Mount: North Carolina Wesleyan College Press, 1989), 121–50.

The paper in this book meets the minimum requirements of the American National Standard for Permanence of Paper for Printed Library Materials. ♾ The binding materials have been chosen for strength and durability.

Library of Congress Cataloging-in-Publication Data

Flowers, Linda, 1944–
Throwed away : failures of progress in eastern North Carolina / Linda Flowers. – 1st ed.
p. cm.
ISBN 0-87049-639-5 (cloth: alk. paper)

1. Rural poor—North Carolina—History—20th century. 2. Farm tenancy—Economic aspects—North Carolina—History—20th century. 3. Plant shutdowns—North Carolina—History—20th century. 4. Industry—Social aspects—North Carolina—History—20th century. 5. Public schools—North Carolina—History—20th century. I. Title.
HC107.N83P614 1990
306'09756'0904—dc20 89-28167 CIP

For

Robert Flowers

1913–

and

Geneva Hollingsworth Lane Flowers

1908–1966

Contents

Illustrations

Preface

"Throwed away" is an expression peculiar to eastern North Carolina. If a piece of land or a person or a stretch along the highway looks "throwed away," it can be in no worse shape. Fields left unattended and overcome with cockleburs are "throwed away." Ramshackly houses with boarded-up windows and rotten porches, or country stores that have bitten the dust are "throwed away." A man and woman are "throwed away" when they've outraged morality; a divorcée may "throw herself away." With less force the term can, however, refer to nothing more ominous than simply a feeling of depression; a woman with the blues might say she feels "plumb throwed away." To say that a friend looks "throwed away" is to declare in the plainest yet most solicitous fashion that he or she looks miserable.

The expression is pejorative, though often but mildly–sadly–so. Used to refer to one's self or a loved one, "throwed away" may convey little more than bemused exasperation, perhaps even affection. Tone is everything. By appropriating the phrase I mean to pay tribute to that capacity my mother's generation had of driving home an idea forcefully with colorful language. Not everybody in eastern North Carolina, of course, is throwed away, but for those who are, no other term will serve.

I am not labeling people and place in general; rather, I am trying to make clear a set of historical circumstances–tenantry and its demise, the coming of the plants and factories, the altered tenor of public education–the effects of which have been devastating to some people. Some are as much the victims of progressive education and industrialization as they are truly enlightened by them, and it is for them that the term "throwed away" is appropriate. For people who have given up on themselves, students the schools regard as unteachable, the workers abandoned when plants close or lay off or go to reduced workweeks, progress is more an illusion than a certitude. No matter that for those getting ahead, as for the region as a whole, the achievements of, say, the last thirty years are real and apparent.

But I am ambivalent about having given "throwed away" such prominence here as I have; it expresses a condition and sensibility for which no better description offers itself, and, yet, perhaps after all it goes too far. Like others calling North Carolina home, I am often of two minds about where we've been and where we're going; it was never *I* who was throwed away—not me, or my family, or anybody we knew well enough to care about—but other people. Always it was *they* who seemingly had so much against them. Nowadays the same kind of thinking applies; typically, no matter whom you ask, it's *other* schools that are bad, *other* plants where the trouble is, *other* families just scraping by.[1] "Throwed away" is, therefore, best used knowingly; as a generalization, exceptions abound. Taken singly, neither schools nor plants nor people fit comfortably under its umbrella. The individual is as defiant of this as of most other attempts to be pinned down.

Still, I'd not want anyone to be dismissive of the kind of impoverishment the term is uniquely capable of casting in relief: the perception of self-hopelessness; the loss of connection with society thus implied; the other abandonments for which a person lost to himself and down and out is responsible. If being throwed away isn't the only truth applicable to the area, nonetheless truth it is—and one not easily arrived at or quickly left behind.

In the twelve years I lived away from North Carolina, from 1968 to 1980, home itself was changing. In ways nobody could have foretold, tenantry as a way of life was ending: farming was undergoing a revolution. Going to graduate school in Ohio and then in New York, absorbed as I was in literature and teaching, little did I imagine that the world I had been born into was fast disappearing, that time had at last overtaken the solid place of my childhood. But memory matters, and the lives of people for whom no record can suffice.

My hometown of Faison hasn't gone anywhere, but of the school my sisters and I attended, nothing remains. Where its grand old building once stood, built in the days when schools were meant to be imposing, the little depot sits, shined up now as the town library. The Greek-revivalist columns once distinguishing Faison High School—in my day, Faison Elementary—now, I am told, grace the home of a former student.

On the old Faison place where we lived when I was in grammar school, our house has long since fallen into ruin; brush and bramble hide it from the road. Where once my grandparents farmed, the rows then straight and clean as type, fields lie fallow.

Memory and experience, reading and conversation have guided me, the truth of the one working to clarify the truth of the other. I am, however, neither a sociologist nor a demographer, a historian of nor an expert in the place and time about which I have written; nor am I simply an observer, detached and disinterested. My obligation hasn't been to tell the whole story, or even both sides of the same story—others having their own forum—but the story I myself, at least in part, lived: that of the tenants and hands, the shirt-tail farmers driven off the land in the 1960s, their transition into the public workplace, their children and grandchildren's coming of age now in the 1980s.

Acknowledgments

I express my grateful appreciation to the people and institutions without whom this book would not exist: the Ford Foundation for a generous grant that enabled me to take a leave from teaching, during which I read and thought and wrote; the Library of Congress; the libraries of the University of North Carolina, North Carolina Wesleyan College, and East Carolina University; and North Carolina Wesleyan College for a leave of absence. The University of Tennessee Press was warmly supportive over a long period, and I was sustained by their continuing interest and encouragement. David Goldfield and Gail O'Brien read the book in manuscript for the press, and the present work owes much to their informed criticism and care. I could not have asked for a fairer hearing. Melissa Rebenstorf was an exemplary copyeditor.

I learned from many school people, certainly the teachers who opened their doors to me, the students who found me in their midst. Principals and headmasters, superintendents and members of their staff gave freely of their time, and I thank them.

To others who talked with me, either face-to-face or by telephone or both – people at area colleges and in the state agencies, working people, employment personnel, dropouts, farmers, parents, former teachers and classmates – I am much indebted. To all those who were themselves in my presence, without necessarily remembering then that I was writing a book, as to those upon whose lives I've drawn, my indebtedness is profound.

The kind and warm response of my colleagues at North Carolina Wesleyan College, on the several occasions when I inflicted parts of the then-unfinished manuscript on them, meant more than they could have known. In particular, I have been glad for the perspective, humor, and gracious care of my former chairman, Leverett Smith.

Ann Keplinger, in Ohio, and Joseph and U. T. Summers, in Rochester, New York, bore more than their fair share of my distress, as did Anne and Jim Wilgus in Rocky Mount; they have my love and gratitude. I thank as well Cyrus Hoy for his unfailing encouragement.

U. T. Summers's close reading of the manuscript and her incisive queries and comments proved invaluable as I revised an early draft; I much appreciate her time and care.

For the teachers I had both at Faison School and at North Duplin, I will always be grateful. Without Ethel Bowden's example of academic excellence I may have been a differently inclined high-school student; without Edna Wilson's love and support, her determination that a way *would* be found for me to go to college, my life would doubtless have taken quite another shape. Their good advice and attention, their integrity and professionalism, I've drawn upon for more than thirty years; the debt is unpayable.

Two people I valued, who stood by me and who believed in this (as in other of my) work, died before I could show them any part of what I had written: Amy Charles and Rowland Collins. I remain in their debt, too.

For their much-needed assistance with assembling photographs, I am grateful to Nancy Jones, Chris LaLonde, Harriett Taylor, and Joe Burnette and the *Spring Hope Enterprise;* as well as Rick Kraft of Kraft's Studio, who kindly made available to me a collection of area scenes dating from the 1940s.

Nothing could have been done without my family. For them, for the lives I've used here mercilessly (as though my own), for my father and mother and the childhood they gave me; for Clara and Rachel, Annie Lou and Dorothy; for aunts and uncles, nieces and nephews; for cousins; for grandparents strong and individual, as memorable as books, nothing is enough, and words as always are inadequate.

But the book's flaws are mine alone; the point of view, the shaping of the story, my responsibility.

Note

Names of persons and schools are usually pseudonymns. Names of places are sometime fictitious. However, the actual schools and places for which I have supplied other names, in fact, exist. Except in a very few instances where for the sake of conveying an impression of an event I give names and qualities to persons who live only within the realm of generalization, all persons named, in fact, exist; none are composites.

It has been neither my desire nor my intention to call attention to those specific schools and persons requesting anonymity; indeed, just the contrary is true. Should my pseudonymns happen also to be the names of actual schools or of actual persons in similar positions, then readers should understand that such resemblances are wholly accidental and that, in point of fact, no real relationship exists between the two.

Photographs are uniquely helpful for conveying a sense of place and time; the private academy pictured in Chapter 8 thus serves my historical purposes. Readers should *not*, however, assume that I observed classes in this particular school.

Throwed Away

Home

An Introduction

The land lies off to the east of I-95, a far-flung quarter moon or a lazy dogleg if you think of starting up in Northampton and Halifax counties, then bearing south down through Nash and Edgecombe, Wilson and Johnston and Wayne, Duplin and Sampson. Fayetteville and Wilmington, Kinston and Greenville, Scotland Neck and New Bern: all are more or less in the vicinity, though not in these counties. From the north, you enter North Carolina for the most part unaware that you've left Virginia; Richmond is but an hour or so behind, and between Richmond and Roanoke Rapids – Emporia, Virginia and Weldon, North Carolina – there's not much to see from the Interstate. Gas stations, the places selling hams and guns and cigarettes, the outlet or two once you cross the state line, not much more.

But from the south, if you pick up I-95 say out of Savannah, then follow it through Florence and Dillon, the entry into the state takes you through vast reaches of land that hearken to an era you would have thought had long since vanished. You see cotton fields, old tenant houses off in the distance now falling down, and roads that run straight for miles through standing timber thinned now by the logging and pulpwood people. And from late April and May through late September, the sun beats down with merciless abandon, the pavement before you, the tin of barns and housetops, the occasional other car or pickup truck shimmering in the heat.

Coming out of New York and Pennsylvania, the Baltimore-Washington area, then Northern Virginia, the farther south you drive the less heavy industry you see. There's the gradual awareness that farms are smaller, the crops different, and the land flattens out as you get into southern Virginia and North Carolina, tidewater and coastal plain supplanting the higher elevation of Pennsylvania. But change direction and head north from Mississippi and through Tuskegee and Macon and Milledgeville, skirting Atlanta altogether, do this and the perspective shifts: now the Commerce Department's designation of eastern North Carolina as "Gold Leaf Urban" or "Highland Plains Urban" will strike you as much less fanciful.

Firestone, Monsanto, Crown-Zellerbach, Burroughs-Welcome, Ingersoll-Rand, Rockwell International, Campbell Soup, General Signal, Cummins, and other national firms have in the last ten or fifteen or twenty years set up major operations in the region. Alongside the textile mills, DuPont and J. P. Stevens, are the smaller cotton mills that once were the mainstay of the towns growing up around them, and the tobacco companies and warehouses for which everybody knows us. These newer industries do much to give the area a look of having been brought closer within the mainstream of American working life. Now in the mid-1980s even this part of the state – the "Down East" region forever caricatured as backward, irredeemably insular and conservative, redneck – has a look and feel inexplicably both different from and the same as that I remember as a child growing up on a tenant farm outside Faison, in Duplin County, forty and thirty and twenty years ago.

East of I-95 is, however, a long way from the more urban, more heavily industrialized and congested Central Piedmont. If Raleigh and Durham and Greensboro, the Research Triangle Park, and those colleges and universities whose names are recognized nationally are closer now to Faison than they used to be, still they are a good ways off; and for some people still, they are as distant, even as unimaginable, as once they were to most of the area's shirt-tail farmers, tenants, small businessmen, women, and schoolchildren. Nobody I knew back then, in Faison, ever thought of Durham or Chapel Hill unless somebody was in the hospital there, was "bad off," this is to say, or else he would have been at Goldsboro or Clinton or, later, Kenansville. To be taken to Raleigh on a class trip in the seventh or eighth grade was an excursion for many of us comparable to that the seniors took the years they went to Washington, D. C.

If some people shopped at Cameron Village or Crabtree Valley Mall in Raleigh, my mother never did, nor did farm women generally. They would go to Goldsboro in August or September when the last of the tobacco had been sold, and sometimes to Mount Olive or Warsaw in the spring; other than this, whatever else that had to be bought came out of the catalogue: Sears or Montgomery Ward, Aldens or National

Bellas Hess. Even biddies the mailman would deliver, their cardboard crates high in the back seat of his car, holes in them the size of quarters.

Except for the places on the Interstate catering to tourists, probably a little less is done here than farther south to play up the clichés still governing outsiders' conception of the South. Confederate flags there are, but fewer than you see in Alabama and Mississippi, and there are magnolia trees but nobody pays them any mind. High-school teams may still call themselves "Rebels," but "Dixie" isn't heard much anymore. Well before the North Carolina line, the red clay of south Georgia has given way to sandy, peach-growing flatlands, and the dirt roads of Mississippi and Georgia and Alabama aren't nearly as numerous here. There is less cotton, as well as fewer Bible colleges, more pine trees, far more tobacco fields, roads that may be a little better. The old tobacco barns for curing are abandoned now; bulk barns, the heat forced around and through the tobacco by a new technology, have supplanted them. There aren't as many dish antennae as in Alabama and Mississippi, but neither do there seem to be as many people living in the worst of inadequate houses.

Except around Wilmington, but also occasionally in fields and towns throughout the region, you won't come across as many mansions of the Civil War era as you will in South Carolina and beyond, although houses dating from the Revolution can still be visited in Edenton and Tarboro, New Bern and Bath.

Nowadays in eastern North Carolina the finest of brick homes are as likely to be found in the country as in the towns; next to them or down the road may be a house with the porch caved in. Trailer parks are all over, as are single trailers off to themselves or in a backyard. Government housing projects have come even to many of the smaller towns. For long stretches in certain areas, there may be no (or very few) houses at all, or much sign of any habitation. In some pockets, what dwellings you do see are pitiable enough; you could be forgiven for thinking the Depression had come again, they look so much like the photographs taken then. Other places, however, you would think had never known anything else but affluence. Poverty and wealth coexist, if not always literally side by side, at least in such proximity as to startle anybody used to seeing the poor (or the black) contained in big-city neighborhoods; here, where life still is essentially rural, unless they live well inside one of the larger towns, rich and poor – and black and white – aren't likely to escape the sight of one another.

Farmers barely hanging on, or whose sons and daughters have given up on farming, and people with land who for one reason or another make their living doing something else, aren't especially against selling off an acre or two to the up-and-coming young professional who then puts up a Tudor or an all-cypress house; a school superintendent, perhaps, or his assistant, a banker or businessman. The family that works at the sewing plant will, as likely as not, rent the same house they once occupied as tenants, the land now leased to somebody else or in the Soil Bank.

Most people of course are not rich, yet surprisingly few, I think, would classify themselves as poor. Despite considerable evidence to the contrary, they will tell you they have about what everybody else has, that, in fact, they are getting along all right: are lucky to have what they do and to be where they are. It's not that such people don't know the struggle they're having just to keep paying their bills, or even that they've never known anything else, but that the reality of life lived any other way escapes them: *everybody,* they'll say, even people with a lot more money, is—when you get right down to it—pretty much in the same fix as they are. The fact that, in 1980, one of every five households in the state was living in poverty goes far to make such thinking explicable.[1] Not only did North Carolina then rank forty-first among the states in per capita personal income ($7,819),[2] but for the families living in the eight eastern counties that are my concern here—broadly, from Halifax down through Duplin and Sampson—roughly 17 percent had incomes putting them below the federal poverty level. The high was Halifax, at 25 percent, followed by Duplin, 20.1 percent, and the low was Wayne, 14.6 percent.

These counties, however, have made such impressive gains, especially over the last twenty years (the advance between 1969 and 1979 being nothing short of phenomenal), that for many people now in their forties and fifties, the present is the best they've ever had it—no matter their hardship—yet this doesn't include everyone. The influx of professional and semi-professional people over the last several years, even in out-of-the-way places, skews the averages, and still there is an appalling disparity between the incomes of black and white, as between men and women.

In 1969, median family income in Duplin County, to cite but one example, was $5,710, and nearly thirty percent of all families had incomes below the poverty level; 2,403 of the county's 9,751 families then earned less than $5,000, and more than 1,500 earned less than $3,000. By 1979 the median had risen to $13,191. For North Carolina as a whole, median family income in 1979 was $16,792; for the nation, $18,255.

To appreciate more fully what these figures mean, we need simply keep in mind that in 1950 more than thirty percent of all North Carolina families earned less than one thousand dollars. Non-white farm families, which is to say black and (considerably fewer) Indian, as late as 1959 had a median income of only $1,213. In 1969, the median for white families was $8,507, but for black families $4,803 was the median income. In 1979, the median for black families was $11,388; $18,182 for white.

When even poor people say, therefore, that times are better than they used to be, they know what they're talking about. Yet, the gulf between rich and poor—or between comfortable and struggling—is probably wider now than at any time since the Depression; for many, there is no catching up. If there is now developing a class of business and professional people who are finding life in the small towns and in the country attractive and affordable, there are also large numbers of people striving against considerable odds to remain simply where they are, hanging on to the rungs of the middle-class and lower-middle-class ladder, no matter how tenuous their grip; and there are others, in sufficient numbers to comprise a significant underclass,[3] who are finding that they are sliding further and further behind.

Especially bleak are the long-range prospects for young people who have no education beyond high school or who dropped out before graduation. The same can almost be said of many who have had a year or so of college or attended (but perhaps not graduated from) an area technical school. Low-skill jobs tend to be deadends and, at that, aren't always available, yet for people without much education, there is nothing else. For some, the disparity between what is needed to hold down even a poor job—presentability, discipline, the ability to talk and often to write intelligibly, reading, arithmetic—and the skills they, in fact, can command, regardless of the level of their formal education, is so great that these jobs, too, are beyond their reach.

To say this, however, is to state a fact of life that will be news to no one: education has always mattered, and some have always failed to take advantage of it or have been shortchanged. What makes the situation different now, in the mid-1980s, is that this is a generation of youth having to make its way in a society where the jobs traditionally open to non-skilled or semi-skilled workers are drying up, and where, on the other hand, without higher or more specialized education, such jobs as do become available in industry and business are closed to them.

Without seniority in the plants and factories, they are the first to be laid off or put on reduced-workweeks; faced with a plant's closing, they have nowhere to turn. And even with a job, more and more people are finding their wages meager defenses against impoverishment.

These are the children, typically, of that first full generation making the transition from farm to factory. Their parents saw such profound changes in agriculture that they left off farming altogether, taking up the jobs that the new industry of the mid-to-late 1960s and 1970s made available. Unlike the jobs now for which the young, as well as everybody else, must compete, not often did these early public jobs[4] require much technical experience or formal education; often the worker was able to transfer skills and knowledge he already possessed to the demands of his present labor. Although the move from farm to factory could never have been easy, at least the degree of educational difference between the two was not (or not usually) insurmountable; the farmer used to taking care of his own machinery, for example, would have found his mechanical know-how applicable to his job in assembly-line maintenance. Nowadays, however, the situation is quite otherwise. Education, frequently of a technical and specialized nature, increasingly is the *sine qua non* for entry into the area's work force.

And this is new. These are not people for whom, historically, education has been important, or, rather, the heart of the matter isn't that education wasn't respected, even idealized – often it was – but that so very few small landowners and tenants had themselves ever been able to carry on with their books and schooling beyond the earliest grades. Formal education was something other people had; as a reality, seldom did it figure in their own lives. Nor had the lack of a high-school diploma necessarily closed them off to what work there was. Their children, on the other hand – the young men and women filling area classrooms in the mid-to-late 1970s and 1980s – have a different story to tell.

Black people and poor whites, farmers who weathered the Depression certainly, have always known that without "that piece of paper," the more desirable jobs, and whatever is meant by "the good life," will likely prove elusive. Theirs was never the insularity, the self-congratulatory boosterism, of the urban middle class. Yet neither did they think of education as anything but an access, an on-ramp to a freeway of less burdensome living.

In this one respect, if none other, eastern North Carolina's rural poor were no different from everybody else.

Part One

Back Then

1. Old Model T

Little girls are playing under the house (where they've been told strictly never to play), a tea set spread daintily upon the dirt and they happily out of the way of anybody's knowing, but the grandfather finds them there, bare feet and overall legs and the yard broom sweeping in upon them, little pink cups and saucers tumbling in the dust. But not the children, not Rachel. From beneath the house they fly, but Rachel flings back at him, Granddaddy chasing them now, "Old Model T!," she screams, "Old Model T can't catch a V-8 Ford! . . . Old Model T can't catch a V-8 Ford! . . . a V-8 Ford!"

The old man (not so very old then) waits on the porch, and when eventually they sidle back in range, out go his quick arms, and he turns one then the other over his knees and spanks them good. The grandmother stands in the door, hands on her hips.

This was 1935, '36 maybe, and Rachel and Dorothy, Clara and Annie Lou lived in the country on the Faison place. Sisters like stair steps, and when they were small, they lived with the people everybody called Mister Jim and Miss Annie–but they were Granddaddy and Grandma, really–and with our mama. Jarvis Lane was their daddy. He had been in France in WW I and now he was dead. Mama had been fifteen when she had run away to marry him and he was a lot older than that. Nobody had thought of me then or of my daddy either, but he was a young man anyway, and hired out to Old Man Will Holly. The Flowerses came from around Wilson to begin with, from Mt. Carmel and Black Creek and Fremont, and Granddaddy Flowers had farmed on the Aycock place close to Pikeville until he moved to Giddensville sometime in the 1920s. Charles Brantley Aycock had been the governor at the turn of the century, and a good one: the "Education Governor," they called him. My other grandparents, the Hollingsworths, were always real Faison people. When Mama was a girl they had owned what was always known as the Cooper place out from Faison, but they had lost it through sickness and hard times.

Nobody had electric lights back then, running water, bathrooms. Grandma–and Mama, too, before we bought the oil stove from Alice Ray's daddy (when I was in the first grade in 1951)–cooked on a woodstove; they stacked the kindling in a box in the kitchen, but first you had to split the slabs into stove-sized pieces at the woodpile. Grandma made lye soap in an iron pot in the backyard, and if you got chips in it or dirt, you were spanked and (worse!) sent to sit quietly on what she always called the "pīz-ah"–the back porch. The front porch was only that, except when sometimes she called it the "verandah," which it wasn't, of course. (*I* knew that!) The house was little but big enough, and unpainted; from a distance, it was an aged grayness, clean and weathered. There were two rooms across the front, then a longer, narrower room where the round eating-table was, and a cot, the radio, and the cabinet with the Sunday dishes, then the kitchen. The back porch ran down this long side, so that the house was almost, but not quite, a square. Rachel, when she was in high school, had a Victrola, and it sat in the room where the radio was. You weren't supposed to touch it. The doors swung out at the bottom, and that's where the records were–"Little Brown Jug" and "I don't care what mama don't 'low, . . ."–but Rachel had the key.

(Years hence, when Annie Lou's Vicky–Victoria–was a child and got out of hand, our way of paying tribute to her volume was to call her Victrola–as in "I *do* wish that Victrola would turn off!")

When Granddaddy died in his sleep they brought him back home in his casket, and everybody sat up all night in the front room where he was. Clara held me up to him, and I patted his suit and tie. Annie Pearl gave us ice cream, putting the spoon in our mouth when it was our turn, but I was bashful and hung back and almost didn't get any. It was Aunt Clara Lee's living-room suite. Bud and Ben and Uncle Herman had brought it on the pickup so the company would have somewhere to sit, but after the flowers and the chairs that folded up and the casket with Granddaddy in it were gone, back to their house it went, and then Grandma put the bed back up. Granddaddy confused "g" and "j" and "d" sometimes, when he was in a hurry or flustered (or had had a drink), and the story they told on him was that when Ben and Bud were little, before they knew anything about the water, he had picked them both up by the galluses of their overalls and flung them into the mill pond. "Swim! Jod-jammed, you! Swim!" But Uncle Herman had jumped in and pulled them out.

Grandma had done his reading for him, signing his name if a paper came to the house, but he could put his "X" where he was told, and he knew how to count money. He had never gone to school at all, but she had–some, through the fourth or maybe fifth grade. (Mama had got to about the seventh or eighth grade before she quit.) "But it didn't matter what we were doing," Clara says, "when six o'clock come, we stopped and went to the house. We had to have them lessons up by bedtime. They'd talk real low . . . real quiet, so we could study. And you had to study, too! Or look like you were. We all sat in the same room where the lamp was. . . . They won't enough lamps where you could get off by yourself . . . and we'd do our lessons, and Grandma and Granddaddy'd be in the other corner, where they could talk and still keep their eye on us. . . . You might *want* to giggle. . . ."

The four of them and Bud (but not Ben, he couldn't be made to stay) went to school at Faison. That was where the men had gone, too, Uncle Herman and my daddy and the rest of them, to sign up after Pearl Harbor. Clara and Dorothy remember the long lines outside the lunchroom that Christmas; but the Army never called them up. By that time, Mama and Daddy and Dorothy and Annie Lou lived in one Faison house, and Grandma and Granddaddy and Rachel and Clara lived across the road in another (Ben and Bud, Uncle Herman and Aunt Clara Lee, in a third). Our house sat at the top of Panther Hill; at the bottom, that's where the Negroes on Sunday would sometimes gather, chipping off the red clay and eating it, taking it off by the sack full. Annie Lou and Dorothy would let me wait with them in the yard for the school bus in the mornings; they'd comb my hair and roll up my sleeves so the holes wouldn't show, then stand me under the cedar tree–and I'd wave (shyly) back at them on the bus, and at Clara and Rachel, at Grace and Esther and Jackie Boy and Marie White. Once in a drizzling rain, knowing they were watching me, I slid down the hill, the bus pulling away, and Mama blistered me good, muddy as I was.

School was fine, Dorothy thought, but a good time was better. She would skip, then have to catch the school bus again in the afternoon before it got back around to our house. But she'd get off it then with Annie Lou, her books in her arms and pretty as you please, and sashay in. The day came, however, that she and her friends–running late!–

drove up behind the bus just as it stopped, Mama looking up from where she was sweeping the yard and Dorothy jumping out of the car and running to link arms with Annie Lou getting off the bus–but it was no use. Mama saw her, and she laid the yard broom on her. Dorothy was seventeen and in the eleventh grade when she quit shool in February and got married. Under her picture in *The Reflector* at school was the rhyme, "Now don't call Dot Lane silly / But she sure is–over Willie!" It was 1949.

Annie Lou was fifteen when that summer she quit, too–and married Willie's brother. She had been a brain down in the grades, but with Dorothy gone and after she met James, school didn't matter like it had before. Annie Lou and James and Daddy had come around the corner of the house. Daddy had been at the tobacco barn when they told him, and Mama was in the swing on the front porch, and Daddy told her, and then they told her, and then all of them were upset. I was five and I cried and cried.

Faison was something then. Saturday nights you'd go to town and stay as late as the shoofly.[1] The people in its little windows looked far away, leaning back asleep some of them, and the high-backed seats all had a white cloth, like a doily, for where a head could rest. (It whistled, too, but you could hear that at home.) Wintertime and Mama and the women would sit around the stove Mr. Joe Parker had in his grocery store and talk. Streets were dark; store light shone out on the people walking by. Jews owned the store that Mama liked.[2] They had cloth in long rolls–all kinds of cloth!–and dresses and shoes, oilcloth like ours on the kitchen table, and overall pants and shirts. Men hung around the poolroom, mostly; the balls hitting against each other rang like bells. Checker players would pull up chairs to the table in the window, and everybody saw them. A girl didn't go inside, but if you opened the door one of the Cottle boys would call your daddy, and he'd come on out. "Miss" Virginia Hatcher ran the beauty shop. She wore a white uniform like a nurse and her fingernails were bright red. Permanents hurt but if you tried not to cry she'd give you a Coca-Cola.

Mr. Pug ran the Amoco station and chewed a cigar; he'd gone to school with Mama, and he'd tease you if he wanted to. Pam and Dewey's daddy wouldn't; he just ran the Pure Oil across the railroad tracks. In the dime store was where Clara had got a job on Saturdays; if you were good, she'd bring you home a coloring book and crayons.

The gin belonged to Mr. Chester, but on a weekend nobody wanted to have to bother with cotton. Nights during the week, the trucks would be lined up; wagons, too. Negroes worked the long hose, moving it over and down into the loose cotton; your turn would come, and you would move up and stop under the hose where it dropped down. You could see the cotton tumbling in the gin, the long trays shaking, the gin roaring like a freight train. The cotton would get whiter and whiter, and then when it wanted to, the bale would fall out on the ramp—like an egg out of a hen. Metal bands squeezed it tighter than tight.

(They called the road that took you to Clinton the "Cotton Highway," but not because of the other gin; there *was* another gin though, and it stood next to a little store, but the road had been paved over a bed made of—cotton! That was during the Depression when you couldn't *give* cotton away, Daddy said.)

Clara didn't work long at the dime store. She would have gone to college but nobody had any money, and the only scholarship she knew about went to somebody else. In 1951 that's the way it was. But everybody knew what she wanted. "She is the first grade teacher now," it says in her class prophecy, and "All the children love her." Instead she went to work at the county office, Mr. John Warren speaking for her. Clara worked and helped Grandma—and waited for Ray to come home from Korea.

(The nineteen seniors in the Class of 1951 had this to say of themselves: "In the fall of 1939," they put in *The Reflector,* "we were fifty youngsters entering the first grade in the Faison School. . . . of that fifty there are eight of the present seniors. . . . By the time we became high school Freshmen, our number had been reduced to thirty-five. . . . We cannot account for all losses of pupils. . . .")

Rachel had graduated in the Class of 1948. Ten of them are in the picture where they're all sitting together on the steps of Faison School, Miss Bowden too. "Everybody in that class was smart," Clara says. "They could all do something. . . . Rachel was sharp as a whip, always had been . . . Moose, Jane Faison, Luther . . . all of them." They were the first at Faison to complete all twelve grades, the twelfth year having just been added.[3]

But it's their ninth-grade picture I like best. Then there were sixteen, and they're standing against the columns at Faison School. The dark-haired girl looking like the others aren't there, not smiling—like this isn't a *school* picture—that's Rachel, hands in her pockets, self-possessed as an heiress. But Rachel, the little girl who had come along first, whose

Grandma thought the world of her (and the world did too), Rachel died in 1974. By then she and John had moved back from Detroit, and their four children were just out of high school.

Dorothy and Annie Lou never went back to school. For years after their children came along, they did public work; Annie Lou mostly at Hamilton-Beach in Clinton, and Dorothy at Hall's Lamp Company, then at the sewing place in Warsaw. Five of their six children graduated from high school. Dorothy has twice won election to the town board where she lives; she's a grandmother herself now, the oldest of her five grandchildren in high school.

Plagued by illness, Annie Lou eventually had to take a disability leave from Hamilton-Beach. Then she kept house for several years and spoiled her two grandchildren. She would take half a day in the summer and early spring and you'd see her with her pole and old hat going to the pond fishing. But in 1986, after a season when she'd felt well enough sometimes to help pack squash and cucumbers, Annie Lou died.

Looking again at Rachel's class picture: the boy in the center, the one taller than the teacher? That's the one everybody called Moose. He belonged to "Miss" Rosa Thornton. He could fix your radio if you took it to him in his shop. When Space Shuttle *Challenger* went up—August 30, 1983—Moose was Dr. William Thornton then, the only astronaut from North Carolina.[4] He invited all his teachers to the Cape to see him lift off, and those who could went. Everybody else gathered at the Fire Station in Faison and watched it on television. It was after midnight. When the thing blazed up and rose like a comet, of course they clapped and cheered.

"Faison's on the map now!" they said. "On the map now!"

2. School Days

Faison School in the early 1950s: the oiled floors and chalk; the smell of lunches and generations of lunches in paper sacks in the cloakroom; bodies; somewhere too there's rain, and the water is sliding down the long windows of a classroom, the children looking up from – What *were* we doing? Pasting red hearts on paper sacks to hang for Valentine's Day? Playing Chinese checkers or Old Maid? Was this our recess? Or could we, possibly, have been reading? In any case, the shades were rolled tight at the top and the long string with the ring at the end of it (that the rod with the hook went into, the teacher on tiptoe, the pole held high and aslant, her head back . . . like the chickens at home when they drank) dangled in the very center of the window: string and ring and sliding rain.

Once when we had oranges for lunch, I tossed mine up in the classroom, nobody there but Jewitt and Kathryn and Judy and me, and the orange had stuck between the concentric metal rings of a light fixture. There we had stood, four little girls gazing skyward, as if incipient Galileos, and the metal bands around the bulb the sun and orbiting planets (which we had studied), but Miss Bowden, finding us there, laughed and got the rod and the orange fell into my hands again.

Alice Ray in the first grade had a red and white checked dress with a lacy white collar; she sat in front of me. The room was deep, and the desks were real wood and real steel and screwed into the floor; the seat was a bench that folded up, and you put your books and papers inside your desk, which had a hole in it for an ink bottle to fit. But in the first grade ink wasn't allowed, and that's where we stuffed wadded-up paper which filled up our desks, our books then sliding out into our laps sometimes, like Santa Claus down the chimney. Steve's daddy was named Alec and he drove the taxicab. One day in the middle of our doing something else, it had struck me as wonderful that being smart Mr. Alec was of course, therefore, "a smart aleck," which I dutifully blurted out—and nobody laughed. Velburn Ray had red hair and his mama and mine knew each other. On the Saturdays when we walked to town for groceries, Mr. Alec driving us home, they would sit in Mr. Wilkes Parker's store and talk about—*us.* Ben's daddy sold ice and hot dogs and barbecue and nobody called him anything but Dilly, except children; we called him Mr. Dilly. Hampton was there, too; Aunt Esther and Uncle Earl were his mama and daddy and he was my cousin. And Lafay and Lynda and Gerald, Billy and Brenda and Buck and Alma Doris. (Hampton and Alma Doris got married later on, but then nobody knew they would. Hampton died before the rest of us, a long time before it was fair, and we didn't know that would happen either.) Kathryn had red hair like Velburn Ray, and Billy was always smart.

In the fourth grade, when "Miss" Ray was our teacher, a fire drill one day caught us by surprise. On the way back to our seats, we grumbled that now we couldn't have the filmstrips—Cinderella, Rumplestiltskin, Br'er Rabbit—but Dewey had declared that if Miss Ray had promised them to us, see them we would. Dewey was a fifth-grader and knew things. At recess sometimes, Miss Ray and the other teachers would bring chairs out onto the edge of the playground and sit there and talk. She would call to first one of us, then another, and we would come and sit on her lap to be held and patted and praised. You would be told then what your sisters had said and done (for Miss Ray had taught them, too, of course) ten and fifteen years before, what you yourself had been reported to her as having said and done, the time you no longer remembered. She was a large woman then, all pillowy, and her complexion was very fair, her arms and face spotted with freckles; never was there a child she didn't love, or who didn't love her. Everybody said so, and long before you got to her room, you said so too. The summer she and "a damn fool bunch of other old schoolteachers, I reckon," Daddy said, went to Europe, everybody talked about what a thing to do when you didn't have to.

Later, when somebody—*Who* was it?—came back from California with a jar of what we were told was the Pacific Ocean, Miss Blount held it before us all assembled there in the auditorium and dipped her finger in it, the prospect of the ocean itself alight in our minds, but among ourselves we said that "it could'a been just any ol' water!" Alice Ray had been to Seattle, and one time Lafay got sent on the train by himself all the way to—Was it New York or Richmond? One of the two.

The auditorium was curved somewhat like a lady's open fan, its proscenium stage being the part she would have held in her hand. That was where maybe once every other year or so all eight grades gathered to see *Heidi* again, the wind in the fir trees as thrilling now as you knew it would be, the old man and the girl and the little mountain shack as heartbreaking. A little less often probably, somebody would show up from the county health department and we would be in for a cartoon-like film where teeth (one of them named Jack) and a doctor's hand and white-sleeved arm were the only characters; the Kenansville person would read the flickering captions aloud to us, and – if we weren't stopped – we read along with him, gleefully making the sentences sound as silly and childish as they were. The floor was elevated, the seats joined one to the other, their rows fixed and immovable. Opposite the stage, the wall was nothing but long, curtained windows; on the white walls at the sides, as in a gallery, hung large gilt-framed portraits of Robert E. Lee and Jefferson Davis and (I am almost certain) Alexander Stephens. Was there, also, a Gilbert Stuart Washington? A Jefferson and Lincoln? Or do I remember pictures from a classroom?

Once, before I had started to school myself, Annie Lou had brought me to see Clara announce a play. Now when I think of this fine old room, much the grandest any of us had then ever been in, I see Clara before me in a soft glow, there in the spotlight against a red-wine curtain, the darkened auditorium hushed and expectant.

Once a new preacher had huddled his children – of whom there were many, their names all out of the Bible – in the cavernous hall, like Noah pairing them off two by two with prospective classmates ("Anybody here in the third grade? . . . Fourth? John, you go with him, he's in the fifth grade, too!"), hurrying them along to where they were supposed to be when school took in. They were Presbyterians. Mary was in my room and soon was as popular almost as Judy. Judy was the prettiest among us and had the prettiest mama. "Miss" Florence wore suits and drove a car, and she would come around selling magazine subscriptions, *Humpty Dumpty* and others for children, and – Was she at one time also the Avon lady? But really they were farmers, even if not like us. Mr. Pete cut hair too, like Alma Doris's daddy did, the one they called Peter Rabbit.

I rode the school bus that Anne Mosely drove. Mr. Mosely Carr had a grocery store, and on long Saturdays, over in the evening when business was slack, he would squat down by the door out on the sidewalk and watch people go by; sometimes we'd see him there, eating johnnycakes out of the box and drinking milk. Anne Mosely went to Duke. Nobody else had except the man who for a short flurry had been principal at Faison, and who built himself a house (hammering in the rain when it suited him) just off the school grounds, but he didn't live in it long. Anne Mosely graduated from Duke, too. Her daddy and her mama–"Miss" Bowden–knew how to dance, and at the banquet the eighth-graders always had, they would waltz alone on the polished court of the gymnasium, everybody standing back and watching.

What grade were we in when the boy we hardly knew, who came and left all in the same year, told the teacher he hadn't done his homework, that he had watched television instead? She turned on him, surprised and accusing, and said, "Do *you* have a television?" as if he couldn't, as if she knew too much about how poor he was for the tale to go unprobed, and he had to tell her no, they didn't have a television, but that he had watched it at somebody else's house–and everything was then all right again. Was it this teacher or another who, having asked us what "class" meant, told us we were all–her, too–middle class? Thus we were conferred a distinction we neither understood nor, understanding, could have accepted; rather, Alice Ray could have, and Judy, two or three others maybe, but not the rest of us, not if money and possessions were the measure. Was it she, also, who had held up for our scorn the country women who threw their dish water out the kitchen door? Some of us saw our mothers behind the splashing, greasy water as she talked, yet we felt as fully superior to the act as the teacher herself. But the little, bitten-faced girl beside me had hissed, "What if *she* had to tote it!" The words stung me with shame they were so right, yet until I heard them, until they caught me up and pulled me back, I hadn't any understanding of the moment; nor did I know that such betrayal can leave even a child for a long time lost.

This was the girl, too, who, when the teacher–Could *she* have been the same?–went on at length one day about the silliness of people believing in Oral Roberts, that his supposed cures were all a hoax, had seethed afterwards on the playground, "God *can* do them things! *She* don't know!"

How to account for such moments? To think of them now is to do more than remember school, incidents and occasions trivial and profound–and who's to say which is which?–teachers, one's own self then; also, memory's having again a sense of where and when, so whole and solid is the past. This intimacy, this special place in our mind where live forever the people in our room at school (always as they were back then), how to understand such depth of feeling? Pain there was plenty, yet hardly do I recall a time when tenantry (when being poor) was anything I thought about at school. For one thing, there were so many of us; for another, everybody in the country lived remarkably alike. Only when the health people came around were you made to remember such imperfections as poverty could cause: eyes and teeth neglected, ears and scalp, and you were paraded no more privately than a hog or a calf to its slaughter. They would leave pictures of bacon, bright bowls of cereal, orange juice and milk, grapefruit, eggs perfectly cooked (Mama's never were), and charts on which you had to put a check beside what you had eaten that week for breakfast. (The boy who had marked everything said, the teacher asking him, "Well, I *could'a* had it all!") But of coffee in thick cups strong enough to walk (Grandma said, smacking her lips), biscuits, fried side meat, grits that stuck in the pan, of eggs fried brown and hard—there wasn't any picture.

Other people had less. The children the hands brought with them to the tobacco barn, some of them went hungry; they would eye the dinner Mama put on the table, quiet and ready. When it was the women's time to eat, the men now talking in the backyard, the babies and children would be fed. The hands would clean the bowls: all the peas and tomatoes, string beans and red beans, squash—everything we grew that by tobacco-barning time we were tired of seeing on the table.

White people went without, too. Willie lived for a month or two on the road where we stayed. The house was brick but the doors were always flung open; screens were torn out, so intricate with holes only a fly or mosquito could have found them purposeful. Everything about the place looked broken—the chair on the porch without any back and the seat missing, the curtain flapping half-in and half-out its window, the old wringer-washing machine at the back steps on the ground. Willie and her brothers and sisters, the baby that squalled when the school bus pulled away: all were dirty and smelly and ragged. But when she smiled shyly, Willie's eyes were bright and the sad little face pretty.

Marilyn, I wasn't supposed to play with (and seldom did); Mama said all of them were so sorry. They stayed on the Cottle place where for a year, when Darrell was little (and didn't believe me that pennies add up to nickels, even dimes), Uncle Edward had tried to farm. Marilyn had the blackest hair and never looked sad at all; if cherubs were dark she could have been one, except for her runny nose, the perpetual aura of congestion in which she lived.

And who's to say what happened to them, the Willies and Marilyns, all the rest of us there, indifferent children of the earth? Some came and went with so little of our attention, their parents sharecroppers moving from place to place; they showed up as if from nowhere, disappeared into nothingness, and, yet, how persistently they linger, how much they are a part of all we mean by "school." Ever on the sidelines, in the lunchroom off to a table by themselves, in every class, they were there yet not there, so rarely did teachers call upon them. Nonetheless, they are as fixed in our memory as if they were some distant versions of ourselves: Dempsey playing soccer and Alice Ray and I following him about until he gave us his B-B-Bats; Willie all the days she had to play with girls who said she stank; Allen with the sores on his arms; Eddie, to whose house our little delegation traipsed – Alice Ray and I, and Woody? Did *he* go? And Velburn Ray? – taking a box one Christmas; Luther and Lillian.

None of them that we knew about after the eighth grade went more than a year to high school, most not that. Curiously, into our midst one day Willie alit, yet, by the next, she had fled again. Odell and Raven, Jimmy and Carroll and Gerald fell away too, and they lived in town; Donnesse and Sherl dropped out; Joe and Cecil, Brenda, Johnny, and Buck.

Thirty years ago, in 1954 – I was in the fourth grade, and the Brown decision was just then in the news – neither Faison Elementary School nor the black school in Faison was accredited by the State Department of Public Instruction; both were designated "non-standard," though Faison High School had been accredited since 1924. Twelve schools in Duplin County were for white students, twelve were for black; white elementary teachers numbered 257 (nine at Faison), and there were 103 black elementary teachers; there were 112 white high-school teachers, 35 black.[1] Rural teachers in North Carolina in 1956–57 were paid an average salary of $2,959; the state average for all public school teachers was $3,132, whites averaging $3,099 and blacks averaging $3,217. For the United States, the average was $4,220. North Carolina ranked fifth from the bottom among the forty-eight states, better only than Arkansas, Kentucky, Mississippi, and South Carolina. In 1957, from the first grade through the twelfth, the state drop-out rate was sixty percent.[2]

Yet, so oblivious were we to such matters, no measurement could have dismayed us; if a cause of grief to some, yet we weren't concerned, for we could have imagined school as nothing other than it was. That blacks rode their bus and we ours, that our schools were different, everybody –

certainly white people—took for granted; catching sight of a bus coming down the road in the morning, you just tried to be sure it was yours before running out to it. Yet, were you standing by the road already as the bus eased along, nobody cared. You waved at Tojo and Rosalee, Gail and Mamie and Jimmy Earl, and they at you. The black school happened to have been newer than ours, and when this was brought up one day in class, our teacher had said yes, and they had surely needed it too, that when she had been in the old Negro school (for a meeting? but why?) she could look through the floor and see the chickens.

Nobody talked about school with more evident relish than the black girls with whom I then worked in tobacco. Long summer afternoons handing and tying the green leaves, and the talk was all of school: those Parker boys and weren't they a sight, how the teachers were, the home economics and typing they liked, and the algebra and English they didn't. School itself we had in common, separate and unequal as our experience there was.

We had no notion that our schools were "non-standard." Always there was this other sense of feeling teachers had, as unlike us as they could have been, and a child knew without anybody telling him that the way he lived and talked at home hadn't anything to do with school. Teachers were different from everybody else, as educated people always were: doctors, and Lawyer Ray, whose fine old house on the corner across from Patsy's daddy's garage "Miss" Ray lived in, too. If teachers didn't happen to be authorities on most matters, nobody told us. My father, apt as he was to mock the women for what he called "foolishness," nonetheless respected them, and a man he would call "professor." (My grandmother when I was a college student a decade hence spoke of me, searching for the word, as a "scholar.") Different as teachers were, however (unthinkable for them *not* to have been), they were never unfamiliar. Like a relative who had left home before we were of age, yet who had kept in touch sending us word of his success, letters and old photographs, a teacher had a claim; long before you went to school yourself, she had become a part of your mental life: a picture in a scrapbook, she reposed in your imagination, leisurely and assured.

Teachers they were, and good ones. We may have had pitifully few library books and almost no laboratory equipment, but if loving and competent instruction counts, of *that* we never were bereft.[3] These were women in whose presence a child didn't want to be inadequate. They knew what they knew very well, and, more important, for them teaching was serious and worthy work. The mark of their professionalism was not just that they had gone to college and now taught at Faison School, but that they *were* teachers. Thus they carried themselves, and thus everybody took them. Their strides were purposeful, their voices edged with authority. Their every appearance, whether in the classroom or on the street or in the grocery store, was public. They dressed for us, and we as proudly wore our best for them.

To be a teacher defined and ennobled; it was what they had set their heart on, and, if ever they had cause for regret, no child knew it. No more likely were they to have revealed such a thing to us, even to have addressed us in our own idiom, or on our own level as if we were their intellectual equal, than to have flown about the room on the broom. Standing before us all those long and peaceful days, they did what they had come to do: they taught the lesson. Our true legacy was that we were not put in the charge of people who couldn't wait to get away from us, or whose real amibition lay elsewhere, school itself having but little bearing on their lives. We were not the objects of a bored and arid mechanicalness. That we stood then, and but momentarily, in that last still spot before inevitably our life, as the world itself, speeded up, of course we didn't know; we were as oblivious to the changes that would shortly overtake public education as our parents were to the new agriculture. There was time then, and teachers were in no more of a hurry than anybody else.

High school, when it rolled around in 1959, wasn't very different. By then there was no longer a high school in Faison. Consolidation of such community schools had taken hold already throughout eastern North Carolina, and new schools—flat, sprawling, and box-like—were springing up as fast as the bulldozers could clear the land for them. North Duplin awaited us, the Class of 1963. That first year we numbered sixty-four, though by graduation, what with many dropping out and few coming in, just fifty of us remained. School buses brought us in from Faison and Calypso, from the outlying farms and crossroads just south of Mount Olive and north of Warsaw, from Beautancus and Friendship, from close to Giddensville and Scott's Store.

Looking back on us then, I think that our class—that 1963 itself[4]—represented a watershed: we were the last, really, to have begun school before televisions were commonplace; among the last to graduate never having attended any but segregated schools; the last generation fully of the farms, whose mothers likely didn't work away from home (although the shift here was already occurring); the last before progressivism forever altered the tenor and medium of public education. Ours was the last class to graduate before the assassination of President Kennedy. We still accepted uncritically—or knew to act as if we did—the values school seeks to inculcate. We believed that you had to work for what you got, that education led, inevitably, to success. Had anybody pinned us down, we would have admitted that what our parents told us more than apt was right, as was their way of getting along in the world. The lessons of the past, we would have said, were reasonable enough for the future.

A girl then still got a bad name if she was promiscuous; not many of us drank; and drugs we knew nothing about. Vietnam hadn't yet anything to do with us, and Civil Rights we still somehow managed not to talk about; neither the murder of Medgar Evers our senior year nor the fire hoses and dogs of Birmingham, engaged us any more profoundly than had the Greensboro sit-in when we were freshmen. The U-2 affair had shaken us, the Russians steaming toward Cuba, the scare over Thalidomide, but —strange to say—not this, though for our parents the mention of Civil Rights was like a red flag waved in front of a bull.

At that age, in that time and place, a fragile innocence possessed us, a naiveté that history, if not the evidence of our own lives, soon would shatter. With what an air of personal discovery did some of us seize on "Look out, World!" as the theme for the yearbook; that as adults it would naturally be we ourselves having to "look out" was an irony then lost upon us. Yet our aspirations were neither very high nor very extraordinary: so unsophisticated were we that we had little awareness of all that it might be possible to *be,* to *do.* Especially were the girls in the class remarkably untouched by the careers that then and in the next ten and twenty years would open up for women. Marriage and homemaking, nursing, secretarial and clerical work, maybe teaching—we could imagine nothing else.

Linda left for Washington, where her sister Elizabeth already worked at the F.B.I.; Sandra went to Raleigh and got a job with Carolina Power and Light; Kathryn and Judy went into nursing programs. The six of us entering college thought no differently of ourselves, really, than they did, than others who were getting married, signing up for the assembly line at Hamilton-Beach, going to the sewing plants. No more than had our older sisters or our mothers did we think of joining a police force or a construction gang, of running for office. One did major in (I think) chemistry and go on to graduate school, but she was much the exception. Of the fellows, nine or ten were eventually to attend college, yet I believe only two or three ever graduated. Donald, who had the best mind of any of us (drawing up his own periodic table and graphing quadratic equations with enviable ease), left State, married, and went to work for a contracting firm in Raleigh; another got on at the telephone company; a third came back home and headed up a family farm.

As for the others, they took jobs at plants and factories, industrialization only then just beginning to make a difference in the area. (DuPont, which had gone up in Kinston in 1953, was among the earliest of the major companies establishing branches here.) Alma Doris clerked for a while at Belk's in Mount Olive; Woody went to a plant in New Bern. Some farmed, the few whose fathers still had land or who were able to rent their own acreage. Women kept house and raised their children. Gary's father brought him into his machine-repair shop in Calypso, and Donald, after he got out of the service, followed his father into the grocery business; Benny, whose father farmed, sold fertilizer. Three joined the Air Force, Alton making a career out of it. Velburn Ray and Tommy went to the pickle plant; Larry, to China as a missionary. Judy, ever the most daring among us, struck out with her husband for Alaska, finally.

Some went to college and some wound up a good ways from Faison, but most didn't. Larry and Judy got the fartherest away, probably, but others also left: Doug (in Weaver, Alabama) and Billy (in Atlanta), Peggy Sue (in Columbia, South Carolina) and Lafay (for years in Richmond, but lately in . . . Jacksonville, Florida, I want to say). There were those staying close to Faison, building a house when they were able and joining the rescue squad, sending their own children to North Duplin, and the ones who moved away, their lives unknown then to any but themselves. For some, happiness would always be, I think, largely synonymous with their career (which is almost to say, with their education), but, for most, employment would never have anything much to do with any essential feelings they possessed, as long as they had a job at all. Yet, familiar as this distinction between professional and working people is, already it was being undermined in the mid-1960s: our generation may have been the last to know that you can't get blood from a turnip, for whom an average job still meant – materially at least – no more than an average life. We assumed we would live differently from rich people, even as we hoped and expected to live better than our parents; that probably we would not have all that plenty of others did, we took for granted. (Yet those staying in eastern North Carolina and going into public work *may,* for once – though exceptions abound – have found themselves in the right spot at the right time; especially could a man hired at, say, DuPont in 1963 expect to be pretty secure there for the next twenty years, if not necessarily until he retired. Women, however, their promotions always few and far between, would have had less cause for optimism.)

Our younger brothers and sisters in the 1970s, our children, no matter how average or ordinary their job, nonetheless expected to live exceedingly well – or, if not truly *well,* at least as they pleased. They somehow knew more sharply than we had the sting of comparison; the gulf had widened between those having a lot and others having nothing, and society, increasingly consumer-oriented and materialistic, accentuated the difference. To have been brought more within the mainstream of American urban life was to have had revealed its broader field of possibility, however little the chance remained of its fulfillment. If expectation now was open-ended, so, too, was disappointment.

Part Two

Working and Living and Getting By

3. The Hands and Us

Tenant farmers themselves were often in a way like landlords. They frequently hired "hands" on their own, men and women and children who knew them to be the boss, and who may or may not have known that, in fact, another man owned the land on which they had been brought to work. In Faison all during the 1940s and 1950s and into, but not much beyond, the early 1960s, white tenants in the summer drove twice daily into Juniper ("nigger-town," they called it) or into the black sections of Clinton or Mount Olive or Warsaw, even Goldsboro, picking up workers early in the morning and bringing them back at close of day. In front of one ramshackly house after another, they would gather: mamas and those grown or half-grown daughters still at home, some with babies of their own; little girls barely tall enough to reach into the slides to hand out the green tobacco that big girls tied steadily all day to sticks, which then were hung in barns for curing; and young men who worked in the field, sleepy-eyed in the morning and sullen, not to be bothered. Summer work was setting out and suckering and putting in tobacco; picking beans and cucumbers and pepper and squash; chopping; grading dry tobacco when it came out of the barn, Granddaddy Flowers telling us we had it easy, that nowadays nobody made you separate the different shades of green, one hue of yellow from another, the trash, as they had when he had farmed. Fall meant picking cotton and gathering corn; winter meant killing hogs, for people lucky enough to have them.

It was my father's part, as that of tenants everywhere, to pay the hands out of his pocket. He might have to borrow from the landlord in order to do so, but they both knew that at the year's end, at the time to settle up, whatever had been advanced would have to come out of the tenant's share. Farming on thirds meant that the landlord deducted from the tenant's two-thirds the expenses of making the crop, a usual (but not universal) exception being that the owner paid part of the fertilizer bill. Labor and gasoline or, before tractors were much in use, horses and mules and feed; cultivators and plows, disk harrows and planters; seed and tools; everything, in fact, necessary for farming, as well as what it took to feed him and his family during the winter when there was nothing to sell and he had to go to the landlord for grocery money, all were the tenant's lookout, whether the crop made anything or not. Some owners of course furnished more than others, even as tenants who farmed the same land year after year (some for the second or even third generation) were more likely to own what they had to have than were those others who kept afloat by going from place to place, shedding one landlord for another as seasonally as molting birds lose and acquire feathers. Knowing this to be the case, the hands might or might not have known, also, that in some ways the tenant's living was about as hard to make, and infinitely as precarious, as their own. The money the tenant counted out to each as he came forward on Saturday when his name was called, the others holding back and respectful, was not, or not yet, his.

To the child of such a farmer, however, nothing was more exhilarating than riding in the back of the truck with these familiar but unknown people, than playing around the tobacco barn all day, or between the rows in the field, listening without consciously doing so as they talked among themselves, their voices cast in a different timbre, the words falling into another rhythm, than when they talked to us. Humored and taken up for by them, saved from spankings by black women appropriating by the sheer force of their person the right to scold even your own mother if she offered to correct you (so long as your offenses, though legion, still fell within the scheme of things), a white child of six or seven, too little to work and in command just of the gentler truths of the world, might have been forgiven for thinking the tobacco barn and these people, the house in which she lived, even the white-hot sun itself, existed merely for her own happiness and peace of mind. Nobody told her any different.

White tenantry in the 1950s was not invariably as crippling as it had been in the 1930s and 1940s, though it was by no conjuring of the imagination ever easy. The days had passed when the tenant's son who could best be spared had to hire himself out to another farmer and cut ditch banks or crop tobacco or break corn, six days a week, for bed and

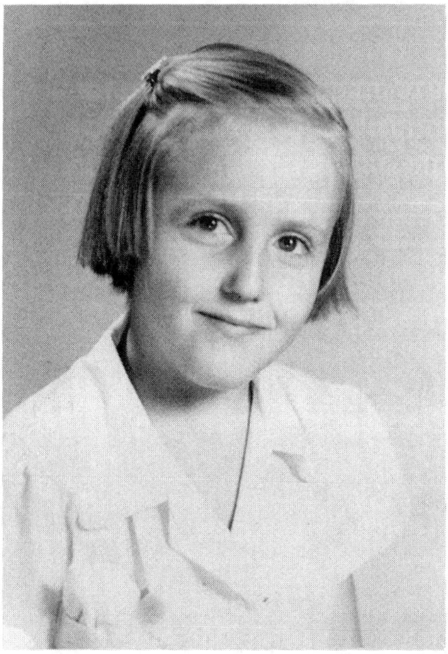

Linda, 2nd Grade, 1952. (Photo courtesy of Lillie Mae Bass.)

Faison High School ninth-grade class, 1945. *Front row, right:* Linda's sister Rachel. (Photo courtesy of Jane Faison. Reproduced from *The Mount Olive Tribune,* August 26, 1983.)

Faison High School, Class of 1948. *Front row, left:* Linda's sister Rachel. *Back row, second from right:* "Moose," Dr. William Thornton, North Carolina's only astronaut. (Photo courtesy of Jane Faison.)

Faison High School, 1949. In Linda's day, Faison Elementary. The school looked exactly the same through at least the mid-1960s. (Courtesy of Kraft's Studio, Archival Negative, Mount Olive, N. C.)

Above: Faison, mid-to-late 1940s. The center building is "Miss" Virginia's beauty shop. (Photo courtesy of Helen Flowers.) *Below:* Faison today. Note the poolroom at the right; farmers and others have played pool here since at least the early 1950s. The town is no larger now than it has ever been—and considerably less bustling. (Photo by Linda Flowers, 1989.)

board and perhaps as much as forty or fifty cents a day. He might have worked for a logging outfit for very little more, and without the bed and board. Fortunes had been made this way. The story is still told in some quarters of the prominent farmer who had, as a young man, been a logger, who had everyday sold his dinner for a dime and saved his money, and whose sons lived to inherit one of the biggest farms around Faison. More likely, however, the day laborer of the 1930s was a tenant in the 1940s and 1950s, or, if luckier or more provident than most, or sometimes just more mercilessly grasping, a small landowner. The tenant, this is to say, who had come through the Depression, who had managed against such terrible odds to hold out, staving off creditors and living at least well enough to keep his children fed and clothed and occasionally in school likely lived better in the 1950s than he ever had before. Especially if he had stayed within a county or two of where he had been raised, if not always in the same neighborhood, he had attained by then something more than is commonly understood by tenantry.

Stability brought with it the kind of security only other people can bestow, the familiarity that, though it may not mean acceptance, is, nonetheless, essential for living in the world. The narrowness of that geographic area in which the tenant felt at home, thirty or forty miles at the most (and more often twenty, if not less), worked to his economic advantage, if to no other: it was the place where his landlord's name had meaning, and, more to the point, where their relationship was an established reality that others, of necessity, had to take into account. Simply by knowning that the tenant lived on Mr. So and So's land, the public transformed the hard fact of his dependence into a commodity upon which he then could presume. Merchants and the fertilizer man, the sheriff and the doctor, as well as salesmen of farm equipment and the men who fixed it when it broke down, these and everybody else saw in the tenant not just the tenant himself but the man behind him; as long as the landlord carried him, so, in most instances, would they. Tenants never were without continual reminders putting them in their place, but, at the same time, they had a place in which to be put. When times were good, such interdependencies could be respected. The larger economic reality directly bore upon every transaction in every place of business the tenant had cause to enter; 1950s national prosperity was the bedrock underlying and propping up the system.

Yet the ironies are such that even other farmers who had known the tenant for years, though perhaps only by sight or name, men with whom he had passed the time of day in town when he had gone after feed or kerosene, may not always have known him to be a tenant, his mere tenure upon the land conferring an assumption of ownership. If his house had been more or less kept up, if his wife made the yard her particular domain, even if it was dirt rather than lawn, which she swept smooth with the yard broom late in the day, if she held her zinnias and gladiola, daffodils and crape myrtles in as high esteem almost as she did her children, daring man or child, cat or dog to intrude upon them, there was often no way to know, simply by passing along the road, who owned his farm and who didn't. Tenant and small landowner alike took at least as much care of their barns and shelters as they did their house; landlords, more. The look of a place was no true sign of who held the deed to it. Houses in the worst shape, the porches rotted and rags sometimes where a windowpane had been, houses without underpinning or septic tanks, running water or electricity, more often than not, however, were tenant homes. Not many tenants had the money for fixing up another man's house, even if they had the will and saw the need; most, because they could do nothing else, took the house that came with the land and lived in it. Besides the lack of money there was, too, an unvoiced but determined resistance to doing anything much to a house that didn't belong to you, and from which you might be told to move after the crop was made; and few landlords, even when they had had the same tenant for years, willingly did anything to improve his dwelling. Panes of glass a tenant might sometimes buy, but not paint; boards to patch a rotten floor, maybe, but not the tin for a new roof. Women knew how far down the list the house was. Subsistence farmers who owned their own land often weren't much better off at the end of the year than a tenant; their houses might look like his.

So much depended upon the kind of people tenant and landlord were. There was no particular shame in walking into town on Saturday morning with your mother and having Mr. Isham Faison give you a Coca-Cola in his drugstore, then drinking it slowly as he shuffled about in the back room getting the grocery money you had come to borrow; you would answer his questions about how you were doing in school, and did you like your teacher, and he would write down the figure in his book with infinite care. Always there was decorum in our reception. It is my impression that landlords who were also among a town's oldest families, those whose fathers and grandfathers had bequeathed the land to them, tended to be the ones for whom, with certain fairly scandalous exceptions, tenants had the most regard. Land often meant more to these men than just the money it brought them. Some had grown up in the tradition of thinking they were not so much businessmen, buying and selling acreage for the profit they could turn, as gentlemen.

Especially if they made no pretense of being farmers themselves, if they sent their sons to Chapel Hill when they came of age rather than making them overseers or giving them crops of their own (thus reducing the land the tenant would have had), were they looked upon as men under whom tenancy might be more than tolerable; but such men were exceedingly rare. The likelihood was that a tenant lived on the same farm, or the one adjoining, that his landlord lived upon, and that he and his family worked the land under the eye and tutelage of its owner. That Isham Faison lived in town and owned a drugstore, no matter the kind of man he might otherwise have been, meant that his tenants enjoyed considerably more autonomy than most others, as well as every responsibility. It was more than happenstance that both my grandfather and his son tended Faison family land for most of their lives, and that my father should, in 1944, have moved onto one of the Faison farms.

For one or two landlords, however, who did business this way, dozens of others did not. For every aged gentleman content with the tenant who had lived on his place for years, there were others every bit as rapacious and underhanded as cliché has them; and the tenant whose misfortune it was to work for such a man, eternally at the beck and call of one, who, with varying degrees of suspicion and meanness, found no aspect of the day's work beneath his scrutiny or beyond his interest, such a tenant lived in another realm from us. But, whether black or white, such tenants were neither so few nor so inconspicuous that their existences, miserable and bitter as they were, did not serve as an instance of what a person might be, or have to be, in the world.

Local people would have said it was the better class of tenant who stayed with the same landlord year after year, and although that was not invariably the case, it was true enough. Honest landlords were as scarce almost as hen's teeth, and honest tenants perhaps only less so; when they found one another, they tended not to let go. On the other hand, those accustomed all their days to having nothing, to being shunted from place to place and looked down upon, always getting the short end of the stick, and with no real recourse for their grievances not infrequently found themselves as capable of fraud as other people when it came to making the system work for them. For the tobacco a tenant hauled off to Clarkton or Whiteville in the dead of night, the corn sold without the landlord being any the wiser, there were a thousand slights, and more injuries to simple justice, not to mention pride, than a person could bear; and if the particular landlord being cheated was not the cause of them all, he was undoubtedly the cause of some, and so could, in a manner of thinking, bear the cost.

About tenants committed to making a crop, with all the debt and backbreaking labor that entailed, not forgetting the storm or drought or flood that could, in less time than it took to tell about it, wipe them out for this and the next several years running; men who saw their wives old and worn and bone-tired from continually working in the fields and houses too, and from bearing and raising children, one after the other—women as unlike the Southern myth of idealized womanhood as it was possible to be, about these tenants the surprising thing was that so many of them did, after all, stand upon the letter of the law, and did so even when they knew themselves to have signed on yet again with an unscrupulous landlord. Honest tenants, those who scorned the shortcuts, and who likely shunned others who would steal the shortening out of a biscuit, nonetheless were quite capable of thinking that old Mr. Whosis, skinned by his tenant, had got no more than what was coming to him. Whatever the shenanigan had been, they would be prone to say, "It won't right . . . course it won't right, but," depending upon the landlord's reputation, "when you look at it, by damn, it won't so wrong, neither."

As for the way it was with us, the two of them, "Miss" Louise at the wheel and beside her, Mr. Isham, invariably attired in a suit with vest (so that to a child he looked like Major Hoople in "Our Boarding House"), drove out in the country once a day, in the summertime, stopping first at one farm, then another: at Sam Fryar's house across the road from ours; at Mr. Price's two-storied house (where the Faisons themselves, or some of them, had once lived); at Uncle Herman's place; at the man's we still called uncle because he had been married to my grandfather's sister when she died; at Mr. Thad Daw's out toward Giddensville; at William Henry Oates's. But the drive mattered to them as much as anything else; always at dusk it would be, when the inside of a barn or house was like an oven, and anybody who had a chance to take a ride, did. They would go by our place, or, if they saw us in the field or on the porch, they might stop then rather than wait to catch us on their way back to town. Conversation was as much a thing of leisure as the almost imperceptible progress of their Chevrolet before, finally, it slipped out of sight down the road. They'd ask about the crops, but not insistently; an outsider would have thought them no more than casual and rather disinterested visitors. They might be taken to admire the dry tobacco packed down in the barn, or the new pepper plants if there was a good stand, but just as often they'd not take even the trouble to get out of the car. Twenty or thirty minutes was as long as they ever stayed, either at our house or at Sam and Rosa's, where we would sometimes spot them parked in the backyard.

The farm was probably a little less than 150 acres cleared; the tobacco allotment, in the early 1950s, about five acres. From one year to the next, twenty or thirty acres would be put in the Soil Bank; the rest, planted: cotton and corn, truck crops such as pepper and cucumbers, lima beans and string beans (once, yellow wax beans), sweet potatoes, sometimes soybeans. Tobacco was the money crop. The idea was to sell enough pepper and cucumbers through the summer so that you would have some money coming in and be able to barn tobacco without going head over heels in debt. If tenants could do that, and if tobacco then brought anything like it was supposed to, then they stood a chance of not being in the hole when they settled up in late September or October, when the last of the cotton was ginned.

But if, as often happened, produce didn't bring enough even to pay for itself, let alone anything else; if beans and cucumbers, pepper and squash, were brought back home – the farmer damned if he meant to give them away for fifty or seventy-five cents or maybe a dollar a bushel (the basket alone costing him twenty-five or fifty cents[1] – and allowed to rot or be fed to the hogs, then the only thing to do was borrow more and more heavily – knowing, as you always knew, that tobacco, its price artificially maintained through government support, might bring but the bare minimum. Farmers didn't have to sell at the support price if buyers for the tobacco companies ("Ligget and Myers, R. J. Reynolds, . . . all such as that") bid higher; they'd talk about bad times, the nights spent on the road going from market to market in the hope of being offered a few cents more on the pound.

"We left Wilson, didn't even head back to Faison," my father says, "went on through Smithfield and around Fedville [Fayetteville], then hit Lumberton, and, hell, they won't biddin' nothing. So we come on back the next day and sold ever' damn leaf of it at Clinton. Clinton ain't twenty miles from Faison, and here we drove all over the country. . . . We'd a gone there to start with if we'd a knowed."

Gasoline cost a man less, in such instances, than the feeling that he had no choice in the matter; that despite having nurtured his crop as if it were the most delicate and precious of living things, more to be prized at times than his own health or his children's schooling, a buyer, who did nothing but walk up and down the rows in a warehouse, could take it for a price that was little more than an insult. Even the most easygoing farmer balked at that. He might be no better off in the end, but for once he would be the one deciding when and where to make the deal.

Cotton prices were so out of line with everything else that, by the mid-to-late 1950s, all but a few farmers (and they the ones with vast acreage) had stopped growing it. Tenants and other shirt-tailed farmers couldn't for long make a go of cotton at $200 a bale, not when it cost $150 to produce and stood a better than even chance of being lost in the field. In the 1930s, cotton had sold for about three cents a pound, whereas in the 1950s it brought about forty cents, yet the fifteen dollars the 1930s bale was worth weighed more heavily in the total economy than one hundred dollars did in 1952. In the late 1930s, a bale of cotton and seed bringing twenty-eight dollars paid for a suit of clothes, shoes, and a hat, and there was change to spare; thus went the first bale my father ever made.

Corn rarely brought more than a dollar and a half a bushel, either in the 1950s or early 1960s, but it cost less to grow and was less of a burden than anything else, and tenants always planted as much as they could.

Tenants still farmed with mules or horses, though some had riding cultivators. Not until 1954 did my father have a tractor, a small, used Farmall that cost him a thousand dollars. Crops, including tobacco, were set out (or sown), tended, and harvested still almost wholly by hand. The machines that would change forever a way of life were, many of them, available in the sense that they did exist, but, in the early-to-mid 1950s, they were, for all practical purposes, largely unknown to the tenants and small landowners in whose care still lay most of the land; and to the hands, whose lives they would make as precarious as a child's toy in a hurricane before rendering them finally and for all time obsolescent, they were but things to murmur about with an uncomprehending but ever increasing foreboding. That these were the years before a revolution, a cataclysm, not only in how people made a living but in how they thought about the natural world, and, inevitably, themselves in relation to it, no one had an inkling. Tenants still went down to their wood-burning tobacco barn at night and added wood to the furnace, checking that the fire neither went out nor got so high that the barn burned. They still cut green corn as feed for the mules and set pepper with a hand transplanter that looked like something off a medieval suit of armor.

The ritual of hiring hands was the same as it had always been. A tenant would pull up in the dirt yard of a black family that had worked for him before, or that he had heard was all right help, and blow the horn, and after a while Eloise or Jessie or Dot—always it would be the mama or a grown girl—would come onto the porch or, if the mama, up to the truck door, and the man, after a bit of the pointless jocularity a white person always carried on with a Negro, would get down to business.

"You gonna' hep me on Tuesdays this year, ain't you?" The question would have sounded like the answer was perfectly plain. The woman would look off across the yard, her head and body sideways to the truck, hands on her hips, and, when she was ready, offer a reply.

"I doan' know 'bout Tuesdays. . . ." There would be a wait. Sometimes she'd say something else, and the man, professing not to believe what he'd just heard, would begin again.

"Aw, don't tell me that. I don't even believe that. You know you gonna' hep me, don'cha?"

The woman might pause, crossing her arms so that she hugged herself, and shift her weight, then deal again.

"Callie gonna' hep Mister Mack Tuesdays. . . . I believe dat's what she say."

The mention of Callie (or whatever the name) was neither irrelevant nor unexpected. That blacks were often reluctant to work singly or where they didn't know the other hands, especially if they had not worked for a particular farmer before, was the stuff of jokes, if not myth. "Every one of 'em up there in Juniper," one farmer would say to another, "knows every other one, so it don't make no difference who you see." Some blacks, however, had helped the same white families, whether they were tenants or landowners, for twenty years; where this was the case, the day for barning tobacco was as well-known to the hand as to the farmer, and as important. It would have been understood that Lillie Belle helped "Mister" Herman and "Miss" Clara Lee on Thursdays, and that day was, therefore, inviolate as far as anybody else requiring her services was concerned.

"Mack Lewis?"

"I believe dat's who she say."

"Hell fire! Mack Lewis's 'baccer ain't even ripe. . . . You can't crop 'baccer that ain't ripe!"

That this was not the truth would have been suggested by the tone, if, indeed, it wasn't so, and the farmer would have known that the woman knew he had not intended it to be taken literally; such was but a way of extending the conversation, of keeping up the half-playful, half-earnest (but essentially patronizing) banter. They would talk more or less in this same vein for ten or fifteen minutes more, neither adding anything of substance, until one or the other would, in some near-indefinable way, capitulate. Usually it was the woman.

"Well, . . . I doan' know. . . . Neece'll prob'ly hep you."

Neece would be her daughter, or granddaughter, as often as not a slip of a girl who may have been, say, twelve or fifteen. She would then be summoned from inside the house where with sinking heart she, no doubt, had seen and heard all, and the involved process of engagement would begin all over again, though this time with the difference that everybody understood what the outcome would be. The mother (or grandmother) had lent her authority to the bargain, and the man could, therefore, count upon Neece being more or less ready on Tuesday when, the sun barely risen and dew heavy upon every blade of grass, he rolled up and blew the horn for her.

The child now having fled back into the depths of the little house, the man would crank up and begin to pull away, in a hurry now, and the woman, for the first time smiling broadly, would, as something that she had had on her mind but until just then forgotten, think to ask after his wife and family.

"How they doin'?"

This not being the time for details, and the woman expecting none, the tenant would call out, shifting into second, "All right . . . all right . . . gittin' along," the dust spun up by his wheels filling the air.

But courtesy, decent and pleasing though it was, should not now, as it did not then, obscure what was at stake here (anymore than, when the shoe was on the other foot, and the tenant had to go to his landlord for five or ten dollars to see him through, any amiability on the part of the man doling out the money canceled the debt). Throughout the 1950s blacks had no where else to work other than on farms, and those had to be reasonably close to where they lived so that even a tenant could afford to transport them; thus, while the whole countryside was nothing but farms, and landowners as well as tenants both sought hands zealously, any one person's chance to work was circumscribed by locale. That in tobacco time or during cotton-picking time, especially, good hands could readily find work, and in that sense chose their employers, never meant that the number of farmers to whom they were, in fact, available was so large, or the farmers themselves so different one from another, that their choice was anything but nominal. The best they could hope to do was hire on with a man who treated them fairly. There would have been little or no difference in the money that was offered; farmers all paid about the same thing: thirty-five or forty cents an hour in the early 1950s, or so much a bushel for picking. If work was slack a hand may have gone without a job, and in the winter nobody had anything.

Hand and tenant depended mightily upon each other. Insofar as it was possible to survive as a tenant, the cost of hiring outside help had to be kept low, and the hands had to be there, wanting and needing to work. Hands, uneducated and, but for their willingness to drudge alongside the tenant a living out of God and the landlord's earth, unskilled, were as bound to the land as serfs. Tenantry was a hierarchy of mutually reinforcing needs and rewards, and each link in the chain was as necesary as the other. But necessity never bred equality, and the sense of having any choice, whether you were a tenant or hand, was illusory.

A tenant was as hemmed in as the hand who relied upon him for work; in one way, more so. Whereas a hand might have had more than one farmer wanting to hire him or her, the tenant whose crop came off a week or two after everybody else's would have found anybody he wanted to hire already taken; hands might be spoken for in advance, but you couldn't blame them for going elsewhere rather than waiting. Only the most stable tenants and hands, those whose working relationships were long-standing, found ways to accommodate each other in such instances. But always it was an intimacy without feeling; tenants and hands knew each other, may have known each other all their lives, but never other than functionally. The same was true for tenant and landlord.

Well into the 1960s, fifty cents an hour was about all a woman could make as a hand,[2] although by then men cropping tobacco made a dollar to a dollar and a quarter an hour. Croppers had always been paid more than others barning tobacco, but never this much more, and the difference here is important. For one thing, since at least 1956 when the minimum wage had risen from seventy-five cents to a dollar, and despite the fact that agricultural workers were not covered, farmers had seen the handwriting on the wall: the day was not long off when even blacks sweating in the fields were going to expect, as they would have a right to receive, considerably more than farmers were used to paying them; and although it was to be eleven years, or not until 1967, before that day officially arrived (and then there would be many exceptions), the dread that it was coming took anchor. There was something almost symbolic in the figure itself; the dollar was a kind of dividing line, which, once attained (once a man made a dollar an hour, having always worked for forty, then sixty or seventy-five cents), changed both a person's sense of self and the way the world reckoned with him. Small landowner and tenant alike, but especially – because they had so much less – the tenant, looked upon such an increase as practically unfathomable. This was not simply another thing taking money out of their pockets, but the compelling, final straw with which some particularly malevolent Fury meant to break them.

Nonetheless, as the 1950s wore on, hands began for the first time to hold out for higher pay. Farmers, their worst fears seemingly confirmed in every tale and rumor that flew, found themselves in an incomprehensibly different world from the one they had always known. No longer could they take for granted a compliant and willing people, eager and grateful for work at any price; nor did their way of doing business with hands any longer serve. The expectancy of something more was in the air, anticipation more palpable than it had ever been before. That people were not just asking for but getting wages that only a year or so earlier they could hardly have imagined making derived from the fact that even more was going on than met the eye: the days when a farmer's chief, if unlisted, assets began with a captive supply of cheap labor and included, if the farmer were white, racial advantage in all things were over. (But nothing is easier to exaggerate than change. Thirty years hence, in 1988, when the minimum wage is $3.35, hands, their numbers much diminished from what they were in the heyday of the 1950s and early 1960s, are lucky to get three dollars, and luckier still if, as some do, they get the whole thing. It is fair to say that a great many work for $2.25 or $2.50, and the situation still is that blacks usually work for whites, and not vice versa.)

Increasingly, in the early 1960s, some farmers found themselves dealing not so much with individual hands, Dot or Jessie or Eloise, as with a crew boss, blacks having, as whites put it, "ganged together" to offer themselves for hire in groups; in some instances, it was the crew boss who paid the others out of the lump sum the farmer had contracted with him, pocketing any difference. There had always been the possibility of something like this happening, but never before had such an arrangement been so organized or politically meaningful. Farmers had found it convenient to be able to count upon one hand ("a good nigger") rounding up others, although they would not have put him in charge of paying them; he and the farmer simply had an understanding, the farmer on Saturday slipping him a couple of dollars extra for his effort. Now, however, the crew boss was more or less self-appointed, and his understanding was with, as it was, presumably, on behalf of, the hands under his charge. He met the farmer as an antagonist, implicit as this may have been, and the stance he took, even his very existence, suggested that from now on things were going to be different.

Yet, it must be understood, the crew-boss system of providing hands never took deep or permanent root, and although it is my impression that the practice was widespread enough to alarm farmers generally, still it was the exception rather than the rule; nor did the sense of structured negotiation it introduced prove lasting. Perhaps the hands the practice was meant to serve were too used to having to look out for themselves, and so they were mistrustful of the whole notion; perhaps too many bosses were scoundrels whose exploitation of their own people rivaled or surpassed that of the farmers with whom they were at odds. More important than the system never quite getting off the ground, however, was the point driven home to white farmers that blacks had more means available to them than they had realized, and that when they chose, they could change the situation dramatically. That blacks might have the upper hand hardly bore thinking. Yet to the farmers who had always known them, it was now plain that hands, uneducated and unskilled and, above all else, black, were indeed capable of putting them in a considerable bind, of "acting up" not just in general (which they expected), but purposefully and for themselves—and if this didn't put the fear of God in white people, it did the fear of everything else.

The talk of hands around a tobacco barn, guarded as it was, even when the only white listener was a child, was different now from what it had been in the early 1950s. Little was explicit, yet nuance and silence, the stories the women told and the weight that unaccountably fell on certain words, the women bending low into the slides, bending and straightening, the green-yellowing leaves right in their hands: this old picture in the mind was shaped then by a significant unease. There was the sense of a people having to settle again where they belonged in the world. Hattie was probably close to fifty, and indignant:

> . . . come tellin' me to call her 'Miss' Susan, like I don't know no better. I knows how to honor her. I don't need no daddy tellin' me how to honor her.

And some stripling of a girl had sassed, "I know what kind a Miss I'd a called her! Uum-uum . . . ," everybody laughing, Hattie too. But a white man a summer or two before would have taken it for granted that a grandmotherly black woman understood she was to address his fifteen-year-old daughter as "Miss." That this father thought the reminder necessary shows his uncertainty that blacks any longer knew their place.

There was the young woman tying tobacco who had worked as a maid in Philadelphia and had eaten at the same table as the white family. "It won't in North Carolina, that's for damn sure," the words tough and stony, and the silence thick. "Them chil'ren treated me just the same as if I was white. Won't no difference."

They talked of other places they had worked, more openly critical now than before. "That ole man? . . . He so mean, he don't eben wan'cha to have a drink a' water, jest holler a'cha all day." And they talked of the things white people said blacks always talked about: weddings and funerals ("She fall all over her foolish self a moanin' an' carr'in' on."); knifings; children; a woman so "eat up with" venereal disease that when she gave birth the baby had to be "pulled out a' her in pieces"; a rape ("all them big mens!"); "the laws"; the reasons a good-looking woman was not married ("She say she ain' gonna' take no lick off no man!"). But of the things history would record, the Brown decision, for example, or what had happened at Little Rock or the tobacco harvesters now appearing in the fields in ever increasing numbers, there was no conversation.

There was the fact, too, that fewer and fewer hands were available for hire at any cost. "I jest be damned if you can git any hep, not these days." The complaint, heard whenever one farmer got to talking with another (or with anyone else), was all too real. Between 1939 and 1954, more than a million blacks had left Southern farms, and in the next ten years alone, from 1954 to 1964, another million left.[3] The Greyhounds and Trailwayses leaving out of Wilmington or Jacksonville and rolling through Wallace and Warsaw and Faison, Mount Olive and Goldsboro, Smithfield and Pine Level and, at last, Raleigh had for years taken on at nearly every stop, nearly every run, blacks going "up the road." Especially the young were leaving, and in large numbers. They would have their belongings in a cardboard suitcase held together with string, or a pasteboard box tied with tobacco twine, which, as often as not, would have already begun to split open, and they'd sway in the aisle as the bus pulled away, trying still to maneuver their cumbersome possessions into an overhead rack. They dug out of paper sacks the fried chicken and cornbread that the women who loved them had prepared, unwrapped the packaged cookies and cakes they had bought, and silently, hunkered in the narrow seats, ate. The look in their eyes said they were scared but had made up their minds; that they might not know the place they were headed, but the sun they had left behind was hot, and the lush fields, somebody else's. Babies might have slept fitfully beside them, the pacifiers loose in their mouths.

As the 1950s ended, however, if blacks were finding life more and more burdensome, so too were white farmers, especially tenants. Higher labor costs and rising prices meant that what an acre of land could produce was worth comparatively less and less; more and more acreage was, therefore, necessary for making a living, even though the more land a farmer tended, the more hands he needed. But tenants had no more acreage than they had always had, if they still had *that*; they had neither the means for acquiring more land nor the money to pay the additional hands they would have had to hire if they had the additional acres, assuming (for the moment) such hands to be available. A tenant or small landowner caught in this no-win situation had but one objective, and that was to make each piece of land he farmed bring in as much money as possible. Inevitably, this meant cutting back on the growing of truck crops—pepper and cucumbers, beans and squash, watermelons perhaps—because they cost so much to house and their market value was so unpredictable. Only the holders of large farms, men who sold a thousand or more boxes of produce every week during green season, could take the risks such farming now entailed.

Farmers on the edge of going under, as tenants always were, had no choice but to grow mostly tobacco and corn and soybeans, and as usual raise a few hogs, since they knew that with its government support tobacco would always sell, and that a man and his wife and children could tend acre upon acre of corn and soybeans, having to pay out to others just for the picking. But the growing of tobacco was by fixed allotment; thus when the bottom fell out of truck farming, farmers couldn't compensate by planting another acre or two of tobacco. Few small farmers had the money to rent somebody else's allotment. Tenants thus found themselves in a squeeze the likes of which only those who had started out during the Depression had ever seen before (and then, at least, hands had been plentiful and cheap). That easing-up they had experienced as the 1950s got underway, had, well before the end of the decade, reversed itself. The dreams with which they had begun each new season, that some of the promises of life might be fulfilled, were now nothing but gall.

There began to be talk in the night of debts piling up and no way to pay them; of again going in the hole; of not knowing how to make ends meet (but the man with a house full of chilren, one day in our backyard, had said, "Looks like me and the old lady done made 'em meet too many times, as 'tis!"). Farmers always talked this way. How else to voice the vague, uncomprehending anxiousness with which they fortified themselves against "bad times." Language made the worries real, but metaphor made them bearable. Everybody knew that if you didn't have a pot to piss in, neither would you have a window to throw it out of, and that that was all right; people who lived in better houses than ours said it, too. But what a child sleepily overheard in the night now was somehow different, more insistent; adding and taking away in the dark, so much for guano, and "sody," something else for tobacco seed (impossibly tiny, and the child got to keep the box like a tobacco barn they came in)–but such figuring was harder than doing the problems in an arithmetic book, and the talking went on and on, and the daddy didn't laugh in the telling anymore, and, when the child got up in the morning, the mama's mouth looked like a knot.

In 1956, after twelve years on the Faison place, we moved to a smaller farm on the other side of town, eight or ten miles farther from Faison than we were then living. My father and another man had signed up with the same landlord, and the other family moved, too. Their plan was to try to farm more or less together, or, at least, swap some of the labor. In their minds, also, was the hope that if things worked out, they would eventually, in another year or two, be able to buy a tobacco harvester and so cut by more than half the number of hands they needed. The new place was just forty acres, but ten of them were in tobacco, which was twice our present allotment. We knew that this landlord's tenants didn't go to him when they needed money; that, instead, every year they took out a loan from the Production Credit Association, and every month they had a check waiting for them in their mailbox.

There was the need for starting over, for taking a chance somewhere else, for seeing how you fared under a new man and different arrangements.

On a day in November, I took another school bus whose number was now mine, and stayed on it, as my mother had told me over and over to do, until it got to the house where she stood in the yard waiting for me.

4. Poor Grassy Farmer

To drive now back along Highway 50 where we once lived and where for miles the Faison land once was farmed by tenants, the houses habitable and the dirt yards walked clean and hard, is to encounter brush and undergrowth where the people once were and fields abandoned but for the occasional crops put in by men who live elsewhere. For a while after we left, three or four years, another family lived in our house and farmed the land, and then they, too, moved on. By the mid-1960s, in fact, none of the people who had made their lives on Faison land any longer did so. Nor did their children.

Sam and Rosa had managed to acquire their own small place, as had the Prices and Daws. An inheritance from her landed father made possible Aunt Clara Lee and Uncle Herman's transformation from tenant to owner, and age and hard times took other families away from farming altogether. Whether because the Faisons were both getting up into age (and Mr. Isham was ill) or reliable tenants were hard to find, or tenantry was too unprofitable even for them, or, what is likely, a combination of these reasons, when those tenants who had been with them since the 1940s left, they were not (or not for long) replaced. The land they had farmed was either rented out or put in the Soil Bank, only to be, eventually, broken up and sold off.

The same is true now for much of the acreage along the road by which we lived and worked after we left the Faison place, and for tenantry in general. With fewer and fewer exceptions in the late 1960s and thereafter, once a tenant father died or became too old to farm or the family moved, the landowner would no longer seek a replacement. No family with whom we farmed on the new place farms today. Nor does a single one of the tenant families I knew back then. As the 1960s took their toll, tenants increasingly found themselves to be unnecessary; owners, especially if they were also farmers, came to rely overwhelmingly on machines, which meant both an unprecedented increase in the number of acres they could farm and a sharp and immediate decrease in the number of people needed to help them.

An owner, therefore, no longer had to take the responsibility (such as it was) for maintaining a tenant family the year around when, in the summer, he could pick up a few extra hands and get his crop in; he needed considerably fewer hands than a tenant without a tobacco harvester or riding-setter or corn picker would have to hire, and then the hands could not have done anywhere near the work in the same time as the machines did. Though "the tenancy rate remained high in the flue-cured belts . . . about 45 percent in eastern North Carolina"[1] as late as 1972, the decline was irreversible. By 1978, the state had fewer than thirteen thousand tenants; in 1930, tenants had accounted for more than half of North Carolina's farmers.[2]

In the 1940s and early 1950s, a tenant son would likely have considered farming himself. In the 1960s, however, he could hardly think of doing so. Young men raised on farms, their fathers and grandfathers tenants and their mothers and grandmothers the daughters of tenants, now looked to the Army or the pickle plant for their living, to the plywood company or the feed mill. They drove trucks, either locally or up and down the eastern seaboard. They tried to get on at one of the sewing plants or chicken-processing plants. They worked on the roads for the state or pumped gas or stacked groceries at the local wholesaler's. Some drove everyday back and forth to Kinston or Goldsboro or Clinton where they may have found a slightly better-paying job, at DuPont or General Electric maybe, or Lundy's. Their sons and daughters would have as little feeling for the land as if it had never been a part of their heritage, and they themselves, the generation that forsook tenantry even as tenantry forsook them, would live to see their kinship with their fathers' way of life, and with their own raising, weaken and grow cold.

The realization that things were now tougher than they had ever been, that nothing was going to be better, and that by moving we had left a frying pan for a fire was not long coming. For one thing, forty acres were not near enough, yet, had we had more land, there would still have been nobody but my parents and me to do the bulk of the work. For another, tragedy dogged us: sickness and pain and error, none of which may have had anything to do with the obvious hardships, and yet for all we knew then (or would ever know) may have had everything to do with them, with never having enough of anything except worry and debt. Illness and error descended upon our lives, blanketing us forever. Such failure we took upon ourselves, claiming it as ours as reflexively as we might have laid another person's ruin at his own feet; there was the inchoate yet deeply ingrained feeling that being down-and-out was somehow morally culpable, that if a man had backbone he wouldn't be in such a fix. Poor people in trouble seldom really know whether having to scrounge for every dime and dollar, and seeing day in and day out the effect going without has on the people they love, causes their drunkenness or running around or madness; or whether, on the other hand, because of their fallenness they squander such chances as may arise and lose all capacity for seizing hold of life.

Not having any answers, and yet, at the same time, proud and used to standing in their own shoes, despising excuses and the shifting of blame more than most people (landlords and others so often using both on them), those tenants for whom the 1960s would be devastating did not take naturally to the notion that there was, finally, nobody in particular responsibile for their losses. That they were the victims of an utterly impersonal concatenation of trends and forces, of history in fact, was not so satisfying an explanation as that somebody somewhere was in charge and had caused the bottom to drop out; there was a secret feeling that everything was their own fault, that if they had but done things differently, if they had been better people and worked harder, they could have turned things around.

It was not that tenants didn't know that conditions over which they had no influence nonetheless shaped their lives; they knew hardly anything else. It was not that other people, landlords of course, didn't sometimes blame them where less partisan observers would have said there was no cause. But tenants knew something else as well, something that made any other consideration irrelevant: they knew that it never mattered what they knew, that they could have as much information as *The News and Observer,* and the right on their side, and if the landlord or the sheriff or the man with money said otherwise, then that was the way it was.

No more than other people did tenants escape the usual ills befalling humanity. Nothing waited for them to get their house in order before overtaking them, neither disease nor transgression, and things they had settled no more stayed settled now than at any other time. Nothing was more hurtful than the expectation that they ought to be able to suffer without being consumed; that nothing was forgivable, not the fact that they could no longer make a living, and not their helplessness and drift once this understanding set in. Some tenants, increasingly fewer and fewer, did stay afloat. Faced with the same economic constrictions as others who buckled and failed, they persevered; a very few managed before they died to rise from tenant to owner.

But my parents and I were like three pieces of paper wadded up in a fist and thrown in the wind. The two other tenant families on the place to which we moved, and with whom we exchanged work during tobacco-barning time, both outnumbered us; thus, there was less saving on the cost of labor than there might have been. My father had to pay the difference between the hours he contributed and the hours seven others worked, as well as the hire of the one extra hand he found he needed. But paying seven people was not so hard as paying the fifteen or eighteen he had had to pay when he had farmed alone and without a harvester, even though wages now were about $1.25 an hour for both men and women; earlier, women had gotten forty or fifty cents an hour, men, sixty or seventy-five cents. Blacks, especially at first when tobacco harvesters were still something of a novelty, were cut out almost entirely: farmers pooled their labor if they had gone together and bought a harvester; otherwise, there would likely be enough white young people in a neighborhood to fill out a crew for those farmers and their families operating alone.

Blacks, if they did not—as nobody did—fully understand what was happening, nonetheless knew that the tobacco harvester was more than simply another way of barning tobacco. Whereas farmers knew only that now eight or ten people could do the work of fifteen to twenty, at less expense and in less time, hands were from the beginning under little illusion that these ponderous machines bode them any good. The feeling ran deep in more than a few white landowners and tenants that blacks were unsuited for working on or around such new and expensive equipment, the setters and combines and tobacco harvesters that now even small farmers thought they had to have in order to stay in business. Blacks, they said, were too slow; they hadn't the sense to keep their wits when the machines broke down, and in their fluster would be apt to do more harm than Rockefeller could afford to make right. Neither tenant nor hand had much capacity for adjusting to the fact that labor so long and intimately familiar to them both had changed. Blacks had sometimes not been entrusted even with tractors; that farmers now looked elsewhere for help, when mechanization was both recent and complex, was therefore not surprising.

There was a certain cachet in working on a harvester, more than there ever had been in working on the ground, and both blacks and whites were quick to sense the difference. Because white crews were small and made up of people who were in and out of each other's houses, if they weren't still in school together, because riding was always better than walking or, worse yet, standing all day in one spot (as women at the barn had to do), work on a harvester now was more evidently an extension of a family's life, and thus had social as well as utilitarian value.[3]

Blacks, too, had enjoyed a similar camaraderie before the harvesters came: white families for whom they had toiled, and who may have worked alongside them, had never had any part in that subtle play of emotion on whose current their words were charged, glance and silence then as eloquent as language. Now, however, none but an occasional hand was ever needed. Yet, for blacks still barning tobacco in the old-fashioned way, and who may have looked up from their work under a shelter and seen a half-dozen white teenagers cutting up in the back of a pickup truck on their way to harvesting in the field, this in the early 1960s when each successive summer brought forth more and more harvesters upon the land, theirs was but the ingrained soul-weariness born of being always the ones done in, left out, and, sooner or later, cast aside. And of the half-grown children in the field, the hazy evening dragging endlessly toward night and the machine bringing the tobacco up to them as relentlessly as if they, too, were steel and ran on gasoline, the day oven-like and no breeze stirring – nothing can be said.

Harvesters helped push the hourly pay for male hands to a dollar or a dollar and a quarter, which provided farmers another reason for not wanting to hire Negroes: if they had to pay a dollar or more anyway, they would pay it to a white man. For the first time even white women and young white people who worked on a harvester got the same or nearly the same pay as men. The machine forced home the realization, grudging as it likely was, that everybody's job was equally essential, and because men and women now labored within a few feet of each other, both riding and neither in the sun, the old feeling that men's work was harder and more onerous than women's, that it mattered more, no longer carried quite the same weight. The truth was that tying tobacco on a harvester, except for the monotony – the dreary sameness – of the conveyer belt bringing the handfuls up to you, was no different from tying tobacco on the ground; croppers, however, no longer having to walk all day bent double under a blistering sun, now sat and rode. Work that had been considered women's, tying tobacco on sticks for curing, remained so; field work had been men's, and men still cropped on the harvesters.

Women still barning tobacco the old way, whether they were black or white, seldom were paid any more than they had always been. Croppers, however, now held out for whatever the going rate for cropping on a harvester was. Black women on a harvester sometimes made no more than if they had been at the tobacco barn.

As much as the cotton gin revolutionized the agriculture of an earlier era, the tobacco harvester single-handedly transformed the growing and production of tobacco in the late 1950s and 1960s. And because tobacco was then, as it is now, the heart and soul of farming in eastern North Carolina,[4] rare was the person left untouched by the machine's influence. Especially were black women and children made the more helpless because of it. If farmers saw their costs go down, their profits rise, once they got a harvester, these people saw a principal means of their livelihood taken from them. No longer did black children have any certainty of working out their keep around a tobacco barn in the summer, with perhaps enough left over for a few clothes when school started. Too small for work on a harvester, and after all but children and unready for the discipline the machine imposed, there was no longer anything in tobacco for them; and their mother or grandmother was no better off. Unless she was either especially young or especially toughened, and, more than this, in the right place at the right time when the few hands still needed (either for a harvester or barning on the ground) were sought out, a job in tobacco would have eluded her. Nor was there any need of saying she could have found something else to do: in the early-to-mid 1960s, by far the majority of black women in the state's eastern counties had only the land and the white woman's house, the occasional café, the cleaning services and laundries, to fall back on.

Yet this isn't quite the whole truth, either. There were farmers without harvesters who gathered crews made up of the old and infirm, of children ten- and twelve- and thirteen-years-old, people who had no other way of living, and drove them mercilessly for perhaps a half or less than half of what hands better situated were paid. Nor were such farmers necessarily tenants.

The machines came so fast that nobody knew, or knows yet, who invented them. By the 1960s, the tobacco harvester was only the most important of many: most important because it affected more people and because farmers were so caught up in the belief that they had to have one, tobacco always taking more time and labor than any other crop. Combines as outsized and cumbersome as dinosaurs, which they somewhat resembled, moved from field to field, one man now able to pick more corn in a day than a drove of hands could break in a week; soybeans, too, were harvested with them. Not many landowners set out pepper or tobacco or sweet potatotes the old way anymore, one person using the transplanter, another dropping the plants, the water toted to them in buckets by a ten- or twelve-year-old kept hopping between the rows as they hollered out to him. Two people on a setter pulled by a tractor now did all that. There were machines on which people rode and picked pepper and cucumbers and squash, and machines later on even for tying tobacco, although these never were widespread. Tractors and all the equipment associated with them, planters and plows and disks, now were more sophisticated: one-row gave way to two-row, then to four-row, which effectively quadrupled the work a man alone was capable of doing.

"If I wanted some money," Ada Martin says, remembering how it was in the early 1950s when she was coming up as a hand on a large farm between Faison and Warsaw, "what I could do was, I'd take myself to the cotton patch or corn . . . we could break corn." But once the machines took over, "they won't nothin' to do no more, 'cept maybe chop," and herbicides soon put a stop to much of that. "They was work, but it won't nothin' reg'lar, not like it used to be. . . . You might could pick some beans."

Tobacco beds, too, still were picked as they had always been, the young plants flat and velvety against the earth, and the women inching along on all fours, pulling up the weeds and grass; such work, however, was soon done, and usually by a man's own family.

It was a religiously-held belief among farmers, one they honored in themselves as much as (or more than) in others, that hard work never hurt anybody; "if it did," they joked with one another, "you and me'd 'a been dead a long time ago!" But farmers were now up against something that work alone couldn't overcome, especially tenants, who stood about as much chance of making the tens of thousands of dollars necessary to buy the equipment they needed as most landlords did getting into heaven. It was one thing to have walked behind a mule ten and twelve hours a day in 1940, when no other farmer plowed any differently, no matter how many acres he had or what he was worth. It was quite another, in 1960, to struggle along, sometimes without even a way of getting back and forth to town, and without any heavy machinery, except a third interest in a tobacco harvester and the same second-hand, one-row Farmall we'd had since 1954. There was only so much borrowing a man could bring himself to do: a riding-setter here, a sprayer there, something else from another place; and a man whose every nickel and dime were already owed knew better than to sign his name again. The most we ever cleared in a year was seven hundred dollars, and that but once, in the early 1950s. More often, we would end up with a couple of hundred dollars, if, as happened increasingly in the 1960s, we didn't actually owe a hundred or so – and then two hundred and three, and then more and more.

Other people, but not many tenants, pushed ahead. Machines, however, separated farmers one from another as they had never been before. There was no way to hide the fact that whereas one man had bought a twenty-five thousand dollar tractor, the tenant just down the road from him had had his tobacco rot in the field because he couldn't pay his hands for another cropping. Of course there had always been rich farmers and poor, but except for those at the furtherest extremes, sharecroppers at one end and landed gentlemen at the other, most country people lived very much alike. Landowners had always had a level of financial security that tenants simply hadn't, money for getting by with, as well as a means of raising money in a crisis, but like tenants they were working people and as worn out as anybody else at supper time. But with increased mechanization, this either changed outright or – just as important – looked to tenants and small landowners as if it had changed: combines, especially, turned their owners into managers and supervisors, farmers who spent as much time in their pickups lining up the next day's work and attending the breakdowns, which were a common occurrence, as actually in the field working. Sons and day laborers were far more apt to be the drivers of the combines and larger tractors than the men making the payments on them.

Tenants had, in the 1950s, been part of a large, rural middle class, cushioned through sheer numbers against the sense that they were any more downtrodden than the next man. Tenant young people compared themselves not so much with those whose fathers owned their own land as with people who lived in town and, therefore, had money: we thought *all* farmers were poorer than town people. In the 1960s, however, this essentially homogeneous, farming class was breaking up, and in some ways a man's interests were as likely to be antagonistic to his neighbor's as private. Land had never before been so crucial. Tenants trying to hang onto the fields they thought of as theirs and the big farmer whose machines devoured more and more acres found themselves, willingly or not, adversaries. Landlords who could make more by renting their land out than they could by keeping tenants could not be blamed for taking the sure profit. Farming was always a gamble, but rent was certain: landlords and farmers who now more than ever needed all the acreage they could get, and who could meet the price of rental, were ready and often eager bedfellows, and tenants seldom were anybody's concern but their own.

In 1959, close to one-third of the farms in the state still were in tenant hands, less than in 1940 to be sure, but yet a significant number; by 1964, however, only about one-fourth any longer were, and by 1969, tenants operated fewer than 20,000 of North Carolina's nearly 120,000 farms. The number of black tenants dropped in this same decade from about 25,000 in 1959 to about 3,500 in 1969.[5]

Moreover, machines were not the only things now separating farmers or coming between landlord and tenant. Federal farm policy itself frequently had a divisive effect. In the simpler days of tenantry, when there were no harvesters or combines and before the large-scale rental of land for which machines were the main impetus, tenant and owner held their livelihoods in common, and each needed the other: the more money the tenant made for the landlord, the more (presumably) he made for himself. By the end of the 1960s, however, tenants had become superfluous, irrelevant both to the new agriculture and, since farming was all they knew, to everything else as well. As iniquitous as tenantry often was, a laid-on paternalism frequently masking the meanest exploitation, there had been some solace in the sense of place tenants possessed: theirs was a necessary occupation, if ignoble, and their value, merely economic as it may have been, was unquestioned. Individuals may have faltered, as men will, but for generations the system held.

When tenantry as a way of life collapsed in the 1960s, ruin was everywhere, but no less absolute and crippling for that. Men and their wives and children were as scarred by the upheaval, as throwed away, as if lightning had struck them. But from lightning they could have taken refuge.

Nothing aided and abetted what happened more than the farm subsidy programs arising out of the New Deal; beginning in the 1930s, the federal commitment to American agriculture proved lasting. The Soil Bank program that Eisenhower and Ezra Taft Benson championed through Congress in the early 1950s had been anticipated in 1933, in the first Agricultural Adjustment Act; then, too, landlords had been expected to share subsidy payments with their tenants, "but noncompliance was seldom punished by local AAA boards, which were themselves dominated by planters."[6] Twenty years hence it was again the planter class, the holders of hundreds and hundreds of acres, gentlemen farmers who of all others were the least likely to suffer privation, profiting most from the federal aid. If the decimation of tenantry was not the purpose of the Soil Bank, it was certainly its effect.

Those who knew nothing of the surpluses such a program was designed to control, the prices it was meant to stabilize, and who may not have cared had they known, found the plan to be, if not a windfall, perhaps the next thing to it. Many farmers of course never participated and, thus, took no land out of production, and many who used the program did so honorably, their tenants (if they had any) getting the payments to which they were entitled. But abuse was rampant, and occasionally inspired, and nobody that we knew ever had much trouble with the law for their chicanery. The most grievous injustice—that whereby tenants had land taken away from them, the landlord putting every crop allowable, and as many acres as he could, in the Soil Bank—wasn't illegal, not exactly. Nothing forbade an owner from dismissing a tenant, and if the next season the fields from which the man and his family had been evicted lay unkept and grown up in cockleburs, the owner collecting handsomely on them nonetheless, who was to be the wiser, much less see to it that the practice was not repeated.[7]

More often, however, a landlord simply kept the tenant's share of the payment or else persuaded him to sign it over, usually as a presumed installment on the debt he invariably owed him. Other and sometimes flagrant abuses arose out of situations where the land in question was rented. Not every landowner took the pains to find out that the Soil Bank would likely have been more profitable to him than outright rental was; corn land, for example, in the early 1960s, rented for as little as ten dollars an acre, whereas the same acreage in the Soil Bank brought about thirty dollars. Elderly owners, especially, and women, as well as farmers who just found it easier to keep on as they were used to doing without getting involved with "the gove'ment," still were apt to rent to a neighbor; then, too, some owners wanted their land to be productive and cared for, rather than left fallow.

"They'd come around once or twice a summer and check on you," a farmer says now of the program he knew in the early 1960s. "You won't supposed to let a field in the Soil Bank be growed up in weeds," but "they won't nothin' done to you if you did. They'd just make you disk it if they caught you."

There was the farmer between Faison and Friendship who rented every available acre a big landowner had for twenty-five hundred dollars and then "the very next damn day," as my father tells the story, put it in the Soil Bank for six thousand dollars, thus clearing a bundle without so much as cranking his tractor—and there was nothing illegal about it. Some farmers, more likely to be owners rather than renters, went ahead and planted land they had already put in the Soil Bank. A well-off landowner on the other side of Faison from us was caught with a field of tobacco on land consigned to the program; but he wasn't alone in the practice. Airplanes, little one- or two-seaters, came in low and circled the outlying fields as we chopped in the spring, their purpose to discover whether or not land in the Soil Bank was indeed barren. Farmers paid fines if a plane found them out, and then they were made to destroy the crop in the field. Discovery, however, was the exception, never the rule.

Tenants whose landlords dealt with them fairly liked the Soil Bank program. The notion of being paid not to work was utterly novel to them, when all their life they had worked and still had nothing, when their labor had never been for payment anyway, but for the prayer of breaking even so that they could embark on the long progress of the next year free from debt. Now, to be offered actual cash money for doing nothing was a temptation not to be resisted. Not many looked far enough ahead to see that down the road, despite their own present advantage, tenants collectively were destined to have their numbers shrink as a result of the plan: no program that made money rather than work the contractual basis of the tenant-landlord relationship could possibly have been in the tenants' permanent interest. That the program was attractive to particular tenants derived from the character of their landlord; any assurance that tenants would be treated fairly proved unenforceable.[8]

There were too many ways a man with his eye on nothing but the dollar could maneuver, and too much money at stake, for tenants to matter. A tenant's value had always been economic, but the kind and quality of his labor were his true currency, the substantiation of his individuality, and in the past this had proved capable of humanizing tenantry. Tenants had been no more interchangeable than landlords. But the money a landlord now got from the Soil Bank (as from renting out his land) depended neither on his own integrity nor that of his tenant; and from that fact alone, much else followed.

A tenant's bond with his landlord was intensely personal, the more so the longer their tenure together. In a hundred ways a year, in matters both trivial and essential, on levels that engaged their deepest feelings and went to the heart of their being, as well as those merely conventional, they faced one another; not necessarily as man to man, but not without the landlord's implicit recognition of the tenant's worth to him, either. Theirs was a trial of will and personality and character, no matter that inherently the deck was stacked, the game rigged. A tenant may have shown himself the superior man and had the satisfaction of knowing that the landlord knew he had, in some fashion still a mystery to him, been bested; the more obvious drift of their conversation, however, was likely to have suggested just the opposite. What seemed to be true or important was not always so; there was often something else equally true and as important just beneath the surface, and coincident with it: the way things looked and the way they really were could be quite different.

Tenants inured to loss, to being beaten down again and again, were still sometimes able to whip a landlord with a quick aside or joke, a story that when looked at another way told him he was not only a crook but a fool. There would be a session with him, the tenant pulling up in his backyard and waiting until the man came to the door and asked him to step inside, or until he came on out and stood there in the yard with him. Then when the tenant got back home, or went into town, he would go over their exchange, adding here, leaving out there, telling it to suit himself. He'd have the landlord down to a "T," the voice and mannerisms, his habits of speech and expression, and while he wasn't apt to lose sight of what they had talked about, his private caricature of the man stood for something, too.

A tenant had no such bond with the federal agencies, the cooperatives administering the farm programs under whose auspices he increasingly, in the 1960s and beyond, came to live. The Production Credit Association, for example, was beyond wit or humor, yet for the tenants using it, Production Credit was a landlord-surrogate, a third-party bureaucracy, which, in making short-term loans to farmers, in fact abrogated an essential function of the landlord.[9] The check that we had envisioned being in our mailbox every month, once we left the Faison place and thus dispensed with the ritual of having always to ask Mr. Isham for the money, was there: one hundred dollars, as regularly as Mama turned over the calendar. My father went to Kenansville and applied for it every year, paying it back mostly out of the tobacco money. For the first time, we weren't much worse off in the winter than we were in the summer.

Production Credit was not new, having been passed in 1933 as an emergency measure to aid farmers during the Depression. We and others were its beneficiaries, especially now in the late 1950s and early 1960s, when the impact of the new agriculture, and of profound social change, was just beginning to be felt in North Carolina's eastern counties. Costs and labor had never been higher, or prices more unpredictable, and without credit nobody could have survived. We were helped by these extensions of credit, but the world was strangely colder and more alien for our owing the government rather than a man. (Literally, we owed the Association, which is a cooperative of its borrowers, not the government, although this difference was lost upon us.)

The bureaucracy, as bureaucracies are, was faceless, not to be thought of when the chips were down; distant, immune to imprecation. For the most awesome debts, the Association was, sometimes, available, and loans could be renegotiated, but for the nagging and continual worries of how to keep body and soul together, Kenansville offered no relief. We seldom saw the new landlord, and, while we knew tenants who would have considered this a blessing, we, for reasons we could not have expressed, felt the absence as a detriment. When he did appear (at tobacco-selling time), nothing in our response to him was natural. He was no more to us than the man who owned the land and by virtue of that, and because now we farmed on halves, got half of all we made. There was between us neither history nor acquaintanceship, and since we owned not him (at least not at first), but Production Credit, there proved to be little means of deepening what was no more than simply a business relationship. Had times been good, probably this would have sufficed; after all, we had left the Faison place, in part, in order to throw off the entanglements of a long association: to begin anew and on a more business-like footing. But times were not good. The last thing we needed, as it turned out, was a new landlord.

Yet, as the 1960s got underway, it is doubtful whether any landlord could have made much difference to us. Farming was now so hard that tenants in general found themselves beyond the help of landlords. Many fell further and further behind and had to borrow more, and from more places, than they ever had before. Some, having taken their pitcher to the landlord's well once too often, took on the finance companies, gambling that when the crop came in they could pay back not just the two or three hundred dollars they had borrowed, but the exorbitant interest it had cost them. Some who borrowed from Production Credit, probably most at one time or another, also had to borrow from their landlord. More than one tenant owed the landlord, Kenansville, Household Finance in Goldsboro, the bank (although tenants and banks were wary of each other), and, on top of everything else, the grocery store and tractor place. More than a few tenants were in the same shape as we eventually came to be in: having to borrow from the landlord in order to pay off Production Credit, so that Production Credit would then lend us the money for another year, during which we would pay the landlord, but again would have to go to him for the last payment to Production Credit; and on and on, until there was no stopping it.

"If it won't for bad luck," as people said, tenants knew they'd "have no luck at all," but they knew, too, or thought they knew, that there would always be another crop, another chance, and that times were so bad already, they were bound to get better.

For us, however, after 1964, there was nothing else. *The Progressive Farmer,* to which we sometimes subscribed, my father had begun to call the "*Poor Grassy Farmer,*" enjoying his play on words, but meaning what he said, and for us, as for countless others, nothing was truer. Still, tenants knew that farming was better than anything else, the only thing, in fact, that a poor man could do and be his own boss. Not even the prospect of almost certain failure changed that; failure that for tenants was a continual presence. Almost without exception, people we knew hung on as long as they could, and longer than reason could have explained, before calling it quits and trying for a job doing something else. Usually it was the wife who first made the break. She would work a regular shift at one of the factories that had sprung up seemingly overnight, then come home and start in on her usual work. A year or so later, typically, the man would follow. He would talk now about having to punch a clock, never seeing the sun in the winter, always having to do what somebody younger than he told him; the woman, however, would say that at least with a public job you could buy the groceries you wanted. Tenants, poor grassy farmers all, understood both points of view; they would not willingly have traded places.

Nobody wants those days to come again, not the heyday of tenantry in the early 1950s and not the years of its decline once everything changed, once the machines came in, in the 1960s. At its best, tenantry still was exploitative; at its worst, it was a kind of slavery. I never lived the worst of it, or anything close to it. For this, as for almost everything else, I have my parents to thank, and other people, men and women whose hard work and fundamental human goodness transcended the lack of money. Scoundrels there were, and we knew them for their meanness, but it is the strength of people that I remember best, the toughness and character. Tenants took satisfaction in the land, and in their own labor, and brought from the earth excellence, as well as tobacco. Never to have attended the fall of night from a chaise-swing in the backyard, work mercifully forgotten, the corn thick behind you, and the voices soft and fine in the darkening, is to have known privation, too.

When the end came, it wasn't people who caused it, but rather an onrushing world so caught up in itself that it never paid anybody any mind who couldn't enter fully into it. Incumbent in progress is, always, loss.[10] But individual suffering knows no comparison, or admits any historical measure, and for the people throwed away by change, left behind, progress is mockery and error and blight upon the soul. Blacks who had seen the harvesters come knew this, and tenants no longer able to survive on the land.

In 1964, once his crop was in, my father left farming never to return. My mother had, in March of the previous year, entered upon a long hospitalization from which she was never to recover or come home. By the time my father left Faison, I had been in college in Greensboro for a year, the scholarship, without which my going would have been unthinkable, having come through. He was tired, hounded by debt, and alone, and there was nothing much to be hoped for anymore. My father's dream lay in ruin around him; mine, although I hardly knew it, had barely begun.

5. "Nothing to Do . . ."

None of us knew then, in the 1960s, that we were a part of the end, that for the few going off to college, as for the many having to look for their first job after high school, life would be an altogether different proposition from that of our parents. Change can be quiet and but vaguely apprehended, as well as tumultuous. No more than anybody else did these children of tenants and small landowners have the means for distinguishing a historical watershed, profound as it was, from the more general and individual uncertainty of those, for the first time, seeking their place in the world. Young men who had never known anything but the land, their schooling like water off a duck's back, and girls still in their teens whose lives were as inseparable from the small frame houses and surrounding fields as their mothers' and grandmothers' had been could no more imagine the future than the young ordinarily can. They could not see that for them, too, the day might come when both land and house, the rows of corn they had chopped and the tobacco they had harvested together, all might either be left behind or sold at auction.

That farms could as effectively disappear as anything else hardly bore thinking; yet tenants, if they had not had to move much themselves, knew of others who had, and small landowners had never been strangers to the prospect of bankruptcy. That the way things had always been might *not* be the way they stayed was, nonetheless, a notion as alien to the old, they with their indefatigable provender of resignation, as to the young. Parents and grandparents had seen worse times than these, not had they forgotten them, and where there was a will, they said tight-lipped, there was a way. Used to being poor, tenants were also used to surviving. If they often didn't have what they wanted to eat or wear, neither did they—if they were of that stable, homogeneous class not much to be differentiated from the small landowner—starve or go naked. Theirs was a determination awesome to behold, and if the past, the tribulation thereof, hadn't beat them, what fear could the present hold? And could not the present, therefore, even the future (when *it* came to mind), somehow be managed? That the hardships in store for the 1960s and 1970s were to be different in kind from those to which tenants and their children were inured was, however, a lesson not long in coming.

For one thing, more and more farm mothers began to take outside jobs in order to help keep their families going. This in itself was not new. Farm families were accustomed to working with and for each other, as well as to picking up other temporary work as it was available. But now the farm mother wasn't to be found at the neighbors' helping in the hog killing, tying tobacco or chopping a few hundred yards down the road, picking beans across the way; she would be stitching blouses and dresses together that had been pre-cut in New York or New Jersey, then shipped to the factory recently opening in the nearby town. When she got off at three-thirty or four o'clock she went home to a house looking just as she had left it that morning, everything she normally had to do in a day's work still awaiting her. The children running in from school, her husband still trying to farm or having taken a factory job himself, they lived now in a household where the unremitting reality of public work had forever altered not just the routine of their lives but also the tenor; neither the woman at the center nor home itself was the same.

Both farm mothers and farm fathers had been physically present in their children's lives; when this was no longer the case, when they both were apt to be out of the house and off the place from early morning until mid-afternoon, children were left unmoored. They may have been in school much of the day themselves, but, nonetheless, young people now were bereft of that solidness of place they had been born into; no longer had they any visual memory of where their parents were during the day, what they were doing. Their mama's work now, their daddy's, was largely inexplicable to them. Conversations widened; both children and adults had to become accustomed to the fact that now there was another significance in a parent's or spouse's life. If farm life had been constrained and insular, the family still was central; work required talk between parents and children, husbands and wives; teaching the young how to work itself implied their essential importance.

Tenant mothers taking up public work undoubtedly improved their

Albert and Vannie Flowers, Linda's grandparents, ca. mid–1930s. (Photo courtesy of Annette Aman.)

The Flowerses, ca. early 1940s: Linda's father with his parents and all seven brothers and sisters. Edward's the one in uniform and everybody's there to see him. Robert's wearing the hat and is the tallest of the three brothers. (Photo courtesy of Fay Darden.)

Grandma Flowers and Fay, ca. late 1940s. (Photo courtesy of Fay Darden.)

Geneva Hollingsworth Lane and Robert Flowers, Easter Sunday, 1939. They were married the next week.

Tenant houses, refurbished and awaiting renters, Faison, N. C., 1989. Robert and Geneva Flowers lived in the house in the foreground in 1941 when it belonged to "Miss" Fannie Faison and sat back in the field against the woods. Both houses have long since been moved. (Photo by Linda Flowers. Courtesy of Will Cottle.)

Above: On the farm, late 1940s. Linda's cousin Darrell and his uncle outside Faison. (Photo courtesy of Helen Flowers.) *Below:* Cousins! Linda's cousins Fay, Frances, and Hampton, ca. late 1940s. (Photo courtesy of Fay Darden.)

children's lives materially, and this mattered. Theirs was not the choice of a more stylish wardrobe over the clothes they already owned, or a house in a more fashionable neighborhood. This first generation making the transition away from the land and into the small factories worked in order to put food on the table, and so they'd have a table. They worked to keep their children in school and so they could dress and be like other children. Their sacrifice was heroic, and deliberate; they knew – nobody better – that what they gained by having a paycheck, they gave up in the splintering of their attention, and that by entering one world they risked losing their authority in another. Farm women had never borne any resemblance to the delicate creatures of Southern myth; the fields they had nurtured were a long way from the verandah at Tara. Ma Joad they would have recognized.

Public work had always been more available in the summer than in any other season, and farm people had sometimes taken advantage of the increased chances then for making a few dollars. Faison, home to North Carolina's largest agricultural market, every summer regularly accommodated not just the local people wanting to work but also tens of dozens of laborers out of Florida and Georgia and South Carolina, people – sometimes whole families – who followed green season north each year. Set amidst hundreds of lush acres of cucumbers, of pepper and squash, beans and tomatoes and cabbage, of potatoes, eggplant, and onions, Faison, self-styled "Garden Spot of the World," was then and still is an important center for the buying and shipment of produce. The market supported both labor and trucking, and the money made off it supported the town.

Area farmers, my father among them, townspeople, and migrants packed cucumbers on the market at night; five cents for topping off a bushel was the going rate in the early 1960s. They graded beans and cucumbers and made perhaps seventy-five cents or a dollar an hour. But always the farmer's own crop was primary; he would work half the night at the market, sometimes into the early dawn, then sleep two or three hours before hitting the tobacco patch. A man took an outside job to try to get out of debt, to make enough on the market to pay his hands for another cropping; he worked to clear up other obligations already incurred or forthcoming. But these jobs were never thought of as permanent, never intended even to be competitive with agriculture, much less supplant it; unlike employment in the factories, such labor was understood as temporary and piecemeal.

Tenants might have talked occasionally of going into public work full-time, but not until the 1960s took their toll did they ever do so in any significant numbers. The migrants they worked alongside at the market may have seemed to them unencumbered; but if area farmers thought sometimes of pulling up stakes and joining the little ragtag bands headed north, taking their chances on the road and living in trailers or cars or improvised campers, very few of them ever did. When these summer people moved on, their ranks were not noticeably increased by farmers having succumbed to any momentary wistfulness, weighed down as they were.

Increasingly in the 1960s and 1970s, however, this pattern whereby farm people worked elsewhere, expressly in order to salvage a crop in the making, changed – radically and forever: by the mid-1960s, the movement away from the land was irreversible. Now, in more and more instances, there was to be no return or working both on the land and off, no sense that, come what may, farming mattered more than anything else. A depleted farm economy practically insured that once a tenant's wife got on at a regular, more or less permanent job, the husband would in short time follow. Two dependable incomes, low as each invariably was, were better than one, and either was more than anybody could count on making in the fields. People who had never done anything but farm, who had never thought of making a living for themselves any other way, and whose connections with the land were presumably indissoluble, found, within a single generation, that such a transition was not simply possible, but likely; desirable, in fact.

Tenants took to public work in greater numbers and on a more permanent basis than did small landowners who, after all, had something more to lose; even so, an owner's wife may have worked for years off the farm, her wages being the difference between keeping a place or having it put up for sale.

Because of the market and the summer jobs it offered, Faison was somewhat better off than many other small towns and communities, at least during the heart of the growing season. Yet opportunity was severely limited, as well as limiting. Except for a handful, primarily those men who owned interest in the market itself, nobody made a year-around living from his association with it. Probably fewer than fifteen or twenty people who actually worked as laborers and lived in or around Faison managed such that their market earnings saw them through all or even most of the winter – and they weren't farmers. Nobody worked at the market with a view toward advancement; except for the owners and a very few others, administrative people for the most part, it wasn't a career.

Men and women may have packed or graded vegetables every summer of their working lives, and they still made the same minimum wage as the person at the belt for the first time; still the same hours were required. Nonetheless, for a town that seemed immune to industry the market was a godsend. Faison offered few job possibilities of any kind, except maybe at the pickle plant; not until 1971 did the town have a single manufacturing firm. The 150 to 300 people the market took on each season throughout the 1950s and 1960s counted themselves lucky, and with good reason.

But something was happening in the 1950s and 1960s without which the move away from farming, which would have occurred in any case, would have assumed a different shape than it did. Expansion in the state's own manufacturing sector, but primarily that by northern and midwestern companies, as well as an occasional relocation by an out-of-state firm (although this was comparatively rare in the eastern counties), coincided exactly with the growing abundance of available and cheap labor, which, if exploited shamelessly, nobody cared: not the state, which did everything possible to promote and advertise the lack of unionization in the area and the right-to-work laws; or the businesses coming in; or, in fact, the workers themselves, as grateful for having a job as they were. The need of one group to survive met head-on with the desire of the other to make a killing. The transition from farm to factory has been aided and abetted by mutually fulfilling, if unequal, imperatives.[1]

In 1940, 33.6 percent of North Carolina's total number of employees were in agriculture (the majority in the eastern part of the state), but by 1979 this figure had plummeted to 3.6 percent.[2] In 1959, there had been 43,000 farms with sales between 2,500 and 5,000 dollars; by 1969, there were fewer than 19,000. (In the same decade, farms with sales between 40,000 and 100,000 dollars increased fourfold.)[3] Where did they go, these tenants and small landowners and hands out of the black communities, who more than any others engaged in agriculture were being squeezed off the land, what did they find to do? For the old and infirm, the ones who couldn't read and write, for those whose efforts to get on as day laborers at another man's farm fell through, or those who for other reasons found themselves unemployable, there was nothing to be done. Aged black women, their grandsons and daughters old enough to leave on their own having gone "up the road," sat on the porch, and when a car passed by, they'd not have even the curiosity to eye it out of sight. Families supported their own, when they could, and the social welfare programs of the 1960s helped those who were able to get themselves signed up.

Others, however, the strong and healthy, the ones better able to meet the expectations of the marketplace, put in applications at one or more of the small factories that, since the 1950s, had begun coming in, seemingly from nowhere,[4] though not in every town or community by a long shot (either then or now). Yet there were enough beginning to be scattered about the countryside that by the mid-1960s they made an appreciable difference in the way many people had come to think about their livelihood. Miserable as they sometimes were, they provided an alternative to farming, and people used to the worry and backbreaking labor of putting in a crop were not daunted by exhausting days now spent at least out of the sun. Some were hardly more than little fly-by-night places where cloth out of the North or the big textile mills of the North Carolina Piedmont was made into piece goods for shipment and sale, ladies' dresses or blouses, children's clothes, men's wear. Women who folded and boxed dresses eight hours a day or else on production, at the sewing factories in Warsaw or Clinton, Wallace, Roseboro, Nashville, would have said that working there was "about like working anywheres else. . . . It don't make no difference." More than one, who as likely as not had left home and got married at fifteen or sixteen, now put her children through high school on the basis of such work.

"It won't the highest paying job," one remembers, "but it was somethin' for women."

This from a woman of fifty-four who worked at a plant in Warsaw for "near 'bout fifteen years," from the mid-1950s through the 1960s, and who knows, as much as anybody can know anything, that such places were "a lifesaver to women. . . . They put a many a piece of bread on the table. We'd punch out some days and come home by dinner. We'd fly on production. They'd have the cloth laid out on the tables, already cut out – they had a cuttin' department – and we'd make the dresses.

"Mary Ann," she adds, naming her daughter-in-law, a waif although in her twenties, "works at one of 'em now, in Garland, but she don't want to learn how to sew. I told her she *better* want to learn how!"

In the 1950s and 1960s, very few manufacturing firms in the rural areas of North Carolina's eastern counties, Duplin, say, up through Halifax, employed more than three hundred people (and most had payrolls of one hundred or less), or required technical training, specialized skills, or much formal education. Except in some of the larger towns, Goldsboro or Clinton, Wilson or Smithfield, Tarboro, Rocky Mount or Roanoke Rapids, no more than a handful were dependent on either heavy or sophisticated mechanization. The most common among them catered to the primary needs of an overwhelmingly agricultural society, as the numerous milling and feed and grain companies still spread throughout the region bear record. There were slaughter houses and meat- and poultry-processing plants, as well as meat and poultry packagers and distributors; lumber and pulpwood mills; furniture companies and cabinet-making places; small machine companies, farm equipment outfits, and construction enterprises; and there were the soft-drink manufacturers and bottlers, without which not many farm people's lives would have been the same, so used were they to the Pepsis and Coca-Colas drunk in the fields of a morning or late afternoon.

There were small textile mills producing dyes and yarns, cord, fibers of all kinds, and fabrics; the fertilizer and cement companies, the clay and brick, stone and glass producers; and in Rocky Mount and Wilson, there were the tobacco-processing companies, at least one of which had been in the business since 1886.

Drugs and chemicals, medical supplies, rubber and plastics, electrical components, power tools and industrial machinery, electronics – not until the late 1960s and early 1970s did the manufacture of these commodities begin to make a dent in the area's economy, and, at that, they tended to be concentrated in or near one of the more industrialized towns, Tarboro or Rocky Mount, perhaps, or Wilson. Firestone in Wilson (1973); Black and Decker (1971), Polylok (1970), and Anaconda (1966) in Tarboro; and Abbott Laboratories in Rocky Mount (1968) in a real sense are still, as they were fifteen and twenty years ago, as remote from Faison and Calypso – from Tin City and Eagle's Nest, Gumberry and Conetoe and Hobgood, Tillery and Weldon, Autreyville and Godwin and Turkey, Pine Level and Four Oaks, Scott's Store and Summerlin's Crossroads, Falkland and Bowdens and Teachy – as, in 1989, the area, taken as a whole, is remote from the high-tech industries of the Research Triangle Park, the diversified productivity of Raleigh and Durham, Charlotte and Greensboro and Winston-Salem.

Few people leaving the farms in the 1950s and early 1960s had, in fact, much choice about the kind of job they eventually wound up doing, or, for that matter, where they worked. For one thing, they often lacked the means for seeking out a job more than thirty miles or so from home; for another, there was sometimes an almost immobilizing hesitation, an unwillingness or incapacity for thinking purposefully, about the prospect of employment beyond one's own town or its immediate neighbors. Small landowners and tenants had "never been anywheres anyway"; their lives had always been governed by the crops they tended and a scarcity of money, and, besides, "people just didn't pick up and go then like they do now." A man resisted the notion of having "to drive up and down the road all day" just to get back and forth to work; he would much rather take whatever was at hand, even if there was the possibility of his doing better elsewhere. A tenant would stay on where he was, maybe farming on the side, or he and the children farming while the wife worked, and then he would get a job, and still the family would stay on until it came time to start another crop; then they might have to move.

Like their forebears filling the mill villages of the Southern Piedmont in the 1920s and 1930s, tenants and other displaced agricultural workers now took comfort in surroundings familiar to them. But the heavy-handed paternalism giving rise to these settlements had, by the 1960s (as so much else definitive of life in the region), disappeared. No company housing awaited the people of my parents' generation then pushed off the land, nor did those moving to town cluster together and live in recognizable plant or factory neighborhoods. The transition was too occasional, too sporadic, for such to occur, and nobody expected a factory to provide its workers with a place to stay. This first generation off the farms kept at least one foot firmly fixed in the same spot as before: people lived on the same place, or near it, in another house in the country, or wherever they could rent in a small town thereabouts. Their children would not be raised in Mayo Mill, for example, or "on" Runnymede, still-thriving mill villages near Tarboro that date from the turn of the century.[5]

The shape that the transition from farm to public work took in the 1960s and beyond differed from that of earlier times: if children in the 1960s whose parents labored at the chicken place, or at the sewing plant or Hamilton-Beach, AP Parts or Lundy's, escaped the ignominy of a stereotyped social inferiority suffered by mill children (not that they did), they missed, also, the solidarity that comes from having one's own turf. More dispersed than mill children had been, having neither neighborhood nor place of their own, they were left far more to themselves, nobody at home waiting for them after school much of the time; nobody in the next house who cared. Mothers at the assembly line all day, who then had the beds to make, supper to fix, and dishes to wash at night, were tired in the evening; they'd have endured the numbing exhaustion utter monotony induces. The pattern of people's lives was such that nobody took up the slack; nobody cushioned the impact. Grandparents typically lived somewhere else, and neighbors stayed within their own confines.

Some people never did adjust to the rigors of public work, particularly men. Farm wives had always lived two lives; the fields were as much their responsibility as the house was. To go to the factory and work there and then have to keep house was in itself, therefore, nothing essentially new to them. But men now found the confinement and rigidity of public work galling; where before they had the open land, the woods and ponds, they now had nothing but walls. Farmers could plow all day if they needed to, or an hour if they chose, but a man with a supervisor over him had to do what he was told, when he was told. Such men, far more than their wives, would have changed jobs; some few moved from plant to plant before taking an early retirement. Children in the 1960s whose fathers had had their livelihoods thus transformed bore a lingering cost.

By the time both man and wife were used to the public work they had taken, close as it was apt to be to where they lived, they would have seen no advantage in moving. Routines had been established; the uncertainty, the dread that they would not be able to find a job at all, would have momentarily calmed. They would have grown accustomed to the house they rented in the country, likely a tenant house, or their new life in town. This was a generation that, except for those least able to adapt (the minority, as it happened), thought long and hard before exchanging one situation for another; a lot had to be wrong before a man or woman moved on to something else.

The feeling throughout the period that "they ain't nothin' to do," which was pervasive, was deepened and lent credence by this pattern of most people staying put. There was, in fact, nothing to do in the smaller towns (and little enough in the larger), and yet it was to the environs surrounding the small towns that displaced farmers and their families looked for jobs. Acutely aware of their limitations, their lack of formal qualifications and sophisitication as employees, they resisted confrontation with what they thought of as alien and superior: better to avoid the chance of rejection than have hope, fledgling enough at best, spent. Even the simplest applications were daunting to people who had trouble reading and writing, or who were middle-aged or older, or who had nothing to show under "Previous Employment" except "housewife" or "farmer"; having to go "hat in hand" and ask for work was hurtful and "made a person uneasy." When they *were* hired, these men and women tended not to be too quick to quit and look for something else, especially since, as all of them knew, there might not be anything else open to them.

Pitiable as area wages were, they were all such people had. In 1959, the median income in, for example, Duplin County was $2,151, making it ninety-third among the state's one hundred counties; 62.6 percent of its families made less than three thousand dollars a year. Neighboring Sampson County ranked eighty-eighth, whereas adjacent Wayne County ranked fifty-fourth. For North Carolina as a whole, 11.6 percent of families earned one thousand dollars or less; only 6.9 percent made ten thousand dollars or more. By 1964, although North Carolina then employed more workers in manufacturing than any other Southern state (but well under a fifth of its workers were in the considerably less industrialized Coastal Plain), it paid them less than any other state in the nation: an average of $1.60 an hour, as compared with $2.58, the national average. In 1979, the average wage of workers in the sewing plants scattered throughout the countryside of, especially, the eastern counties was $3.76 an hour, whereas $4.24 was the national average for the same work. For all workers in manufacturing production, in 1979, the national average was $6.69; in North Carolina, $4.87 – the lowest in the country.[6]

Looking back, however, the remarkable thing, finally, is not how much at loose ends this generation of workers was, but how resilient they were; how much they made their jobs, low as their wages invariably were, count; how unerringly so many of them gravitated into or sought out the places where just their particular skills and interests could best be accommodated; and, above all else, how, in the face of near-overwhelming odds, they took hold of their lives and, as they had never done anything else, kept going. If a native and thoroughgoing insularity held them close to where they were raised and, therefore (from one point of view), narrowed their chances for getting ahead, at the same time they were saved from the heartbreak of invidious comparison, of never being anybody but the worst or having anything but the least; of the self-annihilation that comes sometimes from knowing how bad off you truly are. Throwed away as they were, nobody they thought much of was likely to have been in very different circumstances. Nor were they yet the victims, as their children and grandchildren increasingly would become, of an inflated rhetoric of possibility; consequently, remembering the Depression, those who did, and years of privation thereafter, and not yet corrupted by an acquisitiveness beyond reason and without end, they knew that to be in no worse shape than they were was a balm and a blessing.

A man in his mid-forties, who has been at the same place of employment for twenty-four years, says of his life:

> What choice—in 1958, '59, . . . 1960—what choice did I have? There was the pickle plant, where my brother worked at, and there was Calypso Plywood. They won't nothin' else. . . . These plants you see now, they won't here then. . . . Hell, we didn't have no car. How was I suppose' to get to Goldsboro or some'eres like that to see what they had? I was lucky to get on where I did at. . . . Daddy got sick when I was in the 'leventh grade, and he couldn't work. They won't nothin' else to do but quit school and try to get a job. . . . Yeah, we farmed, but we couldn't keep at it . . . not tenants, not the way things were. . . . Tell you the truth, I didn't care nothin' about school nohow. I was glad not to have to go. Then, too, it won't long before we got married. Daddy and Mama had moved to Mount Olive by then, and when we got married, we lived with 'em. They won't nothin' else we could do.

Beginning jobs at both the pickle plant and the plywood company involved mostly manual labor, and between the two, a young man just starting out might well have seen that he was between a rock and a hard place, especially when he could have had no assurance that either place was hiring at the time he needed the work, or that, if they were hiring, either would want to hire him. The few jobs that came open never went begging for takers.

But a young man who was able to get on at such a place and keep his job was in a position to work himself and his family out of the kind of circumstances in which he had more than likely grown up; he could surpass the standard of living set by his parents. Even if he and his wife both had not finished high school, together they could, in the 1950s and 1960s, still make a reasonably good living. For one thing, they were not competing with anyone very different from them; for another, none of the jobs likely to be available required anything more than what they could offer. If willingness to work was the criterion, they (more often than not) qualified. Nor did education seem to matter; at least the lack of a high-school diploma, other things being equal, was not usually prohibitive. No doubt people who had not graduated felt themselves to be at a disadvantage, but for employment in the plants and factories, personnel officers did not often stick at applicants who had dropped out of school. After all, for rural males in North Carolina in 1950, the median number of school years completed was just 7.2. Nor in the next decade was there significant improvement; the median for rural, white males in 1960 was 7.7 (but for rural, non-white males, a bleak 6.0). The state dropout rate in 1956 was 54.8 per cent. For high-school graduates who never left the area, the future could have seemed no different from that for non-graduates.

The transition away from farming was perhaps hardest on those who had owned farms and lost them. Men and women who had stood in the yard and seen everything they had ever owned in the world sold at public auction could not have entered the labor force with the same feelings as others less encumbered. Some were forced to sell out for a fraction of their land and property's real value; some sold and still had debts in the thousands of dollars above what their farms had brought. At least one man, who in the 1960s lived not far from Faison, lost his farm and home to the same banker who had cut off his credit, thus forcing him into foreclosure. Creditors, the tractor salesmen and farm-suppliers to whom such farmers already owed money and whose pressure for payment had, in many instances, contributed to their bankruptcy, seldom were reluctant to make further sales to them – on credit; they might then sue to collect. Acquaintances and strangers sometimes treated such farmers better than people they had regarded all their life as friends. None would ever live long enough to forget that they, as perhaps their fathers and grandfathers, had once owned the land that now was more alien to them than a foreign country; that the roads on which they now drove back and forth to work ran alongside fields they had once called theirs.

Efforts to cope with such loss encompassed every aspect of their lives. And who was to know what had caused their troubles, whether bad times or a momentary (but oh-so-fateful) lack of attention, or general ingrained improvidence: whether the habits of a whole lifetime had come to one final, awsome ruin, or the culmination of a string of unpredictably grievous luck over merely the last few seasons. If bad times, then how to explain that the fellow down the road had held on, and you hadn't; that others had pulled through, but not you? But if not bad times, then how did a man face his family, those aged uncles and aunts of his father's generation who had seen the land acquired, who knew the estrangements *that* had sometimes caused, and the lives consumed in keeping it; his wife and children, for whom now the future was as shallow as a saucer. Some men faced neither, but receded ever more thoroughly into an inarticulate, impenetrable, pervading silence, for years thereafter as remote from the on-going concerns of their family's daily life together as if they were but guests at the breakfast table, groggy and enclosed, not to be bothered with conversation. Others could talk of nothing else, going over and over every transaction, every turn taken and every one missed, in endless, enthralled subjugation to all the miserable details that had, finally and irrefutably, brought them down.

In 1960, more than 5,300 farms were lost through foreclosure (with tax sales taking close to 1,500 others); in 1965, the figure was 4,375 (and 350 more sold for taxes). Foreclosures dropped considerably in 1972, yet the figure still was more than 1,600, and in 1975 the number of foreclosures rose again, to nearly 2,000.[7] For the state's black landowners, statistics reveal an even more dismal story: from 1954 to 1980, they lost more than 600,000 acres, a decline of 56.8 percent of their land. In 1960 there had been 212,000 farms in North Carolina; in 1980, there were 93,000.[8]

A decade after it happened to him in 1974 or 1975, "some'eres in there," a man out from Faison says (sometimes) that he's "glad of one thing, and that's not to be makin' them payments" anymore, on a corn picker especially, but on other equipment too; and on days in July and August when the temperature hovers in the high nineties, he says (sometimes) that he "don't miss the worry" of "messin' with" tobacco.

The farm, some two hundred acres, had come to him from his father and ultimately from his grandfather, and it was his part of a much larger, plantation-like acreage that had been in the family since well before the turn of the century. Tenant houses on the old homestead, where generations of black (and some white) families had lived, now are all falling in, those that haven't been pushed over and broken up, hauled off to clear a field. The homeplace, empty though still stately and well-maintained, is owned now by a stranger.

But his wife, shaking her head, says that for her part she "just hope[s] nobody else ever has to go through it, . . . not what we did":

> You don't ever know who your friends are until you go through something like this. People stopped coming. . . . And then after they found out that both of us were off from home working, trying to make a living, stuff started getting gone. Rakes, hoes, anything that was setting around. Stuff that we had tried to hang on to, . . . for a garden, or just to have. It was ours.
>
> [One woman] saw me at church the Sunday after this place was sold, and she wanted to know where I was living at now, . . . as much as to say that I'd

> left [my husband] and had moved. I looked her right dead in the eye and said, 'I live at home, where do you live?'
>
> That next spring, we rented land here and there, were going to farm anyway. But that didn't last but a year or two before we saw we just couldn't make it. Not with things like they were. They won't no way. . . . Then [my husband] got out and looked for a job.
>
> He had several jobs . . . first one thing, then another. At the filling station, . . . then he drove a truck before he got on where he is now.

For men of no more than middle age who could do something besides farm, who could drive an eighteen-wheeler or knew something about engines or machinery, the chance of picking up a job, although it might not have paid anything or may have been temporary, was relatively good, at least during the summer ("But you look for somethin' in Feb'ary or jest before Christmas . . . Damn!"); for most, however, an area plant was the only real alternative.

The generation then coming of age, those sons and daughters who, in the mid-to-late 1960s and early 1970s, may have been thirteen or fourteen years old when the farm on which they had been raised was sold, faced a world quite different from the one they had been led to expect. Sons nurtured on no other belief than that one day they would take over and run the family farm now had no farm. Nor did most of them have much of anything else in the way of marketable skills or interests. For many, the first acknowledgment of what had happened to them, wishful as it was—"I'm gonna buy it back . . . one day . . . I can work it out agin!"—had to be let go as the fuller realization set in of just what buying it back meant. Like their fathers, they too had jobs to find. Some rented land on their own and put in a crop or two, even as they were finishing high school; others took whatever was at hand—the local 7-Eleven or Zip-Mart, the Esso station or the log-woods, the Army or some other branch of the service. Girls, if they didn't go off to school or get married (and even, typically, if they did), worked at a mill or plant or clerked in a store; some, never more than a few, became bank tellers or secretaries.

"There I was, just settin' on the side of the road," says a young man who was fifteen when his father's farm was sold at auction in the early 1970s, "and everybody else was goin' off to college or had a job. They were doin' *somethin'*, but I . . . I just waved at 'em goin' by. They thought I had it made, livin' at home and not workin', . . . and I was goin' under for the third time."

He could have had no realistic chance of ever buying back the family farm. He and his peers entering the job market in the 1970s outnumbered the men and women leaving it by about two to one; area young people faced tough times. Not only were more white youth remaining in North Carolina, but also there was beginning to be a reversal of the trend whereby so many black young people left the state seeking a better life in the North.[9] By the mid-to-late 1970s, there were simply more people competing for increasingly fewer jobs; especially hard hit were the eastern counties, where there had always been the highest concentration of rural blacks (as of rural whites), and the fewest opportunities for public work. On the one hand, such plants and factories as had come into the area contributed toward keeping the population stable and intact; on the other hand, almost nowhere did the number of jobs in fact accessible to young people just off the farms keep pace with the actual number looking for work. More even than their parents in the 1960s, youth now were to find time and again that hiring was at a standstill; that gains in employment over recent years were not necessarily going to remain constant, much less increase; that aside from seasonal labor on the farms and at the produce market (and no more than a relative few ever got on at either), if they had no job, they might not—or not for a while—get one. Not until 1988 did unemployment in the area drop significantly.

Tenant sons were of course no better off than the young men whose farms had been sold out from under them. They may never have had any land to have thought about inheriting, but many had never had any other prospect but farming, either; when farming went bust, they were as much without anything to fall back on as the sons of men who had owned land, and like them there was nothing to do but turn to the fast-food places and small businesses, the armed services, the mills and plants. Many did what they could to remain farmers. They rented land or, much less frequently, signed on as tenants themselves once they were on their own, but seldom could they hold out more than a year or two before circumstances forced them into another kind of work.

Three sons of a former tenant in Sampson County, men now in their early thirties, each dealt with the transition differently. No more than boys when, in the early 1960s, their father gave up farming and went to public work (their mother already at the sewing plant), they lived at home for several years, or as long as they were in school, without any fundamental dependence on agriculture although they still helped out sometimes on neighboring farms and lived in the country, no more than a few miles from the place their father had last tended. Of the three, two found ways to stay more or less in farming; the other never had much interest in it. The youngest, now thirty-one, is a day laborer at an agricultural experiment station, a test farm owned and run by the state; having worked here since high school, he seems the least touched by the changes he and his parents and brothers have seen.

After a hitch in the Army the oldest boy worked first at Young Squire in Mount Olive, where he spread material for the making of men's and boys' suits and coats; then at Futorian in Turkey, a maker of reclining chairs, upholstery covers, and the like. Both jobs he found too confining, as well as "hard and boring. It won't nothin' but push, push, push—come here, do this—all day. You couldn't do nothin' else."

It was a matter of a year or two here, then there, of weeks sometimes in between jobs, and of summers when inevitably he would be back helping somebody farm, before he got a chance to farm himself, on contract: for a set wage he farmed another man's land. Unlike tenantry, which contract-farming resembles and into which it can evolve, here the farmer typically gets no share of what the farm makes, but, at the same time, he has little or no financial obligation for producing the crop; some set-ups allow the farmer a share of the profits if they exceed expectations, although he will then have to shoulder more of the costs. For men who spend more time in the woods hunting than with other people, and for whom now a job in a factory seems the equivalent almost of a stretch in the penitentiary, contracting is an attractive, although still uncommon, alternative—even if their wives routinely have to get out and find public jobs in order for the family to make it.

In 1987, however, this son called it quits. Falling out with his landlord and facing up to the more or less penury even of contract farming, he got on at a turkey place in the area—poultry-growing houses and processing plants now, in the late 1980s, as much a lifeline here for people without education as the sewing places had proved to be in the 1960s and 1970s.

But it is the second son whose expectations have been most often disappointed in the marketplace, though not because he hasn't been able to find work. His checkered experience is instructive. From 1972 to 1983, which is to say from when he finished high school at eighteen until he was twenty-nine, he had ten different jobs—not counting various periods when he was without public employment and worked here and there, catch-as-catch-can, on local farms. His story provides an inventory of area jobs and reveals much about the way younger people, those of the first and now second generation off the farms, often look at work.

For six months he was at Hamilton-Beach in Clinton, then for eighteen months at Young Squire in Mount Olive, and from there he went to Faison Manufacturing Company, where for six months he "toted cloth to the women."

Then for five years he worked for the Department of Transportation, the regional office in Clinton, but quit "the day they put me cuttin' ditch banks by myself . . . cleanin' out ditches like a nigger, and it *hot*!" Next, he was at West Point Pepperell in Clinton, eight months; Cook Machine Company in Clinton, five months; Clifton Enterprises in Faison, two months; Futorian in Turkey, a year; Georgia Pacific in Bowdens where he stacked lumber, three months; and, finally, Quinn Wholesale in Warsaw, where for eleven months he was a stock-boy filling orders put in by area grocers. Significantly, the periods of his longest employment – at Young Squire, Futorian, and the Department of Transportation – were spent where, probably, his chance for promotion and job security, insurance and retirement, was best, though a number of his other jobs paid better.

Nonetheless, since 1983 the drift from job to job has continued. Along with weeks and occasionally months of unemployment, he has gone from Cates Pickle Company in Faison, where for two years or so he seemed to have settled down, to his present job at a poultry place in Duplin County. This pattern whereby a man works here and there, picking up and leaving jobs once the routine is learned, the numbing and draining physical labor established, is now quite common.

On the other hand, what is, in fact, most significant here does not lend itself readily to objective measurement. Were this young man not a local person, white, the son of Ed and Letha Oates who used to live on the Cottle place between Faison and Turkey; in short, if he were much different from what he is, an average fellow perfectly familiar (as a type) to every employer he sees, there would be little likelihood of his moving with such relative ease from job to job – not these particular jobs, certainly: an outsider, for that matter even a man with more education, could not have done so. But because the jobs available required little except physical labor, and since his employment history, erratic as it is, may, in some instances, have worked to his advantage, he was frequently hired where another would not have been. Nobody expected more of him, apparently, than the six months or year he was usually willing to give. Employers concerned as much with keeping wages low as with keeping their employees would have found him to their liking. For jobs requiring little training or skill, a high turnover is less costly, in the short run, than maintaining the same workers, with periodic raises and accrued benefits cutting into a company's profits.

This generation was, in any case, less apt to hold on to a first or second or even third job than those people more immediately off the farms had been. They had overcome their parents' dread of being poor, and they had left behind forever the rural sensibility that having public work was cause for gratitude. Jobs were harder to get, and some were beginning to require more education; competition was becoming keener, and yet, at the same time, younger applicants wanted and expected more. Despite the fact that often there was little meaningful difference among the kinds of jobs available to them – or because of it, perhaps – they were unlikely to stick for long with a situation that had gone sour. Farmers and farm wives had, typically, counted themselves lucky to have managed the move away from the land successfully, but their children, most of them never having known serious privation and – increasingly – never having worked before at all, saw in the mills and plants, the Friendly Marts and Super Dollar stores, limitation and duress, not a chance to make something of themselves.

Parents, too, wanted more for them, and, yet, there was nothing else; between this wearying sameness and the pride of life, compromise galled. In light of such a lack of choice, even more schooling sometimes looked good.

By the summer of 1969 I had completed a year of graduate school. As the Trailways bus I took home inched along farther south and east, Ohio and the mountains of the two Virginias, the brick and concrete of the huge university I had just left, seemed scarcely any more to exist – much less *Paradise Lost* or the Anglo-Saxon I had spent months translating. The land flattened out the closer to Faison the bus brought me. I was coming home because it was summer and there was nowhere else to go, and because, also, I needed a job until September. My thinking was that I would stand a better chance in familiar territory than in Columbus where I knew nothing and (outside of a few other graduate students and professors) no one. I knew, too, that the factories at home took on extra people sometimes in the summer; my sister Annie Lou was a line-supervisor at a plant in Clinton that often hired more hands in the summer.

As it happened (but another of the small factories would have been the same), it was at Hamilton-Beach where I and perhaps fifty or so others found ourselves standing around waiting to see if we would be called to work or not; eight o'clock on a June morning, and already sweltering. Applications had been put in a few days before, we had been called, and here we were: women mostly, more black people than white, some young but most middle-aged or older, everybody eyeing everybody else.

Then the personnel man began to call out names, and as the minutes passed and the crowd thinned, as a few were chosen but many still were not, the place and what happened next seared itself in my mind. Talk that until now had been decent and easy died down, and in its stead hung the silence of a customary knowledge as shaped and fully present in the yard as we ourselves. The black woman at my side spoke softly out of the corner of her mouth, she and her friend hugging themselves as hot as it was, muttering without looking up from the ground:

"They sho picking' 'em, ain't they?"
"Umph."

Their words were tight and resigned, and it was only then that I noticed what was happening: the whites were all being called first, no more than two or three of the blacks having gotten the nod. And I knew that when my own name was shouted out I would answer to it, no questions asked, as if no wrong had been enacted and nothing to be remembered had occurred.

And there was the summer five years earlier when I had known that in the fall I'd not be going back to Greensboro, that because I had failed this course and that my freshman year (or had come close to doing so), the scholarship with which I had been honored had not been renewed. The man in our living room had said, speaking to my father as if I were not there, "Most of 'em that quit, they don't never go back." Try as I did to make the words go away, I knew them to be true.

That was the June I had left Faison on the bus headed for Raleigh, there being no thought of looking for a job closer to home; summer work was one thing, but the prospect of permanent employment was something else. Especially was there nothing at all for women in the small towns. I had worked a summer on the market pasting labels on bushel baskets, as well as (the summer after high-school graduation) at the pickle plant, where if we had the cucumbers the line would run deep into the night. (We'd get out just before the birds started up, in that last full darkness before light, and the parked cars and pickups, the produce trucks loaded and waiting to pull out, would be as wet with dew as if it had rained, and the air cool and damp.) But not many temporary workers stayed on after green season. All of us knew that there were women in the canning room who had been there for twenty and twenty-five years, as had some of the men who worked the vats and stacked, and that they'd not be quitting; younger workers hadn't much of a chance displacing anybody, and the number of new full-time employees was always low.

Finding a job even in Raleigh was no piece of cake. Waiting rooms and personnel offices were full of girls eager to be secretaries or clerks, many of them with business experience or training. Raleigh was a magnet for young people from outlying farms and small towns, as I was quickly to discover. The rooming house on Blount Street where I stayed for ten dollars a week was one of several in the area near Peace College; almost without exception, occupants were girls like me – young, single, and dependent on the city for our first real job. We slept two or three to a room and were out of the house from before eight until after five; kitchen, bathroom, and the all-important telephone were communal. Most of us worked, once we did latch on to something, for nothing else so much as to get an apartment, a move that usually required at least one roommate, if not two. Yet the house was clean and comfortable enough, the girls a motley crew; life was sufficiently interesting, the group supportive. We were all too poor to be truly in debt, and thus what money we had was, in fact, ours.

There was Rita who had an office at the Capitol; the only college graduate among us, she came from a farm in Gates County. Her father didn't buy anything on credit, she told us, not even a tractor or car. She had a Ford Fairlane he had given her, which as far as we were concerned – we who had either to walk or take the bus – proved his point. Mickey, who at last got work with an insurance company, was from Enfield, and her father was a pharmacist. Ruby came from a tenant farm near Tabor City and was a secretary for the Red Cross. There was a child-like girl from a farm near Louisburg who almost never left her room and, for the year I lived in the house anyway, was without work; we slipped her money from time to time, and, little as it was, it may have been all she had. Kathy was a receptionist at a used-car lot. Four girls from Goldsboro were telephone operators.

Annette, who was taking a business course at King's, had a husband in Central Prison and a boyfriend who drove a white Cadillac – a match for the one his wife had. Annette's parents lived in Raleigh and kept her two children. She knew the projectionist at the Ambassador Theater, and when we trooped downtown with her, he would let us all in free. Once we went to her parents' home where she played the piano and we sang hymns.

The forty dollars I had after I paid my first week's rent lasted a good while, but it had to be replenished by dribs and drabs from my father before, in August finally, Branch Banking and Trust Company hired me as a clerk in the transit department for 220 dollars a month. For most of June and all of July, however, I had walked the soles out of my shoes following the want ads, most of which led to jobs that were nothing like they had been made to sound – when, that is, they existed at all. There was a public library on Fayetteville Street that, as the weeks went by and still there was no job in sight, I sat in and read; lunch counters and diners were more interesting, but they took money to frequent, and at least in the library nobody looked very successful. Books, the way they looked and felt, were more familiar and certainly more comforting than the streets; parallels could be found in them to my own situation. I knew the ones to read.

(I had not then discovered Alfred Kazin's *A Walker in the City,* but when I fell upon it some years later it was with instant and total recognition. For this summer of 1964, it was the American expatriots that drew me – not so much their works, as their lives, as books and essays about them. If Paris was infinitely more alluring than Raleigh, still Raleigh was a city too, and for a young girl on her own there and without a job, enamored of books, nothing was easier than falling under the spell of this "lost generation.")

Meanwhile I had registered with an employment agency, and it was through an interview it set up that I was finally hired – at a cost of ninety dollars, half of what I cleared in my first monthly check. But college seemed far away, more an impossibility now than ever it had been before.

6. ". . . But Go to School"

Young people in eastern North Carolina in whose mind the notion of going to college had never before entered found themselves during the mid-to-late 1960s reckoning with the possibility that for them, too, high school need not be the end of formal education. The kinds of students who had always gone to college still went, and in ever-increasing numbers; now, however, they were joined there by the sons and daughters of tenants and small landowners, laborers and clerks, of the out-of-work and the down-and-out, of black also, now. Or if they were not so much joined *there,* at Carolina and Duke, Davidson and Meredith, at what everybody still called WC,[1] then at one of the community colleges or technical schools then beginning to spring up. Nothing was more fortuitous than the General Assembly's authorization, in 1957, for the establishment of industrial centers throughout the state, out of which was to emerge, in 1963, a Department of Community Colleges under the State Board of Education.

Especially in the eastern counties where employment for everybody was precarious; where, in pockets, poverty was endemic; where the children of the poor very rarely went away to college or, if they did, seldom came back afterward, here a community college or technical school was a godsend. Everybody knew that an education was "somethin' nobody can't take away from you," but as the period unfurled, a year or two at James Sprunt or Wayne Community, Nash Tech or Sampson was apt to be looked upon as an alternative even to the willful capriciousness of life: to the new agriculture undermining the chances of hands and tenants to make a go of things; to the public work that sometimes was but another form of servitude, the plants and assembly lines that workers were beginning to realize "ain't all they're cracked up to be." As the 1970s got underway, an associate degree came to embody the hopes and aspirations of young people for whose parents and grandparents "the colleges" had ever belonged to somebody else.

This was a generation that wanted more than it had, more than its parents had had, more than most of its own members could reasonably ever expect to have, especially if between high school and the factory lay but a last summer's momentary lull. Pay in area plants seldom exceeded the minimum wage; in the slaughter houses, dime stores, machine shops, and in some offices and banks, it may have been less; and as for moving up, being promoted, none but a few ever were. For young people impatient to get on, who in high school had gloried in a recognition their parents had never had the time to acquire—playing ball, going out for this or that, cheerleading—and that they would likely never see again, the labor awaiting them could only have seemed an abyss into which they were powerless to keep from falling.

The boy whose job now at the pickle plant was sometimes no more than putting nuts and washers on bolts, the boxes in front of him, he sitting on a turned-up bean basket, yet who but a few weeks before had run under the lights to the cheers of a crowd, what could he have thought had happened to his life? Or the girl on the line at the appliance factory, did she ask herself before the whistle finally blew, the belt of mixers stopping—in each mixer she may only have tightened a screw, wrapped a wire—did she ask how she had come to be there? The fact that people without jobs, middle-aged as well as young, would eagerly have traded places with them, and their knowing this was true, couldn't have mattered much on ceaseless afternoons after the talk died down and they no longer heard even the roar of the place. Come August or September, school may again have seemed worthwhile.

In 1954, nearly forty percent of the state's public high-school graduates continued their education at a college or trade school or by entering a nursing program or going to business school. By the end of the 1960s, this figure had risen dramatically, to nearly sixty percent. Throughout the era, however, considerably fewer students in rural areas than in urban sought additional schooling; "Down East," certainly, attendance was lower than for North Carolina as a whole. In Halifax, Edgecombe, and Johnston counties, in 1954, less than thirty percent of all high-school graduates entered college; in Nash, Wilson, Wayne, and Sampson counties, less than twenty percent of all black students then went to college, although in Nash County over forty percent, and in Wayne, Wilson, Sampson, and Duplin, between thirty and thirty-nine percent of the white graduates went to college.[2] For both races—though everywhere the difference was stark—the educational boom years were the mid-to-late 1960s: a national phenomenon. From 1964 to 1970, the percentage of all of North Carolina's high-school graduates going off to school increased by about eleven points (from 48 percent to 58.9 percent), whereas the increase between 1970 and 1980 was less than four points (from 58.96 percent to 62.3 percent).

But it was in the 1960s that for the first time the impact of massive amounts of federal aid to education began to be felt. Congress, having rejected comparable measures in bill after bill during the 1940s and 1950s,[3] passed finally, in 1958, the National Defense Education Act; the Russian Sputnik of the previous year accomplishing what nothing else had.[4] There was, as a result, an availability of money for academic purposes such as the nation's students had never before seen, short-lived as some of it proved to be. Influxes of federal money into the schools themselves, and at all levels, most of it for the sciences, trailed such strings that in the next decades government and education would be wary partners in an increasingly uneasy alliance, but for the students of the period nothing could have been more advantageous.

Money alone, however, would have been insufficient; crucial as financial access was, legal access was even more fundamental. Without the Civil Rights Act of 1964, which put teeth into the Justice Department's capacity to combat discrimination in the public arena, education being a primary beneficiary, many students would have found the doors slammed on them no matter how much money they had. Blacks and other minorities, as well as women, gained an unprecedented access to colleges and universities, technical schools and trade schools and public institutions of every kind, as well as to federal loans and grants.

This isn't the place to document all the ways in which the 1960s changed us. It will be enough to say that at no level did education remain untouched by the aspirations the decade unleashed; possibility was in the air. For hundreds of thousands of the poor, people ordinarily as closed off to public sentiment as to political action, the dream of living more decently may have seemed capable of, if not fulfillment exactly, at least its approximation. Misery was still misery, but poverty had had war declared on it. Especially did the young enlist in VISTA and the Peace Corps, and the symbolic nature of their doing so far outshone either their actual number or eventual success. People who had never before thought of themselves as part of the national life, for whom history had always been the province of other people, awakened to a new sense of what their place in the world, in their neighborhoods, and even in their homes might be. This feeling of being connected with what's out there, such that a person's place, where he lives and works (*if* he works), is an arena in which his enlarged sense of self may be defined: nobody was more fully responsive to such an excitement, momentary though it was, than the poor. Political consciousness then meant that you knew your own struggle for the redress of a racial or economic, or, later, sexist grievance was also, and inherently, a struggle for historical redress of profound dimension. Not just for civil rights did men and women and children march, and live in Resurrection City, or not for civil rights alone: at stake was the nation's capacity for empathy and shame, the government's will to act.

The same rhetoric galvanized us all, the same pictures in *Life* and on television; if we were attentive and cared. Kennedy's inaugural ("Ask not what your country . . ."), Martin Luther King's evocation of the promised land, as if it lay just barely beyond our outstretched hands, close enough in fact for our effort to reach it not to seem absurd; the plain and sometimes splendid speech of simple people who, in the crucible of their pain, shaped the heart's utterance—at Montgomery and Selma and Birmingham, all over the South, words stung into being a new era.

Eastern North Carolina white people, however, were as immune to such promise as they were everywhere shaken by the turmoil accompanying it; the white poor, and certainly tenants, believed as thoroughly in segregation as their betters. Children of the farm, the plant, or the factory may have had no more use for Kennedy than for King, whose speeches, even if they heard them, wouldn't have moved them. Twelve years of sitting in schoolrooms they'd likely not taken personally; as the 1960s rolled on, however, they might nonetheless have been affected in ways unknown to them (and against their will had they known) by the times in which they lived. Even they might sometimes have driven more slowly home from the field, the mill, the factory, the notion opening within them that they were due more than they were getting; that there ought to be something else.

Passing one of the many technical schools in the area or a community college, the buildings having gone up almost overnight it would have seemed, off a bypass or in the country skirting a small town—Kenansville, say, Weldon or Smithfield—a boy might have wondered if he could handle school again; if it would make any difference in the long run even if he could. A few years earlier and the school wouldn't have been there; a few years earlier and the boy would have had no capacity for imagining himself a part of it, had it been. Nor his sister, either.

For them to think now of going, the school of course was necessary, but of equal importance was that the repercussions of idealism had had time to set in; by the late 1960s, the imperviousness of institutions had been forever cracked. Just how vulnerable colleges were had by then become plain, the evening news bringing campus demonstrations and protests, and hence "the colleges" themselves, into everybody's sitting room. A college was no longer off limits. Moreover, so many young people were now going to college that even the ones who weren't knew others who were, knew *them,* this is to say, not merely *of* them. Especially accessible was the technical school or community college just down the road or in the adjoining county. Moreover, open admission and cut-rate fees insured that neither poverty nor previous academic record would, ordinarily, keep out those wanting to go. Blue-collar people and tenants, black and white, cared about education too. That these parents wanted for their sons and daughters the same chance in life as the children of affluence enjoyed is amply demonstrated, if proof is needed, in more ways than one.

"I want her to learn *something,*" such a mother might have said of a daughter about to graduate from high school. ". . . Not just jump off here and get married. She'll be married all her life!"

"He can do just as good by going to Wayne Community," she'd have said of a son. "That way, he can stay at home and not have to pay out all that money just to live."

Ever-rising enrollments well bear out such attitudes. In 1969, more than forty thousand students across North Carolina were enrolled full-time in the Community College System, and thousands more picked up what courses they could, perhaps at night or, their employer willing, a couple of hours or so a week. In just ten years, from 1969 to 1979, full-time enrollment shot up threefold; in 1983, nearly 130,000 students were engaged in full-time study. Of all the state's high-school graduates from 1980 through 1983, some twenty-three percent opted for a community college or technical school.[5]

What were they like, these students who, in all probability, were the first in their families to go to college or, often enough, the first to receive their high-school diploma? A 1969 survey of 11,184 of them, representative of forty-two community colleges and technical schools, provides what probably is still the most comprehensive statistical study for the period.[6] Its figures are illuminating. For one thing, more than eighty-five percent were white, only about twelve percent black; this in a state where, in 1970, blacks comprised 22.2 percent of the population. Over sixty percent were products of either the general or the vocational track in high school. More than two-thirds were men. Over sixty percent of their fathers hadn't gone as far as the twelfth grade; neither had about fifty-four percent of their mothers. More than a third of their parents earned less than five thousand dollars a year; about a fourth earned less than four thousand dollars. Over half of the students surveyed worked either full- or part-time. In age, they ranged from seventeen to over fifty; nearly three-fourths, however, were between eighteen and twenty-two.

Thirty percent reported that if the school they then attended hadn't been there, they would not have gone to college at all. What may seem a surprisingly high number of them—thirty-eight percent—said they planned to enter a four-year college and work toward a degree once they finished their current program.

But pride isn't quantifiable, and neither is the financial sacrifice that going to college may have entailed, despite its low cost and its convenient location. People on the job who had been in the same spot longer than by rights they should have been, clerks and managers and secretaries, knew that if ever they were to move up, they would likely have to demonstrate improvement in (say) grammar, in what is now called "communication skills." Mechanics, technicians, junior-grade laboratory assistants, machinists: if they could get more sophisticated training, perhaps they would not be held back or let go. It wasn't, therefore, only the young person just out of high school or the dropout who looked to such schools for a way out of a predicament, as it is not today. For the older, more experienced worker seeking advancement or increased job security, as well as the person without a job who wants to be more employable, an associate degree may be the answer. Employers, knowing that specific job training is frequently available, neither have to accept whoever turns up nor to retrain employees they can do better by replacing; competition, this is to say, is at a higher and more intense level than it once was.

The cycle is familiar, though no less distressing for that. More heated competition for jobs makes education that much more essential, but because enrollments in the 1960s kept rising, more and more people gained the credentials for intitial employment. This being true, because now enrolling at the technical school or community college is so typical, many graduates inevitably find that jobs in their field still are elusive. Unlike their counterparts going away to the four-year college or university, many of whom never return to the area, the overwhelming tendency of these students is to stay as close to home as possible. One result is that often they must necessarily continue their education; they pick up another course, enroll in another program. Hence the thinking of that thirty-eight percent surveyed in 1969 who indicated they would likely seek additional schooling.

There was the growing realization in the 1960s and 1970s that mere willingness to work wasn't going to suffice anymore; that a young person needed all the particular training he could get to make a decent life. Especially if their parents had owned farms did young people discover they weren't likely to make any better of a living themselves, that they might not do nearly as well. To be locked into a low-paying, seldom secure, always precarious job or series of jobs was becoming the average case of the average person in the area, young or not. But what may have been more disheartening, as the 1970s got underway, was the realization, also, that graduation from a college was by no means a guarantee of economic security.[7]

Particularly if the graduate stayed in the area, he or she may have had as little choice about where they worked as the high-school graduate two or three years their junior; they would have been competing with older men and (increasingly) women who could offer work experience, dropouts who would take less, and professionals with considerably more education than they, people who had found that their degree, sometimes an advanced degree, was worth more in the rural areas than in Raleigh or Chapel Hill where everybody, it might have seemed, was similarly equipped.

At least one survey of the time, a 1972 questionnaire returned by forty-three graduates of an area technical school—a small sampling, to be sure—suggests just how bleak the outlook could be. Eight of the forty-three surveyed reported incomes of less than eighty dollars a week, and more than half (fifty-five percent) earned less than a hundred dollars a week. Fourteen percent had a weekly income higher than $120. Moreover, more than a fourth (twenty-seven percent) had jobs "not related at all" to the training they had received in college, and—the most telling detail of all—fifteen percent worked at *two* jobs. (Yet the author says that probably her findings are biased in favor of the more fortunate graduates. "This is indicated," she writes, "by the percentage employed [91%], those who feel that their present jobs were directly related to their training . . .[73%], and those who believed that their training . . . was necessary to getting and keeping their present job" [56%].)

The two older sons in a Duplin County family, boys who grew up with no other thought than that the farm where they lived, which their father had inherited, would one day be theirs, found out the difference losing a farm can make, yet they've done remarkably well. Interests that likely would have gone unnurtured had the farm remained in the family were, instead, encouraged, a life's work for the older emerging out of a boyhood fascination with electricity. Upon graduation from high school, Michael in 1977 and Timmy in 1983, they went to Wayne Community College in Goldsboro. Michael then went to James Sprunt Technical College in Kenansville, and Timmy took a course at Sampson Tech in Clinton. Their mother tells the story:

> Michael took Electrical Engineering Technology and got his associate degree. He'd always, ever since he was little, been interested in 'lectricity. He told us he might not never do nothing with it, . . . but he wanted to learn about it. He went the whole two years and then an extra quarter . . . there was something he still needed, that he had to pick up. Then he got the job at Whiteville with that 'lectric company, but in . . . 1980, I reckon it was . . . when it just went ka-fluey, and the economy went bad, he got . . . not laid off, but they had him doing something else for less pay, and he just couldn't live down there anymore on what he was getting. So he came on back home and took Electrical Installation and Maintenance at James Sprunt for a year and got his diploma there. That was just a diploma program.
>
> CP and L [Carolina Power and Light Company] hired him as an electrician two or three months before he finished at James Sprunt. They were waiting for him when he did get out. He's been at Southport about three years now, and he likes it, I think, real well.

As for Timmy, Mrs. Moore says that he will "have an associate degree from Wayne Community when he finishes up the course he's taking now at Sampson Tech:

> His is in Electronic Data Processing. I don't know just what, but they was a course at Wayne Community he needed . . . communications and writing, or something like that . . . and he didn't pre-register, and so he got closed out of it. That's why now [in 1985] he's going two nights a week over to Clinton. He'll transfer that course back to Wayne Community and get his degree that way.

Mrs. Moore remembers a good many things about the boys' academic preparation for college; her conviction is firm that without Wayne Community (or a college like it) they couldn't have gone.

> Neither one of 'em had to take any remedial work at Wayne Community, although I know a lot of them that do. But they were lucky . . . Michael got put in the high math. But they won't no electronics taught at Coastal Plains, like it is at some big high schools, and so all the lab work, the hands-on experience, was new for him when he got to it.
>
> They both had real good grades, but Timmy had to dig harder for his than Michael did. It was easy for Michael when he got to James Sprunt. He'd already had a lot of the work at Wayne Community. He made a four-point every quarter he was there and was on the President's List.
>
> Timmy'd study every night . . . three hours a lot of the time, and stay at school too, in the evenings, to work in the library.
>
> Michael, when he was at Wayne Community, would come home and say that the servicemen from the base [Seymour Johnson Air Force Base] would help him in lab and he'd help them on the bookwork. A lot of retired service people—I reckon they're retired—anyway, they go out to the College and take things like electronics, and Michael said they found the labs easy, but it was just the other way around with him.

About the prospects for employment now, in 1985, Mrs. Moore says that "they's still a lot to be desired . . . here in eastern North Carolina." Young people, she adds, "have got to branch out and get away from their roots" if they expect to find the job they want. "They still needs to be a whole lot more [job openings]. . . . I believe it'd be harder for a girl." Mrs. Moore continues:

> A course now, the girls do the same things as the boys, . . . but I believe they's still sometimes some . . . they can't *say* so, but I believe a lot of people'd still rather hire a boy. There's fifty or more 'lectricians where Michael works, but they're all men.

"They still ain't a whole lot of jobs around . . . not here in Duplin County. . . . It used to be that people, even if they were middle class, had to be motivated to go to college. Maybe ten percent would go when you came along," Mrs. Moore tells me, referring to the early 1960s, "but nowadays it ain't like that. You just about have to go somewhere now.

"Timmy wanted to go to State, but I told him . . . I didn't say nothing much one way or the other . . . but he liked it at Wayne Community, and he likes it at Sampson Tech. I believe he likes Clinton better."

Students like Michael and Timmy, however, are the exception. There are thousands of others each year who leave the Community College System without completing their program; thousands more whose performance is, at best, marginal. Retention, of course, isn't a problem confined to the technical schools and community colleges, any more than are ill-prepared or uninterested students; however, because the System was created for the purpose of reaching just such students, it attracts more of them than most senior colleges.[8] From the beginning, its students have tended to be average or below, the superior student going to the more traditional four-year school. (Superior students who came along before the Community College System got off the ground, and before there was much scholarship or loan money available, if they happened also to be poor, simply got left out. A woman with as good a mind as anybody, who was a first-rate student at Faison High School in the early 1950s, and denied college only because there was no money for it, says, remembering how it was then, "If James Sprunt had been going when I got out of school, I could have gone. I know I could, when I worked at Kenansville.")

The difficulty some have of finding work even after graduating is suggested by a second 1970s survey. Forty-four of the 1974 and 1975 graduates of an eastern North Carolina technical school, again a very small sample, responded. The average age of the group was 24.8 years. Fifty percent had found full-time employment, yet nearly forty percent worked outside their professional field. Fourteen percent reported that a job in their speciality wasn't available. Eleven percent said their college training wasn't "helpful at all" to them. "Significantly more white (fifty-five percent) than black (thirty-eight percent)," the author concludes, "and female (fifty-eight percent) than male (thirty-one percent) found a job in [their] field." (I assume that women graduates in nursing account for the higher figure here, the town having a hospital.) Of those employed either full- or part-time, thirty-one percent of the blacks and nineteen percent of the whites earned between 51 and 100 dollars a week. Forty percent of the respondents earned between 101 and 200 dollars. Twenty percent said they planned to enroll in college or in another training program within the year, and forty-three percent indicated they were uncertain about whether or not they would continue their education.

A more substantive study, however, was conducted for 1977 through 1983 at yet a third area technical college; some 420 graduates from the seven graduating classes responded. Based on a five-year average, about eighty percent of the graduates were employed full-time; of these, eighty-five percent still were also going to school. Of this same eighty percent employed full-time, however, nearly forty-six percent were already working in their present occupation before ever attending college, and this number increased to more than half in 1981 and 1982, then dropped to about forty-three percent in 1983. The school's true bearing on a graduate's chance for new or initial employment was considerably less significant, therefore, than at first glance we may think. Not eighty percent, but more nearly thirty-four percent of its graduates may have been hired as a direct result of having attended college. Moreover, in 1979 and 1982, nearly a fourth of those working said that their present job wasn't related to their college training. From 1977 through 1983, nearly thirty-eight percent reported gross monthly earnings of more than a thousand dollars, but about forty-six percent earned between 600 and 999 dollars a month. Sixteen percent had gross incomes of five hundred dollars or less a month.

A computer listing of more than five hundred students tracked by an area community college in 1985 is here instructive. Of the 462 who reported their income, more than two-thirds (341) earned five dollars or less per hour; just sixty-seven men and only twenty-two women reported earning more than five dollars. Two men said they earned fifteen dollars, the highest hourly rate reported; ten dollars an hour was the most a woman earned, and just one woman earned that. Of the two men earning fifteen dollars, one was self-employed, the nature of his work not given; the other worked in electrical maintenance for General Electric. The woman making ten dollars described her work as "Self Employed/ Cleaning Service." Northern Telecommunications, UPS, GoldTex, the Air Force, Buehler Products, and CP and L were the employers reportedly paying at the top of the scale, eight to twelve dollars an hour; graduates in sales, automotive especially, and in health care made about the same. In North Carolina as a whole, in December 1986, manufacturing wages averaged $7.01 per hour; only in Mississippi was the average lower.

For the early 1980s, the definitive survey is that of students who left the Community College System during the 1979–80 school year; the largest study "of its kind . . . in the United States," with 24,441 responding.[9] Students polled include those in all the curricular programs except General Education – a significant omission – and College Transfer. Findings are remarkably corroborative of earlier, more piecemeal studies.

More than four-fifths of the more than seventy-seven percent then employed had been employed prior to enrolling in college, and "almost one-half of these were in similar work." The average salary of all respondents was $6.18 an hour; of graduates, $6.01 and of dropouts, $6.31. ("Dropouts" likely included the mid-level manager picking up a course or two, as well as the student leaving school without completing his intended program. So many students enroll just for particular courses that the distinction blurs between them and the traditional dropout; typically, not even the schools themselves separate the two.)

Yet these students revealed a very high rate of satisfaction with the school they had attended; just four percent thought their "occupational training below average." Also, "more than half the students who attended and more than seventy percent of the graduates said [their] training . . . [was] related to their present occupation. Nearly eighty percent are meeting their objectives," yet, of those not meeting their objectives, "less than five percent indicated dissatisfaction with the institution."

"Early leavers and dropouts reported lack of qualifications as a major reason for training not being related to their job," the study concludes, "while graduates cited lack of jobs in their field as their major reason for unrelated jobs." The "most prevalent job codes were secretary, registered nurse, wholesale and retail trades supervisor, production work supervisor, licensed practical nurse, teacher aide, bookkeeping and accounting clerk and auditing clerk, general office work, and machine operator and tender."

But such surveys are to be read with caution. Here, for example, a fifty percent rate of employment doesn't mean, necessarily, that the true unemployment rate is fifty percent also. Graduates not considered as employed may have gone on for further schooling or married and left the job market, or no longer sought work for other reasons. The really throwed away don't much respond to follow-up studies asking how well they're doing any more than do those whose whole life in schoolhouses hasn't yet enabled them to read and write; the studies aren't fully representative.

Institutional surveys do not ordinarily cover students in special programs, particularly programs under the umbrella of the college but officially not a part of the curriculum. Many people enroll part-time or take courses for no academic credit, and they aren't usually considered either. Such chronically unemployed people as those enrolled in HRD programs (Human Resources Development) typically fall between the cracks, yet the number of these surpassed thirty-two thousand statewide from 1973 to 1982. *Their* average individual earnings throughout the 1970s and into the 1980s was under twenty-five hundred dollars a year.[10] Nor are people who have completed or dropped out of GED programs (high-school equivalency), learning-resource programs, and the like routinely included.

The point isn't that schools in the Community College System are inferior or that employment coordinators don't do all they can to place their graduates, but that as the 1970s came to a close, work was hard to come by. Finding the job you want has never been easy "Down East"; changes since the 1960s, the revolution in farming that has forced large numbers of people off the land and into public work, exacerbated a situation that was never good. For many people, aging hands and tenants and their children and grandchildren, educational and personal deficiencies may still be of such magnitude as to make life itself tenuous, even problematic, employment precarious. For some, a two-year program may be undertaken more to fill the time between high school and the reality of embarking on an adulthood of public assistance or low-skill, low-wage labor than, in fact, for actually preparing themselves to go out and snare something else. For the young the gap between what employment counselors and high-school teachers are asked to do and what anybody at this juncture *can* do is frequently so wide as to make the usual rhetoric defining effort and success sound empty as a drum.

And, above all else, there is the continuing fact of pitifully low wages: the pattern emerging in the late 1980s is that unemployment may be less the probelm than wages falling considerably below national norms. Analysts are seeing another kind of poverty; people are working, many at more than one job, and still not making ends meet.[11] What difference the community college system will here be able to make remains to be seen.

Students arrive in the System (not the Michaels and Timmys but others whose mothers also have stories to tell), their aspirations shriveled by – what? – lifetimes of inadequate housing, poor nutrition, hit-or-miss health care; by previous schooling that had no more effect on them than if it had been a television running continuously, on and on and on, the house empty, the family off somewhere else. Asked what she wants to become, *to do*, a girl in a sociology class sits on the teacher's desk and swings her legs, her jeans thin and sweater on wrong-side out, and she says she wants to be a secretary, "the boss's boss . . . the one that tells him what to do, who to see, where he has to go. . . ." They complete a program in, say, Criminal Justice, and get a job in a snack bar; in Cosmetology, and wind up at the mill; in Accounting, and clerk at Belk's. Yet some do indeed become policemen and beauticians and accountants.[12]

Completely shaken, however, is the assumption that their parents and grandparents had that school and success are, inevitably, synonymous (although by "success," people still usually mean no more than money).[13] For the children of the poor who stay close to home, be they black or white, boy or girl, whether they have gone to a community college or not, the professional fields remain as closed as they have always been. Data processing, working in electronics or as a diesel mechanic, being a dental hygienist or a teacher's aide: these are the occupations for which they train. Eastern North Carolina technical schools and community colleges aren't the schools supplying our Research Triangle Park with its more sophisticated technicians and theoreticians. College is no longer the be-all and end-all it was held out to be in the 1960s. Access to higher education has provided more people, and more groups of people, with an associate or other degree, but the same economic and social and racial demarcations remain pretty much in place. That idealism with which the period began has by now, in the mid-to-late 1980s, flickered and waned.

It took the 1960s to make the distinction between "work" and "meaningful work" a public issue; to make even marginal students and others for whom college had never before seemed an alternative think education might be for them, also; but the open-ended promises of the time are a long way from fulfillment. Young people for whom school was then proclaimed the way out and the way up, the open sesame into the mainstream of the best that life has to offer, have now lived long enough to see that it isn't necessarily so.

Yet never has a degree been more important for entering the work force than now; at a time when high-school and college students alike seem more disinterested in education than ever before, school is more essential to them than it has ever been. But neither has the relationship between school and income ever been more demoralizing, nor the prospect of what going to school can eventually mean, less heartening. Young people whose friends, having had some college or perhaps having completed a two-year program, still work at jobs that may be appreciably little different from those they would have had a shot at straight out of high school, or even if they had dropped out, aren't to be blamed for asking the worth of school. That education might involve something more than training for employment, nobody much considers; take away the financial benefits presumably to be derived from college, and people who have never thought of the advantages of a degree in any other way will be at a loss to value it at all.

What has, in fact, happened since the 1960s has been the emergence of a layer of workers and potential workers a cut or two above that of unskilled labor, but, also, several cuts below that necessary for competing on an equal basis for the kind of employment now increasingly available, especially in the Piedmont cities. These are people who, despite their efforts to better themselves, are still on the periphery, their jobs as likely to be wiped out by a changing and ever more sophisticated technology, by shifting emphases in the workplace, as the farms their parents and grandparents knew that disappeared in the wake of the new agriculture. And there are others whose lack of education and marketable skills already put them well out of the job search. Some manufacturing workers may have found a niche[14] for the time being, and then only *some*—certain tradesmen, para-professionals, and small businessmen—but for people whose education lies primarily in their having acquired just a technical skill, the likelihood is that that alone won't suffice.

But if the competition for jobs has always been a definitive aspect of life in the region, since the mid-1960s young people have seldom had to compete for admission into area colleges. Besides the eight technical schools and community colleges just in these eight counties, there are three private senior colleges, as well as two more private senior colleges in nearby counties: in Greenville there is a large public university. *All* draw upon primarily the same high schools for their entering freshman classes. The National Merit finalists, Morehead Scholars, Katharine Smith Reynolds appointees, others receiving prestigious academic awards will, as they always have, go to State and Duke, UNC-G and Carolina, Wake Forest and Davidson, and a very few will elect Emory or Virginia, Princeton perhaps. Graduating seniors just below this group ordinarily consider East Carolina and other colleges within the University of North Carolina system, Wilmington say or Fayetteville State. As for the others, they have the community colleges vying for them, as well as the area's other public colleges and, increasingly, the private colleges.

More than likely, money proves decisive. When an eighteen-year-old from Fremont can go to Wayne Community College ten or fifteen miles down the road from him, and for fifty-seven dollars in tuition a quarter; or a student in Weldon can enroll at Halifax Community College for forty-four dollars a quarter, why, he may well ask, should he pay two thousand dollars in tuition alone for a semester at a private college?[15] Yet a good many of the poor *do* enroll in the area's private colleges, and for reasons that bear examination. Unless they are academically superior, the children of welfare, as those of the working poor, young people who traditionally haven't gone to college at all, have just this choice: the local technical school or community college, or, if enough financial aid can be mustered, the closest private college. Why a private college, rather than a public? It is the area's private colleges most assiduously going after even the average and sometimes the below-average student. Enrollment here may be so crucial that virtually every student receives some financial aid and is guided with some care through the intricacies of an application. Besides, the state's public universities lie outside the experience of these children of the small, rural high schools; larger by far than the private colleges, they are also urban. The small, rural private college, whether in the country or a small town, is thus more familiar, not as off-putting.

But the private college whose student body is now comprised of disproportionate numbers of such students has a new row to hoe, and perhaps one it had not anticipated. The fact that neither these students nor anybody else in eastern North Carolina has any other conception of education than as training for employment, and that the surrounding technical schools and community colleges have as their expressed purpose preparation for employment, means that these colleges will likely be called upon to reconsider their own mission. Institutional identity will be hard, if not impossible, to sustain when the private college offers courses and programs similar to those available at schools with which historically it has had nothing in common; even the baccalaureate may be threatened.

Because the pressure for such change is profound, deriving from the area's need for skilled workers to meet the needs of a marketplace where an education now matters so much more than in the past, the private liberal arts college remaining true to its heritage will be rare. As more and more students seek *both* a college degree *and* training focused upon specific and immediate employment, not knowing just how opposed these two pursuits are in the traditional liberal arts setting, the private colleges that have gone out and sought just such students will be edged into having to respond; hence, even here such curricular additions as majors in Criminal Justice, Food Service and Hotel Management, Business, Nursing, Fish and Wildlife Management, and the like: necessary pursuits, but strange bedfellows with the professions, with the academic disciplines. For the technical schools and community colleges, neither offering the baccalaureate, no comparable demand is made.

Where there's nothing to do but go to school, and, consequently, everybody goes, colleges can hardly remain unaffected. Competition, however, can be insidious. The serious student now enrolling in an area liberal arts college may discover that he will be unable to take a degree in, for example, a foreign language; that the school offers neither a humanities program, as such, nor intensive course work of the kind possible only where academic standards are uniformly high; that others in his classes will be as intellectually incompatible with him as if he had entered a technical school or community college. Large universities have a capacity for absorbing change that a small college simply doesn't; the risk of its becoming the same as its competitor is high.

The irony is hard to miss: in an insular and circumscribed, rural locale, the more colleges there are and the closer their proximity, the more intense the competition for students is, and the more likely that all differences will be eroded. The result is a narrowing of the kind of education available, even as the number of colleges remains constant or increases. Eastern North Carolina young people may find that it hardly matters which local college they attend: private or public, community or technical; all may be remarkably similar. The poorest among them, those going to school in the Community College System merely because it's the only one financially open to them, may already have found how empty the word "choice" can be, yet even limited choice is better than none at all—and they will know that, too.

I had a choice the year I stayed out of college and worked in Raleigh, although at the time I hardly knew it; rather, I was so determined to show Faison that I *could* do it, that, like the young men whose fathers had family farms auctioned out from under them, I was going to get it back, that the possibility of my not returning wasn't as real to me as probably it should have been. Another college was unthinkable; for reasons I could not have articulated, the same college that had found me wanting had to be the one to say, on some day in the future I then but vaguely apprehended, I was all right; that I had met its expectations.

Money was, however, another matter. A year's tuition, room, and board then at UNC-G cost $850. Strange to say, it was but *one* year that shone before me, that I allowed myself to consider; thus I wasn't undone by a sense of impossibility. Had I dwelt upon the *three* additional years I needed, who is to say what would have happened? I still had a North Carolina Prospective Teachers' Scholarship Loan of $350 a year; the difference between my being a college sophomore in Greensboro rather than a transit clerk at Branch Bank in Raleigh wasn't as great, therefore, as it might have been. Five hundred dollars was a lot of money, nonetheless; that I would need even more than that, of course, for I had to support myself during the year, didn't bear thought, either. Take-home pay was in the neighborhood of $180 a month, out of which I saved sometimes ninety or a hundred dollars.

With some unexpected help from my father's brother late in the summer before I entered upon the 1965–66 school year (which made possible some of the amenities), it turned out to be enough. For my last two years, there was another scholarship, which this time I saw that I kept, as well as a small loan my last semester that enabled me to do student teaching. Luck and happenstance account for much, of course; had I known enough that year in Raleigh to know how close I was to going in another direction, probably I would have tried that, too. Ignorance may be as much a cause in our lives as anything else.

That I might go not only to college but, also, to graduate school, teach in a college or university, did not then occur to me. Being a college graduate was prospect enough. Not until Professor Amy Charles nominated me for a Woodrow Wilson, just before Christmas of my senior year, did this too enter my thinking. She knew very well I would not get anything so distinguished; that the nomination itself was important, however, she knew, too. But did she know, also, that the gesture alone lent encouragement and purpose of a kind enlarging to my sense of self, defined a choice I had not known was mine to make? Perhaps.

Leaving Faison for Ohio State in August 1968, the bus pulling out of Warsaw and Dorothy and Clara waving up to me, more or less—they were so fearful of departure—boxes and books already mailed ahead, little did any of us know that it would be a dozen years before I would come home again for good; or that returning, in August 1980, I would see fields and towns long known to me as different places, people living here now of whom I had never heard, the houses of families alongside of whom I had been raised abandoned and falling in. The young, especially, I would find alien, their apparent familiarity masking profound differences between their generation and my own, between them and my students in Ohio and New York. Some were the children of people with whom I had gone to school; they belonged to families whose older members I had known or whose names I recognized. But they had in their short lives undergone transitions that eastern North Carolina as a whole still was in the process of confronting, and that I knew I would have to understand if I was to be able to stay here. They were, some of them, my own nieces and nephews, young men and women whose lives now nobody had imagined or could have foreseen when they were little.

Much had been acquired since 1968; as I was increasingly to discover, much also had been lost.

Part Three

Nowadays

7. School Days

Coastal Plains High is a small rural school, and its students are the children of the outlying land, of the small plants so many of which have just within their own lifetime come into the area. It was their parents, typically, who first made the transition away from farming and into the work force. They were the ones who provided the labor when, for example, in 1968, Hevi-Duty opened up on Highway 117 between Mount Olive and Goldsboro and The Boling Company and Burlington came to Mount Olive. Now often supervisors and department foremen, likely enough they are the ones plant managers hold accountable for production quotas, for the lines running. For their children still in school, as for those who have already graduated or dropped out, these are parents for whom public work has been everything. The idea they had of themselves as farm people, owner or tenant or hand, they've had to abandon. It wasn't simply the empty house that, when they were small, these young people had come home to, or that they come home to now, but parents whose lives have, in ways still to be reckoned with, broken apart.

Not all moves away from farming were painful, of course. For some, the initial uncertainty neither lasted long nor cut deep. Yet, this being my home, I cannot recall the names or look at the students in these classrooms—at Coastal Plains and Henderson, Wexler and Edison—without seeing in them the heritage forever now unclaimable. To their grandparents who twenty years ago may have worked a public job on the side, the old folks still tending a few acres, holding on to the land, or who have now lost it all, these teenagers occupy a fundamentally altered if not antithetical world. They had seen it coming, they'll tell you; everybody had known that for most people farming was a losing proposition. What they had not seen ahead to, however, was the changed tenor of their lives. But these black students' forebears likely worked the land as hands for the parents and grandparents, and great-grandparents of the white students with whom they now go to school. Black and white now work alongside one another in the plants as, in the 1960s, they worked together in the same fields. And industrialization itself, minor and sparse as it continues to be, has already done much to call into question generations of economic and social, if not racial, distinctions.

At Coastal Plains alone, of the dozen or so students whose families I know, all have parents now in public work, and all come from farm people making the shift away from the land fifteen and twenty years ago. Anna's mother is a practical nurse, her father drives trucks, but her grandparents on both sides farmed their own land, and a great-grandfather had owned hundreds of acres; her father had tried farming for a while. Mark's father is now in law enforcement, his mother a cafeteria worker; both sets of grandparents, however, were tenants. Neither his father nor his uncle, who is a truck driver, ever seriously considered farming themselves. Lisa's mother works in the office at Burlington, her father at Calypso Plywood; her grandparents farmed, her mother's family owning land, her father's family tenants; what land is left in her mother's family, an uncle still farms.

Thomas's father has been at Hevi-Duty since he lost the good-sized farm he had inherited. His great-grandfather had amassed a considerable plantation, the land passing down to his sons fifty or sixty years ago. However, in the years since his father sold out, two of Thomas's uncles have had to give up their farms as well. More than half of the great-grandfather's original plantation has long since been lost to the family. None of the farms, as one after another have been put up for auction, have been bought by men who came and lived on the place. Land now is owned by one man, rented out to and farmed by another; any house still standing will be occupied, perhaps, by the family once owning it.

Larry's father works at DuPont, the Kinston plant, but his grandfather still farms. Talissa's mother cleans houses and helps out in other ways, mostly for the white families on whose farms she once worked as a hand. Even now she goes to the fields when there's work for her. Alice, Carl, and Sharon's mama has been at Boling fifteen or more years; their grandparents were tenants.

Untold others could as easily be cited. As the 1970s came to a close, it was the children of people first making their living in public work who filled the area's rural high schools. For many such families, more money was coming in than ever before, if still never enough. Low as

Alongside the produce line. A picture that might have been snapped anytime between the late forties and early sixties. (Faison, N. C. Photo courtesy of Hazel Rackley.)

Above: Waiting in line to sell your stuff at the Faison Produce Market, 1947. *Opposite page, above:* Barning tobacco, ca. late 1940s. The scene would have differed little even in the mid-1960s. *Opposite page, below:* Grading and packing cucumbers, Faison Produce Market, ca. late 1940s – but the scene remained virtually unchanged through the early 1960s. Note the "women's work" and the men's. (Courtesy of Kraft's Studio, Archival Negative, Mount Olive, N. C.)

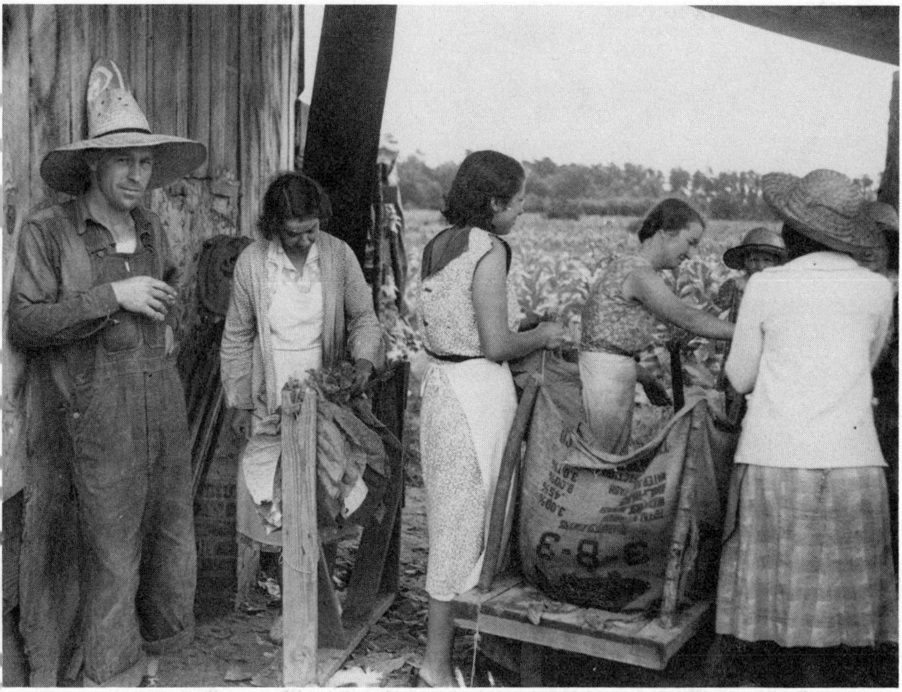

Along Highway 50—the Faison land today. Note the ditchbank grown up in weeds, the woods thinned, the land sown in grain (Photo by Linda Flowers, 1989.)

The Faison-Fesperman House, 1983. The home of Isham and Louise Faison, who owned the Faison place on which Linda and her parents lived from 1944 until the late 1950s. (Photo courtesy of Nan Fesperman.)

The house to which Linda and her parents moved upon leaving the Faison place in 1956. Then the highway in front was a dirt road and there were woods across from the house itself. (Photo by Linda Flowers, 1989.)

wages in the sewing plant, chicken-processing plant, or electrical-appliance or furniture plants were, they were more or less dependable, which farming never was. A man and his wife, both of them working, could likely provide a higher standard of living than either had ever known. Inherent in public work, people thought, was the promise of a better life.

Schools, too, the eleven public and five private schools that I visited in 1982 and 1983, seemed to have more to offer than had been the case in 1963 when I graduated. From almost any point of view, public education has the capacity for being better now than it was then. Even in the poorest high schools, laboratory equipment in the sciences is far more sophisticated than we had, and there's more of it. Equipment for the teaching of trades such as auto mechanics, carpentry, drafting, bricklaying, electrical wiring, and the like is modern and well-maintained; business and home economics thrive. Teaching materials of all kinds usually are more than adequate. More than this, there has been a proliferation of support-personnel that, twenty-five years ago, would have been unthinkable.

For me, however, not having been in a Southern school but a time or two since 1963, the most crucial difference is, of course, integration; that, and the realization that public schools nowadays more accurately reflect the realities of American life than at any time in our history: integration accomplished this and, at another level, the broadening of the curriculum.[1]

Before integration, before the swollen enrollments of the mid-to-late 1960s, in the days when the poor, when black children and white, had to work on the farms for much of the school year in order that their families could keep going; when children unattuned to books and classrooms quietly fell away, dropout rates sometimes topping fifty percent: then the public schools taught everybody there, and in the same classes. Graduating classes were homogeneous. Down in the grades there was remarkably little ethnic or cultural – and no racial – diversity. Then the young, as the school people I met reminded me, were "teachable" in ways that today they no longer are. Nonetheless, other factors kept the number of high-school students low; poverty more than anything else, and the fact that girls routinely married at fourteen and fifteen and sixteen, of course quitting school when they did.

But nowadays students are more diverse, coming from such different kinds of homes and such different cultural expectations; furthermore, we now have more sophisticated diagnostic tests for determining intelligence. So say the schools. In the 1950s, however, nobody in Faison had ever heard of "tracking"; high-school students all fulfilled essentially the same curriculum. And the closest we had come to "grouping," to separating students on the basis of academic ability, was in the first and second grades when we had been either a Red Bird or a Blue Bird – the two reading groups.

Patsy left us for part of the morning but came back after lunch; she attended Mrs. Clifton's class in – I think in – the lunchroom, where she and maybe a dozen others "got out of" school for what was then called Special Education. Standardized testing was familiar to us, though I cannot recall anything much ever happening as a result of our scores.

But since at least the mid-1970s, tracking and grouping have become routine, definitive of the academic experience a child now has in school. It wasn't just another progressivism overtaking us, schools having long been objects of reform, but the fact that now for the first time education would found itself upon this rock of scientism: the quantification of learning, as of the presumed capacity for learning, as measured by standardized tests available nationwide, the scores then used for determining the grouping of actual students into actual schoolroom classes.

Picking up on what was then a national mania for categorizing students into as distinct groups as possible and then teaching them "at their own level," schools in eastern North Carolina found this a bandwagon they too could ride. A decade hence and the professional literature on both, but on tracking especially, is decidedly mixed,[2] yet I saw no sign of the schools here abandoning or even of rethinking either practice. Even in schools small enough to employ fewer than twenty-five teachers, students still were assigned or led to select different curricula: college-bound, vocational, general. Multi-tracks aren't unusual; beginning in the lower grades, students still were placed in advanced or average or remedial classes. The difference is that between taking consumer math or algebra, remedial reading or honors English, general science or advanced biology, world studies – courses labeled "studies," I was to discover, frequently were for "low" students – or world history.

The difference is more than this. When, in February 1982, I met with a half-dozen parents whose children went to Jackson High School, an urban school considerably more sophisticated than Coastal Plains, grouping was very much on their minds. "It came in when the schools integrated [late 1960s, early 1970s]," our host said, "and it really was a way to segregate the classes, but, at the same time, not keep out the one or two or three blacks who could do [accelerated or above-average work]."

"That way, the rich white kids could be kept together in mostly white classes, and the poor whites and almost all the blacks would be together."

"Children who've been placed in low classes down in the grades," a mother insisted, "can't compete out of them. . . . They just can't."

"Yes," another agreed, "they're not given a choice until the ninth grade, and then they can't keep up with the higher-level classes because they've had no preparation."

Following the argument, which I knew I could have heard at other dining-room tables in the vicinity, I was moved by its intensity; and though I myself do not connect grouping with integration, the fact that the two occurred at roughly the same time makes such a linkage, to those needing to see it, plausible. More to the point is that the classes I was then to observe, in the early 1980s, still were racially definable.

"'Show me the occupation of the student's father,'" the host quoted a school administrator as having said, "'and I'll tell you what group he's in. . . . My hands are tied . . . I'm not going to fight it anymore.'"

But a woman quieter than the others, who told me later that she was a teacher, disagreed. "It's *not* done by who you are. They have to keep records. They can be taken to court!"

"All of our children do not excel academically," she added. "We have to accept that."

When later I asked an assistant superintendent for Jackson about such perceptions, he confirmed some, denied others. "When I came to Jackson in 1976," he told me, "it was clear that ability-grouping was going to be done. . . . I still have a reputation as being anti-grouping. I had some questions about it . . . went to the school board and expressed concern. . . . Now [at least] the principal can no longer just deal with the teacher or do the placement by himself."

There's a placement committee, he continued, to which parents can appeal, and in high school, "It's completely up to the student and his parents and what they pre-register for." In the lower grades, he said, "Six or seven kids in a grading period may go from one group to another."

Mr. Sullivan recalled, however, that when he and his family first moved to Jackson, his child was placed in the higher group immediately, despite the fact that her previous school records hadn't yet arrived and no placement tests had been administered. "Now," he insisted, "this kind of thing wouldn't happen."

Of the Jackson principal, Mr. Sullivan said that he had heard criticism on this score before. "He's an advocate of the old system of 8–9 track grouping," he concluded, and he "cares more about the college-bound than the others."

Coastal Plains is one of many schools in the region that came into being in the mid-to-late 1950s when the movement toward consolidation began. Like others of that era, especially in the country, its long central building is narrow and flat. Only the gymnasium inclines to any kind of height, and that not many feet above the arc a basketball thrown by a boy might make. For everything else—the cafeteria, the vocational-agricultural shop, even the trailers behind the main building that have been turned into classrooms—there is rather a look of holding close to the ground. The neatly-tended lawn lends grace to the spare buildings; the school has stature almost despite itself.

On a winter morning in 1983, Mrs. Johnson's class in Remedial Reading is about to get underway when I arrive. "Get those activities out you were working on yesterday, so you can finish 'em," she says. Four students are present.

It's cold this morning in the trailer. The four boys, who range in age from about fourteen or fifteen to probably seventeen, work silently at their tables.

A boy coming in a few minutes late is sent to the end of the room and told to listen to a tape of exercises he missed earlier in the week.

"Get out your contracts," Mrs. Johnson prompts them, preparing to check homework. They rummage through their workbooks until they find the section she has in mind. She goes from one to the other examining what each has done.

"I'll let you go through this junk," one of them tells her, but "I don't know what you're talkin' 'bout hardly."

These are students whose scores on the California Achievement Test put them well below the average for their grade level. The juniors in the class have all failed the North Carolina Competency Test, and not until they pass it can they graduate from high school.

Mrs. Johnson is today not in the best of moods. She sounds tired, almost listless, and she fusses, yet without much heat, at the boys as they take their time showing her their work. At one who is especially sluggish, she nags, "You don't have any respect for yourself or anybody else," and to the boy at the tape recorder who now joins the others, she says, "And I don't even think you listened to the tape that quick."

"Lord, Jesus Christ," he mutters, teeth clenched.

At Coastal Plains again the next day, I sit in on Mr. Christopher's class in United States Studies. A young man, thirty or thirty-five maybe, and personable, Mr. Christopher is also an assistant coach. He begins by reading aloud a mimeographed sheet from the office of the district's congressman, whom he calls "Brother Charlie."

"Let's see what Brother Charlie's got to say today," he drawls. It's by no means certain, however, that his charges know who "Brother Charlie" is.

Nineteen or twenty students sit at desks placed three rows deep and twelve rows across the long side of the trailer. They are gangling youngsters, many of them, and they are too large for their desks, which seem to have been made for children. The teacher stands before them, looking them over, but unless he turns deliberately toward each end of the room, he can see only those in the center rows.

From Congressman Whitley's memo, somehow the discussion comes around to the day's lesson, "Immigrants: 1880 and Before." Mr. Christopher reads questions aloud from a manual and the students call out the one- or two-word answers, which he checks against the list he has.

"Why did some people want to cut off the flow of immigration?"

A boy leans across the aisle and reads an acceptable response off somebody else's paper. The matter of immigration itself is not pursued.

Finally, Mr. Christopher asks, "What did [a local town] do this weekend? Who reads the [local paper]?" Two or three students wave their hands, but they are thinking of something other than the article he has in mind, about the way the mayor has just filled a replacement for the town board, and he takes a few minutes to air the controversy. They listen politely enough, yet the issue doesn't engage them.

We return to "Immigrants: 1880 and Before."

The room is very cold. Some students are wearing gloves and scarves, even hats; almost all have on their coats. But these are mostly poor kids, and, as bundled up as they are, their clothes are too thin for February.

Plessy versus Ferguson is mentioned. No one, however, underscores its importance or connects it with civil rights.

At last Mr. Christopher has everyone open their books so that he can "go over right quick" with them "what'll be on" the test tomorrow. They flip through the chapter dutifully marking the passages he wants them to know.

There is no more instruction. It is twenty minutes before the bell.

Proponents of grouping – and there are many – have a case to make; the issue is complex, and few observers can be confident they see the matter clearly and whole. My sympathies, however, lie with the other side: for the vast majority of the more than one hundred classes I attended, nongrouping would have been preferable to grouping except in those classes for the mentally handicapped and those for the truly academically gifted – though I saw too many instances where students, especially in the advanced or honors groups, seemed inappropriately placed. Children and young people cannot be sorted with as little harm to them as the leaves of tobacco that people in my grandfather's day graded (some bright leaf, some ruddy, some green, some "trash"). Labels carry with them expectations, and for both teacher and student, the likelihood is that grouping becomes self-fulfilling. Students here are being failed by such measures, throwed away by the very reforms some educators still tout as redemptive.

Like their grandparents victimized by the new agriculture, their parents by the promise as yet unfulfilled of the new industrialism, young people today in eastern North Carolina know that in the schools, too, success can be elusive: a chimera that fewer and fewer, their lives ingrained with defeat, any longer pursue; that failure wears many guises. Nothing could be less democratic or less democratizing than a system defined at every level by test scores, scores that are in large part a function of a child's earlier schooling, which has itself been shaped by a yet earlier battery of standardized tests: a self-perpetuating cycle that effectively locks students into the respective groups; for those always in the "low" classes, the process is apt to be, also, self-annihilating.

Procedures for appeal there may be, but the parents of students most likely to be placed in a lower group are the same ones least likely to know how to challenge the decision or to think of doing so. Poor, frequently black, seldom a part of a community's mainstream, often unable to read and write effectively themselves, perhaps a single mother: these are people for whom making a living takes everything they have to give. Accepting of authority in the plants and factories, they are not prone to question that of the schools, at least not formally. Get them by themselves, however, and another side may emerge.

On the day that Jeannette Phillips talked with me in Jackson, sliding into the booth at the Golden Corral a little after five o'clock, straight from her work at the utility company, she knew what she wanted to say.

"Shirley ain't gettin' what she's 'sposed to be gettin' out a school.

"At Jackson, they's just a very few people runnin' ever'thing. . . . It all boils down to specific interests of a specific group of people. . . . You hate to be at a point where you can't trust nobody, but when they don't give me the opportunity to prove myself, who's gettin' robbed? Who's doin' it?"

Mrs. Phillips was certain that in the Jackson elementary school her little girl attended grouping was based "more [on] social standards than [it was on] educational standards.

"It hurts me to my heart," she lamented, "to see us put a damper on talent."

Black, ill-educated, struggling to keep the bills paid and her family afloat, Jeannette Phillips knows what it means to sacrifice for a child's education; well does she know the importance of school. She wants for Shirley no less than what any parent would want: the chance for her to make something more of herself than she has known. Thus her shock and anger when a friend at Shirley's school had called and said to her, "You think Shirley's in the first grade, don'cha?"

"Come to find out," Mrs. Phillips told me, after kindergarten Shirley had been put "in somethin' they called a pre-primary class," not in the first grade at all, and that, although her teacher thought she had been notified, in fact she had not. Upon subsequent testing, the little girl had gone into the first grade, but in the lowest class.

"Some chil'ren are in ever'thing," Mrs. Phillips murmured. ". . . Shirley don't get to do ballet, modern dance, . . . gymnastics . . . Group I [students in the "high" class] can, but not Group II. . . . They don't get to do none a that."

White, educated, middle-class, Edna Michaels would seem to have little in common with Jeannette Phillips. Yet a half-dozen or more years after her sons graduated in Jackson, in the late 1970s, her anguish at what she considers "was done to" the younger is unabated. Tom's low self-esteem, the problems he has had finding work and then keeping a job, she attributes to his repeatedly being placed in a lower group. "Without any doubt," she remains convinced "to this day" that Tom is marked for "not having had a chance in school.

"I *trusted* them," she tells me. Looking back on the experience, nothing hurts her more than this sense of having been betrayed. "'Mama, I wanted to learn, too,'" Tom had said.

A Jackson graduate, Randy was twenty when I met him in 1982, although he looked more like fifteen. He had been a student at Pitt Community College for a while after high school, less than a year, but he had dropped out and was then unemployed. "Maybe if I'd a been encouraged more," he said of his school days, or "hadn't been in Group II . . . I could'a done better. . . . Group II didn't really prepare me."

Randy admitted to having "a bad attitude toward education," largely, he thought, as a result of "what happened [to him] at Jackson." He wants some day to go back to college. "I can do better," he insisted, than work on a line.

Randy, little Shirley, Tom Michaels: I heard their stories many times over. Yet parents with whom I talked may have known almost nothing about their children's academic experience; others, if they said anything at all, likely expressed unease. No conversation was atypical. Details varied only in the names and places; for the rest, there was a predictive sameness: a sense of separation from schools and all that schools might represent; the frustration that "You can't get past [the principal] no matter what'cha do, . . . It's like a wall, and they [school people] all stick together"; the belief, which is widespread, that school officials listen just to those having stature and influence in the community; the feeling that school people regard the schools as *theirs*, as belonging to them exclusively; the conviction that children nowadays can't read and write like they ought to, that they're not learning all that they should.

Yet so much has happened in public education since their own school days that many parents, some of them not having graduated, shy away from voicing specific criticism. There is, rather, a throwing up of hands, an exasperation with "the schools," even when they have no particular problem in mind. These are not people having the vocabulary necessary for ordering opinion. All they know is that they want their children to have solid instruction in reading, writing, mathematics, and perhaps history; and this whether the schools find them to be average, below average, or gifted.

"Not like 'the brains' maybe," a mother in Johnston County said of her son, "but so he can at least read and write, so he will know *somethin'* when he does get out!"

Exactly what graduates should know, such parents leave to the schools.

And if they live in houses without books and magazines, if they themselves don't read and write, nonetheless they care about their children's education. Knowing how hard they have to work, the days they clock-in whether they want to or not, and sensing in their every encounter with educated people the gaps in their own lives, working people here need no persuasion that a diploma matters.

For large numbers of students, though – at Coastal Plains certainly, but everywhere else too – education is not very important. They like school well enough, but if they don't they may not worry about it; "it's awright . . . ," they'll murmur. Few have anything very bad to say about going to school – or anything very good, either. By "school," however, they are likely to mean nothing more or less than the friends they see there, the activities in which they participate: band practice, athletics, cheerleading, chorale, annual staff, the newspaper. On the other hand, thousands aren't involved in anything at all. These you see off to themselves; when everybody else is at the pep rally, they're catching a smoke behind a trailer, in the bathrooms, at the far end of a hall, in a doorway.

Students "don't appreciate education anymore . . . not like I did," an English teacher at a local technical school tells me. "They don't relate work . . . having to work in order to accomplish a goal or to learn . . . to school. When they find out that work is involved, that scares them away."

Other than as something more to be endured, classes may be perceived as relatively meaningless. On the whole, not even students in the advanced placement sections I attended seemed especially excited about learning. I saw excellence occasionally; enthusiasm, seldom. What specific criticism students had, however – that school is boring, that they don't like to read, that there's no "use of" algebra or *Macbeth,* that the teachers are "down on" them, that school has too many (and "too many picky") rules – surprises no one. Parents and teachers, as every generation of students, can recite the litany as well as they.

Talking with students underscored my impression that education no longer meant to them what it had meant to my generation; observing them in class was even more confirmatory. At Coastal Plains and Wexler, the other schools I visited, students using their study period to talk with me were broadly representative both of the area's realities and its aspirations. Despite my strong sense that these were not young people for whom learning itself especially mattered, most said they wanted to go to college, either the community college nearby or a four-year school. Teenagers taking the vocational and general curricula mentioned college nearly as often as those in the college-bound track, although they were much less likely to mean a four-year college or to be thinking of going to college immediately after high school.

Overwhelmingly, these were students of that first generation in their family for whom at least some further schooling was possible. "College," however, was hardly anybody's initial response when asked about his life "two or three years from now." For nearly everyone except seniors in the college-bound curricula, the future was unplumbed territory; for seniors who weren't then going on to college, who hadn't been thinking of taking their college boards and selecting colleges at which to apply, the prospect of graduating was daunting.

Corrine, a senior, hadn't thought much about what awaited her beyond high school. Vaguely, she mused that probably she'd "get a job . . . like a sales clerk or something."

Susan, a pale and diffident tenth-grader, didn't like to read, didn't much like her teachers. Especially did she "hate being made to read an hour" in homeroom on club day, the others–those in various organizations–being excused from such sessions. Graduation, however, didn't bother her. All in all, she laughed, hers was "just a plain middle-class family."

Alicia, pretty and well-spoken, was in the eleventh grade. Her father was "a plant foreman in Greenville," the family having moved to North Carolina when she was four. She thought she might "go into the service at first" upon graduation, then perhaps "go to college . . . and major in English."

For Larry, a senior and on the football team, the notion of graduating, of no longer being in school, wasn't anything he liked to think about. He wondered now, in January, if in August he might try to get into the Marines. "Yes," sometimes he "thought about college," he told me politely, but he "didn't have time to take" the Scholastic Aptitude Test necessary for admission. His mother worked at the local pickle plant, his father at Georgia Pacific as a laborer. Larry was the youngest of twelve children.

Like Corinne and most of their friends, Mary, an eleventh-grader, hadn't given her future much thought. Maybe she would get a job, she said, "something to do with computers." Yet when I asked if Wexler had computers available for students or if the school offered computer instruction, she wasn't able to say; she didn't know.

Four girls arriving together were almost wholly silent, although two eventually did come forth with the admission that they wanted to go to college; mostly, however, they stared at me. Asked what they thought they would be doing in five or ten years from now, the two mentioning college agreed that whatever it was, they certainly saw themselves as "not living *here*!" All four tittered and shook their heads, and it occurred to me that they were laughing as much at the question as at their answer, ten years from then unfathomable to them.

At the bell, they lagged behind and softly, patiently, volunteered their names and addresses, as if by then they had decided – Denise and Dorothy, Annette and Stephanie – that being put in a book might be just fine.

Milton and Lewis wanted to get on at Firestone in Wilson. "It's got the best pay of any place around," they agreed. But "you don't really have to have a job," Milton suggested. "You can buy stocks."

Joanie was twenty and still in the twelfth grade. Unable to pass the Competency Test, she will graduate not with a diploma but with a certificate of attendance. Her mother made her stay in school, she told me, although that was what she wanted, too. She thought perhaps that "later on" she might "try to be a nurse." (A counselor confirmed my impression that EMH students – Educable-Mentally Handicapped, Joanie for example – "very rarely drop out of school," most leaving with a certificate.)

Daphne, in the tenth grade, wanted to be a cosmetologist. Laughing, she announced that "North Carolina's backward!" Asked about her school work, she insisted that she would "do better" if she were "up North in a school that [she] really wanted to be in." Her father was in the military.

Tamala mentioned that her father lived in New York, and that when she graduated – she was a senior – she was going to the John Powers School of Fashion, in Raleigh.

Marcy and Carol came in together. Carol said she was "very familiar" with young people being out of work "even after" they graduated. For example, her brother still was trying to find a steady job, and "he got out of school last year." Marcy agreed, adding that her mother hadn't been able to find a job since 1980 when Sylvania in Smithfield, where she had worked for fifteen years, closed.

Johnny and Luther had just passed the Compentency Test; they came in joking about how easy it had been. Johnny said his father was "a body man," and that after he graduated, he would be also. "Some weeks [there] ain't no cars, and we don't eat much," he admitted, but "some weeks we have a lot of work." Luther said he would likely go into "the service." Both disliked being in classes where the students were all at the same academic level, Luther especially; they would rather their classes be "mixed-up."

Monica, a senior, drove a night school bus for dropouts coming back in the evening for classes. "A lot of kids who drop out," she said, "wish they hadn't. . . . Most who drop out," unlike those she saw on her bus, "just stay out. They don't go to any kind of school." Monica was looking forward to joining the Army, although she would rather have been going into the Air Force, she let me know, "but the Air Force is full now and has a waiting period." She didn't want to have to wait.

(It was the opinion of a Navy recruiter at Coastal Plains, certainly exaggerated, that "Ninety percent of the students in this area flunk the Navy entrance test," whereas "kids up in Guilford County with just a GED [General Education Development, a certificate of high-school equivalency] do better than those 'down East' who have a high-school diploma."[3])

Small for a tenth-grader and unusually intense, Craven could hardly wait to be seated before launching into a criticism of the emphasis Coastal Plains placed on sports. Resenting "all the attention the athletes get," he was incensed that "money could be found to clear land for [a] football practice field, but "not for FFA, . . . not for crops. . . . They can put in lights for sports," he said, but "they won't do anything for us . . . [and] farming matters more."

(Craven isn't alone; not every student I met was infatuated with school-sponsored athletics. A good many appeared alienated by what they saw as the misplaced commitment—affection and approval—of adults. Like Craven, they wanted their own interests to be taken as seriously as they thought school people took athletics.)

Six of the boys, their blue corduroy FFA jackets almost a uniform, liked taking most of their courses in agriculture, in welding and small-engine repair, as well as the work-study program under which two of them worked in the afternoons at an auto-repair shop.

And the others, the tens of thousands for whom these few must stand: Tina and Carlton whose fathers were unemployed, both seniors, Tina thinking she might become a nurse, Carlton perhaps a welder; Mitchell, a tenth-grader, maybe he would be an auto mechanic; pretty Felicia, then about to be the first in her close family to finish high school, applying for loans so she could go to North Carolina A & T; Denise, wanting to be an airline stewardess, though her friend Karen, "just a plain housewife"; Annette, who was thinking of the business course, maybe, at James Sprunt; Ralph, intent on becoming a highway patrolman; and there were the three ninth-graders who told me, laughingly, that though school was boring, probably this was their own fault, not their teachers'.

But when have students not found school boring? The transition from high school to another kind of life, unsettling? Are Craven and Corinne, Larry and Susan and Milton, Mary—are they really that much different from their predecessors a decade ago? Twenty-five or thirty years ago? For the majority, has learning ever especially mattered? And whether it has or not, have those going off to college usually done so for inherent academic reasons?

With some important qualifications, I think not—not essentially; however, so much has the medium changed in which the young now live that these human constants take a different aspect, have other dimensions, than even in the recent past. Beneath the surface of an ordinary school day, young people here may, to those adults knowing them best, resemble the students of another era; but the likeness isn't what matters. What does matter, and matter profoundly, is the surface itself: a school world that locks some students into failure as surely as it enables the academic self-realization of others; that is fragmenting to the intellectual sensibility of students generally; and that too often simply is dull and deadening.

To think of these small rural schools as they were in the 1950s and early 1960s and then to see them as they are now, thirty years hence, is to do more than set one description against another: it is to take the measure of a profession. If schools were gentler then than they are now, in the 1980s, they were not always so. Stories my father told of the goings-on when he was a boy evoke a school world no longer imaginable. In the 1920s and 1930s a "professor" had seldom had more than a term or two in college; the man, single, having with him just those books out of which the lesson came and his clothes, boarded in the community, moving from one pupil's house to another; a woman, she was just "the teacher." Nobody had to be more respectable. Schools in the country were apt to be one-room; a coal or wood fire warmed you in winter. Teachers had to keep the stove going, the water bucket filled, the school clean.

Then, as now, teachers had other confrontations than with the lessons. Gangling, near-grown boy-men, still pupils in the seventh and eighth and ninth grades, would be kept home in the spring and early fall to work in the fields. They would "whip a man-teacher, if they could," my father said, "make him leave. . . . A woman, they'd just try to make her quit. They'd do all kinds of meanness . . . jump out the window, . . ." Children were whipped, too, "the blood running down in their socks" at one school where, along in the 1930s probably, a particularly memorable schoolmaster had been employed.

By the 1950s, however, teachers and principals and superintendents had acquired a different sense of professionalism. During the next thirty years, education itself would be transformed. As much as the new progressivism would come to define the school days students would experience in the 1970s and 1980s, it changed, also, school people; as how could it not? Or perhaps the change occurred the other way around, the new breed of men and women then nurtured in the nation's schools of education being responsible for introducing and inculcating the new aesthetic. Which came first no longer matters; the point is that neither could have taken hold without the other.

A teacher entering the profession in, say, 1960, not only stood at the threshold of a new era, she was a different kind of teacher from her older colleagues: more tutored in methodology than they, more likely to think methodology important; less likely to have had as much, or comparable, instruction in her academic area, but more apt to have taken courses in other disciplines; far likelier to have majored in education than in English or history, mathematics or chemistry. Yet no more than anybody else could a teacher then taking her first job, at Coastal Plains or Timmons, Edison, say, or Wexler, have known what awaited her and, especially, her colleagues teaching down in the grades: open classrooms, mini-courses, learning-for-life enrichment, multi-tracking, look-see reading, new math, ability-grouping; and more. Standardized testing was even then becoming the basis of a new scientism having profound repercussions.[4]

Education was to become ever-increasingly professionalized; no aspect of school would be untouched by the change. From the Ed.D. angling to be superintendent, to the newly-minted B.A. with her first class; from the teacher now going back to college for her master's, to the M.S. in educational administration hoping to become a principal or work in the central office; for everybody, credentials mattered now as never before. East Carolina, Fayetteville State, Campbell, and Atlantic Christian were the colleges drawing the area's teachers, men especially, and women who would drive over once or twice a week for an evening class and during the summers, gradually building up credits toward a second degree.

In Raleigh, in the state's 144 central school offices and eight regional centers, the bureaucracy commensurate with the profession's enlarged sense of itself was developing. By 1987 the Department of Public Instruction would employ, in Raleigh alone, nearly one thousand persons: program specialists, analysts, planners and researchers, statisticians, directors, coordinators. Few statistics would seem too incidental for compilation; few problems, beneath study. Education nationally had turned its light on itself, and if knowledge was not always what was illumined, at least schools were to establish the vocabulary for a continuing public debate.

There was developing, this is to say, a cadre of other professionals ancillary to instruction itself: a managerial and executive class more prestigious than teaching and considerably better paid, comprised of people who may once have taught, though usually not for long, and from whom the classroom teacher has become increasingly separated. Professionalization is never without cost, of course, but in public education its toll has been heavy indeed. The more administrators and teachers have divided into these two groups, their different roles accentuated, the one rewarded, the other not, the wider the distances have grown between the classroom and the decisions affecting the curriculum; the more the flow of ideas has been from top to bottom, and the more we define administrators as being "at the top," teachers "at the bottom"; the less autonomy teachers have over their professional life, as over their personal life at school: then the more is a teacher's authority eroded, her capacity for being perceived by her students as significant, diminished.

To address these issues, however, is to define another sensibility than that which prevailed in the 1950s and early 1960s. If my teachers saw themselves as bureaucratically oppressed, as powerless and beleaguered, we didn't; we would have hooted at the notion that Miss Blount was downtrodden, that she or Miss Bowden, Miss Edna, or Miss Ray were fearful of anybody. Principals then may have "ruled with an iron hand" if they "kept the school board happy," as a retired administrator rather wistfully reminded me, but as far as we and our parents knew, the teacher's classroom was her own domain. Some people may occasionally have gone over her head, but not if they were poor, not if they idealized learning as my family did. Nor did it occur to us that teachers were badly paid, tenants having so little cash money that to them, as to many others, a person getting a check regularly was well-off.

There was no sense then that either teachers or principals,—and principals were teachers, too—wanted to be somewhere else; superintendents weren't the hired guns they have since become. Mr. O. P. Johnson had been superintendent in Duplin County for as long as anybody much could remember; Miss Dail, Miss Martin, Miss Davis, Miss Ray had all taught at Mount Olive or Faison Elementary for years and years, as had Miss Blount, Miss Edna, and Miss Bowden. Principals were harder to keep, a new man coming in every other year or so. He would teach the eighth grade.

But for the man twenty years ago who made the central office his own fiefdom, staying there the greater part of his career, there is now the superintendent whose tenure may last no more than five or six years; who may bring his own men with him, an assistant or associate or program coordinator, occasionally smoothing the way for them to be tapped for a superintendency elsewhere. This is to say that bright young Ed.Ds now in positions of authority have quite another view of themselves than their predecessors did. Capable in things pragmatic and, for the large part, well-intentioned and personable, even dedicated—but they could as easily work at the telephone company as for the schools. Men they would most like to resemble aren't at the university but at the local bank, perhaps, or the fast-food headquarters. The corporate manager more nearly fulfills their ideal than any scholar; Lee Iacocca, say, rather than a Louis Rubin or a John Hope Franklin.

This is to affirm nothing more or less than that school officials now are indistinguishable from businessmen and government careerists and junior executives; that the school establishment behaves generally like any other. Administrators, if they are not directly responsible for the curriculum, may have no particular connection with learning,[5] no more than if they had hold of some other commodity; too often, they've lost sight of the intellectual tradition entirely. Appearances do little to suggest that ideas and books, what man has thought and said and done, are their stock in trade. Neither the principal whose office is full of reports and manuals, attendance profiles and institutional self-studies, nor the superintendent whose week is spent reviewing accreditation reports, State Department of Public Instruction guidelines, and finances—statistics being available on every aspect of education lending itself to quantification – on a late and weary afternoon when the spirit flags may be able to walk across the room and put his hand on a real book.

In none of the offices where, in 1982 and 1983, I talked with administrators, do I recall there being a volume of history, of literature, philosophy or economics, nothing on art or music, chemistry or physics or mathematics, no poetry, no drama – no books at all. The omission is enough to constitute a repudiation of the life of the mind; an abandonment or sidestepping of the content of the curriculum, of the intellectual heritage, at the most serious level possible. Insofar as these successful men would seem to be concerned, there is here reflected no necessity for Shakespeare, for Mozart or Einstein or Descartes, for Aristotle or Marx, Galbraith or Faulkner or Freud.

Teachers inhabit another world from administrators. Central offices are marked by the special quietness necessary for serious work, by the civility that leisure can provide; here, or so the feeling is, there's both work and reflection. Schools move to another rhythm. Teachers may seldom have free even the twenty or thirty minutes granted them for lunch. They are pulled this way and that from the time they arrive in the morning until they are released in the afternoon by students needing attention out of class, by another questionnaire from Raleigh or the central office, by the principal's latest memo, by non-teaching duties such as cafeteria patrol, hall-watch, the Quiz Bowl, the science fair, the school paper, practice for the senior play, and on and on. Lessons are routinely (and in some schools constantly) interrupted by the intercom with its incessant chatter, announcements predictably trivial. For the area's average teacher, professionalization hasn't yet made the school day more conducive to the serious engagement of learning. Nor has a more enlightened leadership yet instilled the kind of changes that would make teachers feel as though they are a vital part of the new order. Teachers and administrators are no closer as real colleagues now than thirty years ago; they may even be further apart.

The doctorate increasingly differentiates this administrative group from the vast majority and in fact from teaching. The advanced degree will almost certainly be in school administration, rarely in an academic discipline. Of the 7,147 doctorates in education awarded nationwide in 1983, for example, 34.6 percent went to people planning careers in administration – for the most part, public-school administration (we may assume, higher education drawing largely on Ph.D.'s). On the other hand, of the 37.7 percent indicating that teaching would be their primary employment, most undoubtedly had in mind teaching education at the college level, not—or not for long—teaching in a public school.[6] In eastern North Carolina, classroom teachers with doctorates are scarcely any more evident now than in the 1950s. I encountered just one in the sixteen schools I visited, though there were also two principals with doctorates. In the central offices I visited, maybe a dozen superintendents and other personnel had their doctorate. But this low number is itself misleading, for the urgency is that the schools acquire a leadership having ever higher credentials. Impoverished as well as affluent districts now want their superintendent called "Doctor."

Edison High School is hardly larger than Coastal Plains though it is set within a small town rather than in the country; the outlying fields are barely out of sight even on main street. Since the early days of integration, schools here have been victimized by "white flight"; eighty-five percent of Edison's students now are black. Nothing is more revealing of the dearth of jobs, the depression of Talton County as a whole, than that only about five percent of the seniors, in 1981, said they would be seeking full-time employment after graduation or that the annual dropout rate holds at about 8.5 percent (which, however, doesn't include students who don't return after the summer).

I attend Miss Pruett's class in United States History. There are at the outset twenty-seven students, all black. Others trickle in, having been dismissed from the Competency Test a few minutes after the bell. The room is large and attractive, but the students seem almost to be in each other's laps, there are so many; aisles between the long rows are narrow, and there are only a few feet left at the front of the room where no one sits. Miss Pruett puts them to work on a set of mimeographed exercises. Using their books, they are to fill in the blanks of sentences, which have to do with culture.

The class is orderly and quiet, but from time to time the teacher gets after first one then another for "running off at the mouth." Perhaps ten or fifteen minutes pass.

Miss Pruett then reads the sentences aloud, the students calling out their answers. They have so many wrong, and so oddly wrong, that I wonder at what level many of them can read.

The teacher's voice, while not unpleasant, hasn't any energy in it. Speaking always in a drone, she stumbles over some of the vocabulary. "Architecture," she pronounces as "ar-chee-tecture," a "ch" sound instead of a "k." "Millenium" becomes "mill-yum." "Artisan," she calls "ar-tee-sian," the emphasis upon the "tee." She reads without conveying much awareness of syntax: meanings run together, blur, are lost. But nobody asks for clarification; nobody seems to notice.

The next forty minutes, Miss Pruett records the grades, having assigned pages 14–29 of the second chapter for them to read now at their desks. It is October seventh. For more than a month the class has been meeting on days like this, sunlight softening the brown, blue, and red tops of the desks by the window.

Perhaps one-third begin the reading; several of the others are without books. Most look around; some talk quietly. Four have their heads on their desks. A boy reads a magazine, looks through it anyway. Three or four of the girls pass notes and giggle behind their hands. A boy looking out the window has a face as old as a man's.

Miss Pruett finishes at her desk, passing back the papers. The bell then sends them on their way.

"Many of the ninth-graders when they get here can't read and write," Edison's assistant principal tells me, "although a lot are extremely street smart." Reading teachers "down in the grades," he explains, are "now pointed toward competency remediation," and "kids get lost in the cracks. . . . Until they flunk the Competency Test at fifteen or sixteen, they get no real help at thirteen or fourteen if they can't read."

Of those Edison eleventh-graders taking the Competency Test in October, 1980, 25.6 percent failed reading. More than thirty percent failed math.

"Then, when we get 'em," Mr. Adams goes on to say, "some will do badly in order to get in Mr. [Bennett's reading] class," where they can get "individualized instruction and make As and Bs and graduate.

"A lot of the parents can't read and write," and that's why "they don't always sign the notes" that students take home with them. Ten years ago when he was new to the classroom, Mr. Adams recalls criticizing the grammar in a note a student had brought from home. "I told him I knew his mama hadn't written *that*," he laughs, "but she had!"

Mr. Adams is interrupted constantly as we talk. Teachers turn in attendance reports; they stop in to check the whereabout of students, to see if they've been suspended or otherwise are subject to disciplining, to find out any changes in the day's schedule. Students needing passes get them here—to be in the library, to be in the hall on the way to or from the library (or bathroom, the gym, their locker . . .), to make a telephone call, to wait by the front desk for their mother coming after them; and on and on. One and all, Mr. Adams handles adroitly and with good humor. That he remains poised tells me that probably this is an ordinary morning.

"We have managed to breed a couple of generations of people who believe that whether you do it or not, the payoff is still there," he reflects. "The same things are not important to them as they were to me. Education is not important to them."

I observe Mrs. McKinsey's Senior English class. She has twenty-one students today; one is white. There is a television in the room, as well as stacks of much-read paperbacks. Ten vocabulary words are on the board: "bathos," "banal," "biased," "chauvinistic," "circumspect," . . . , and Mrs. Mac, as everyone calls her, reads them off, the class pronouncing them with her.

"Get rid of that gum!" she admonishes. "Now you owe me some time after school!"

The lesson is on *The Canterbury Tales.* Lively and alert, Mrs. Mac is in her fifties, probably; authoritative enough to be called old-fashioned, motherly, she keeps her eye on them. Moving between the rows of desks, she pats one on the shoulder, closes a notebook of another, looks them in the face as she talks. Assigning the characters, she explains that she "will be Chaucer," they "will be the pilgrims," and that "come Monday" – a week away – they "will stand up here" and begin telling the tales they've read, and in their "own words." Everyone is to be responsible for knowing the portrait Chaucer drew of his character in the *General Prologue;* students are to keep it in mind as they prepare their roles. The paperback text they're using is in Modern English prose. Mrs. Mac ordered it for the class on her own, she tells me later, the selections in their textbook being insufficient for her purposes.

Everybody laughs – the boys whoop – when Mrs. Mac announces that on Monday she will appear "dressed like Chaucer." Warning that they "cannot wait until Sunday night" to start ("after swapping spit for thirty minutes"), she begins now getting them into the poem. "The same type of people exist today," she tells them, "they do." Not the same professions they represent maybe, but "the same type," and "that's important."

They are confused, hesitant, not sure what's expected of them; Mrs. Mac soothes and comforts. Fully responsive to all the uncertainty, she's able with no undue fuss to carry on several exchanges at once. She praises this one, teases another, chastises a third. The class isn't especially quiet, but it is attentive and, despite itself, interested. One or two are even shyly intrigued by the whole thing; they listen intently, silent and bright-eyed. A mixed group academically, the class as a whole is closer to being "below average"–as the standardized tests measure achievement–than not.

The period a little more than half over, Mrs. Mac has a student move a projector into place (film strip wound and ready for showing), and they have a short film on the literary and social background of the poem. Interest has waned, however, and not many pay the cartoon-like figures on the screen much mind. Notes get passed; talking picks up; bodies stretch. Perhaps seeing a film is too much like watching television to be taken seriously; perhaps they're just tired.

Weariness long ago settled into the lines of Mrs. Mac's face. The full knowledge of what a teacher like her is up against can be read there. Her mouth may tighten from time to time, and eyes that have seen it all may no longer have any capacity for surprise, but she's fiercely determined–prodding, admonishing, loving–and she gives little quarter. She wears the school color, a green ribbon in her hair, and on Friday she's driving the activity bus to the football playoffs. There are other things she tells them: that she had a flat tire on her bicycle, that her dog won the ugly dog contest, that the Competency Test is tomorrow.

But she teaches the lesson.

Timmons, another small though rural high school in Talton County, has had, like Edison, to bear the consequences of racial inbalance. About one-fourth of the county's population, as the 1980s got underway, fell below the poverty line: more than 25,000 people. According to a Timmons internal report, 397 of the school's 552 students qualified for the free-lunch program in 1979–80. As at Edison, having to do without is normal for most of these students.

Such figures surprise nobody in Talton County. Never an area of much industry except the railroad and three or four small mills, farming has been all that people have had to do. Now not even the mill towns flourish and no trains stop. Competition abroad and foreign imports have taken somewhat the same toll as did the new agriculture in the 1960s. Laborers still lucky enough to have jobs in the spinning mills, often enough uprooted tenants and hands and small farmers, come out to their cars to go home in the evening, white with cotton, the lint and dust sticking to them; now they must contend with the likes of Taiwan, Korea, and the Philippines. The loss of jobs, the unease and worry are devastating; Edison and Timmons both see the results in the lack of local funding for education, as for much of anything else; in students whose homes reel from the impact; in the broken will of the communities.

"Many students only come to school to eat," the Timmons report quotes a Talton County principal as saying.

In one high school, fewer than half of the students surveyed in 1977–78 lived with both parents. Over one-third of the girls had babies. Twenty-three percent of the fathers who had jobs and more than 30 percent of the working mothers worked in area mills. More than one-third of the mothers were unemployed, some heads of households.

Just 26.2 percent of the students' mothers had graduated from high school, and 28.5 percent of their fathers, though 2.4 percent of the mothers were college graduates, as compared with 2.0 percent of their fathers.

The week I spent at Timmons in December 1982, signs everywhere about the school exhorted, "If you think staying in school is tough, talk to someone who quit."

In the few minutes he has before the start of his EMH English class, Mr. Karl stands in the doorway, the students gathering in the hall slowly making their way into the classroom. I notice both how boisterous and how gentle they are; unlike most, these clamor to know who I am, but they ask their teacher my name, not me. In 1981, the Educable-Mentally Retarded in North Carolina's schools numbered more than thirty thousand.

"All I'm tryin' to do today," Mr. Karl tells me, "is keep 'em quiet."

Fourteen or fifteen students, all but two of them black, are set to work copying what Mr. Karl tells them is a short story. Writing covers the room's five blackboards, and the class is instructed to number the words as they copy them down.

A girl promptly puts her head on her desk, asking—telling, really—the boy next to her, "When time to go home, you wake me up?"

Most students talk continuously, though softly, and look around; two or three get up and mill about, sharpening pencils, bothering their friends, playing with the blinds. A few, however, perhaps even as many as half, are copying the passage. Their writing is slow and laborious.

Much of the steady hum, the "talk," I begin to realize, comes from their voicing to themselves the words they're struggling to get down on paper.

On the board is "A Visit from St. Nick." Mr. Karl doesn't read the poem aloud or say anything at all about it; nor does anybody ask to have it read. Nobody appears to recognize it – "'Twas the night before Christmas, and all through . . ."; they brood on the white words silently.

Mr. Karl comes over to where I'm sitting and says that he has "two LDs in here," two students who are "Learning Disabled." They "are the real hard core," he explains, the "ones who are unteachable." The state's "Learning Disabled" came to more than forty-five thousand in 1981.

To illustrate the point, Mr. Karl sends a boy to a wall map and tells him to find Florida. The young person, who probably is sixteen or so, begins by looking intently at the continent of Africa, and the teacher turns to me and laughs. Nobody else can find Florida either; some of them now laugh, too.

"Do you know why you're not having a Christmas party?" Mr. Karl asks. "Figure it out."

Nobody challenges him. Looks are exchanged, mouths tighten, but the remark alone, without query or discussion, fills the room.

"Some of them could learn a lot more than they do," Mr. Karl has told me, "if they'd apply themself."

"At Henderson High, a relatively large urban school with a reputation for excellence, I happen upon a history class where today there's a substitute teacher. Apparently, however, Mrs. Clark has been with the class for much if not all of the week because she announces that since they've not yet discussed the news, today they'll do that. Students have the responsibility, evidently, to keep up with the headlines.

"Is picketing a successful means of protest?" she asks. The reference is to an article in the local paper about a man in Washington, D. C., protesting nuclear build-up.

"If you have time to waste," a student declares.

There are twenty-five in the class, eleven black. In the manner of schoolrooms immemorial, pictures of presidents line the wall. Mrs. Clark's a kindly-seeming, older woman. She speaks well, is clearly interested in what she'd doing, but she's also what used to be called "prissy," and the students more or less ignore her.

"Can you believe everything you hear, everything you read?" Mrs. Clark wants to know.

"*Sports Illustrated*, you can," a boy pipes up. Several of the girls wince. The boys laugh.

Henderson is an affluent school generally, though a sizeable minority is as poor as anybody at Edison and Timmons. Considerably larger than they, on the whole Henderson has withstood the ravages of "white flight"; rather, black and white both seek to enroll their children here, the school offering academic programs and a degree of sophistication unavailable elsewhere in the immediate area. But what happens now reveals something of the abyss still separating the classes, politically as, of course, socially, which is to say, also, racially.

A black student mentions the soup kitchen a local church is running; Christmas on the way, people in need are making the news. The student doesn't say so outright, but plainly the piece in the paper has touched her; she's shyly approving.

But another student, a white boy of fifteen or so, breaks in to say that "all this is just taking away the American will to work," that if people are given food and clothes, they won't do anything but take them.

"Shee-it!" Helpless not to say it, the young black keeps the word under his breath; only his immediate seatmates hear it.

"Gettin' somethin' for nothin'," the first boy plunges ahead, his resentment manifest. From what source we cannot know, whether personal affront or because this is all he hears, in any case, a compelling fury hurtles him forward.

Seeking to defuse the issue, I suspect, Mrs. Clark frames a question having to do with unemployment in general; again, however, the class divides along the same lines. Some can't quite admit that even in Henderson people are without work; others know only too well the truth of the matter.

The black students are all very quiet, their silence purposeful, heavy. White students from families living as close to the edge as a good many of the black now find themselves torn: for them to argue against the kitchen would be to deny their own homes, whereas if they speak in its favor, they will call attention to the very hardship they've doubtless tried to hide, as well as align themselves with the blacks. Thus this air of boredom, which for some is real, food lines and soup kitchens being a long way from anything they've ever had to know, for others is assumed as a necessary alternative to self-revelation.

Finally, the dainty little girl who brought up the kitchen in the first place offers a compromise. "It's comin' out of our tax money," she says, an olive branch for the boy still flushed and angry, "our" most delicately put, but "the church is having a hard time."

"Ever'body's down there," another of the black girls says softly, as if to herself, "winos, people without jobs, . . . people with jobs. . . ."

Classes were different in the early 1960s when my generation came of age. In ways difficult to articulate, at levels forbiddingly private and subjective, there was then another quality of academic experience—and not just for me, not just for Billy and Donald, Alice Ray and Sandra, those of us who loved reading and going to school, but, also, for Hampton and Alma Doris, Kathryn and Jewitt, Woody and J. D. and Ben and Velburn Ray. For one thing, we were never grouped; for another, we were not near as regimented, as blatantly and pervasively subjected to discipline, as students nowadays routinely are. If the small country schools of my childhood hadn't yet been taken over by an educational bureaucracy bent upon ability-grouping and tracking, if standardized testing was only then just beginning to come into its own as a force ultimately determining the composition of classes, then we were the beneficiaries of our area's backwardness. A class like Mr. Karl's was unknown to us; teachers like Miss Pruett and Mr. Karl, I never had.

Nor were we yet the objects of any philosophy of education, national or otherwise; the latest theories, we hadn't heard. We had failure, and dropouts by the score—54.8 percent statewide in 1956. But no state competency test did we have to pass or else be placed in classes where the drills and test-like examples are endless, the workbooks and filling-in-the-blanks all anybody ever asking of us. For my generation, the curriculum still was content-centered; lessons were taught as if they mattered inherently. That there were certain things an educated person ought to know and be able to do nobody doubted; *students* may have questioned such an assumption from time to time, but nobody paid our criticism any mind. Discerning critics of our own education, nobody thought us to be. That schools might be brought to respond to the criticism of the young was a lesson of the 1960s to be sure, but not one that anybody graduating in 1963 would have caught.

We had the incalculable benefit of our peers, and our peers were everybody going to school with us. Our lives forever bear the imprint not only of those classmates smarter than ourselves, but also, and as memorably, of those less capable; not because any teacher had us try to teach one another—they would have smiled at such a notion—but inevitably, as a consequence of being in a room where students of varying interests and perspectives, of widely diverse abilities, had a part to play. Thus we were saved from the assumption that only we had the answers, Billy or Alice Ray, Sandra or Donald often enough outdoing us; or that only we never knew anything, we too, even if usually we were wrong, being sometimes right. Donald's brilliance in math and science, his sheer economy in working a problem or balancing an equation, mattered profoundly to us, subtly altering the academic timbre. Real intellectual ability wasn't something that weaker students only heard about; this abstraction they were somehow being measured against wasn't segregated from their daily experience. Nor was it something only teachers possessed.

Despite our individual capacities and talents, we inhabited but one academic world. Arriving in the morning, we knew we would be attending many of the same classes throughout the day. Neither were we the victims of an ineluctable sameness, the arid and alienating sense that we were unteachable. Being neither grouped nor tracked, we were spared the invidious labels, the public demarcation of our academic status, and we escaped, also, a teacher's expectation that the class we were in may have been pitiably deficient and thus, in all likelihood, beyond her help.

But this isn't the whole of the matter. The truth is, also, that even in the early 1960s area high-school students underwent a less rigid, less systematic kind of tracking than has since come to be. Some classes the less academically-inclined never took—algebra, trigonometry, physics, French—just as certain boys never took agriculture or shop, or certain girls never took bookkeeping and shorthand. If we were spared the ignominy of being in "low" classes, nonetheless everybody knew who was smart and who wasn't. School was always inimical to some; poverty wasn't the only reason students quit.

But failure was not then, as it is today, a function of school itself; there were disappointments, and students suffered for their inadequacies, but the process wasn't deterministic. Students at least stood some chance of learning whatever it was holding them back and then reclaiming their place with the others. There were not then significant numbers of young people still in school for whom the day might be spent in going first to Miss Pruett's class, then to Mr. Karl's, then perhaps to Mrs. Johnson's—a day, a year, twelve years; thus a generation for whom failure is irreversible, who are singularly ill-prepared for either a job or further schooling, young men and women as throwed away in the world as they have been in school.

Huckleberry Finn thought the world was right, however far away from it he tried to run; the burden for feeling different, he took upon himself. Young people, especially if they're in trouble, characteristically make the same assumption. Out-of-step with things as they are, with what seems to be working for other people, the source of their distress must be themselves. That boredom may be, in fact, legitimate, isn't a conclusion many students want or are able to reach. They may express rebellion in other ways, accusing anybody else who's handy, but at the level where it truly counts, the conviction of their own guilt likely remains entrenched, solid and unshakable. The fact that, no less than the rest of us, they *do* sometimes cause their problems merely confirms the point. For the average teenager, blaming one's self isn't necessarily harmful; but for the others, the ones silent and always on the periphery, the disengaged, those in whom there's nothing but a lusterless passivity, the mechanism is important. People in trouble always have a hard time, of course, separating themselves, their own fears and imaginings, from the literal facts of the matter. The boundaries here are as tenuous as they are profound.

And such young people are everywhere in the schools—and out. Glenda, for example, dropped out of Jackson, though it could as easily have been Coastal Plains or Timmons, Edison or Henderson. She was in the eleventh grade, she told me, and failing. Listen to her:

> Teachers would say, "What are you doing here? I thought you dropped out." . . . I wasn't a very important person. . . . The year I quit [in 1982], fifty-nine students quit. I hated it so much. I had skipped sixty days and never got in any trouble for skipping.
>
> I had a few good teachers . . . art and English. And [Mr. Williams] really cares. If he was principal, I'd go back.
>
> Most teachers at Jackson High School are so secure in their jobs they can do about what they please. [The main faults of most of them are] not giving a damn, not caring, and—'Their way or no way!'
>
> [The principal] is a joke. All he cares about are preppy students and the football team.
>
> In the tenth grade is when it started getting bad. You're supposed to enjoy school! . . . I didn't enjoy it.
>
> My friends that quit, they're not stupid. It's a matter of just despising it.
>
> I love to read. I read everything I can get my hands on. I didn't drop out because I was stupid. I kind of wish I had that as an excuse.
>
> I wouldn't go back for anything in this world.
>
> [But Glenda worries that her brother in the ninth grade] is falling into the

> same trap at Jackson as I did. I'm not going to let him quit. At least I caught him early. He wants to be a baseball player. He'll have a chance at college, but not me. I have the technical school.
>
> . . . I hope you don't think bad of me for dropping out.

When Glenda dropped out, having failed the eleventh grade, her mother got her to enroll in the high-school equivalency program at the local technical college. "Getting my GED was real easy," she says. In June 1983, Glenda was thinking of going into physical therapy or, perhaps, computers – "somewhere the money's at!"

But rarely does a story such as Glenda's have a happy ending. Two years hence, in June 1985, she was still at home. She had done some part-time work here and there, but for the most part she hadn't found anything to do; that is, until the last month when she had gotten on at Glenoit Mills, only to work five days, then break her foot and have to be out again. The brother she thought she had talked into staying in school dropped out in the tenth grade, in 1984. For a while he had a job doing carpentry work, but for weeks he was laid off. Yet Glenda still insists that for herself she doesn't regret dropping out "not one bit. . . . If it'a been a good high school, maybe I would, but not Jackson, not like it was, I don't."

Glenda and Ronnie, both now in their twenties, both unemployed and close to being unemployable, live at home with their mother, a supervisor at a fast-food restaurant.

Throughout the 1970s, more then 30,000 of the state's high-school students dropped out each year, 36,000 in 1971; yet the rates *were* edging downward, if slowly, from 34 percent in 1971 to 27.1 percent in 1981. In the 1985–86 school year, 27,700 students dropped out, 27.7 percent.[7] They leave because they can't cope, because for them school no longer has any validity. They want to be treated differently. "Taking names in high school!" Glenda can hardly believe, "just like in elementary school!" The rules and restrictions, the regimentation that defines every aspect of the school day, the hours of seat work, of lessons that seldom speak to them, either because they're neither challenging nor important, or the teacher's demeanor is off-putting, or because the student isn't equipped or willing to respond; all of it they find shriveling to the soul. Passed along from grade to grade, failure about them like a cloak impossible to doff; always on the outside; in Group II or the "B" group, many of them, or that for the educationally disabled (called "PCs" at one high school, "Privileged Characters"); some of them never having learned to read, others much brighter than average. Facing it all again day after day proves, finally, to be too much. Education as an intellectual endeavor capable of exalting the spirit, filling the mind, something emotionally and mentally satisfying, this they've not experienced, and, yet, they know that in school, too, as surely in themselves, something's missing. ("I didn't drop out because I was stupid," Glenda said. "I kind of wish I had that as an excuse. . . . I love to read. I read everything I can get my hands on.")

"Young people drop out of school precisely for the reason people drop out of life," Ernest Boyer, president of the Carnegie Foundation, has said. "They lose their way."[8]

"Academics just get lost in high school." Donald Jenkins was twenty-eight when he made this statement to me in 1982. A graduate of an area high school that might have been Edison or Timmons, Jackson perhaps, Donald says he can barely read and write. Married now and the father of a baby girl, unemployed, he's enrolled in a program for teaching associates at Nash Technical College. He wants "to work with" elementary school children, maybe as a teacher's aide.

"Blacks don't know any better than to take vocational courses, play sports. . . . They don't realize . . . just don't realize . . . that if you can't read and write how tough life's gonna' be for you."

Donald thinks that in high school, because he was black, his father a tenant, because he didn't seem very capable academically, and probably not much interested, he was "sloughed off into vocational courses . . . shop, and all like that." Now at the technical college, he worries that the same thing is happening again, that because he reads so poorly he's being nudged into a trade rather than encouraged in the career he would like.

"When you just in high school," Donald says, "you don't know nothin'! You don't know any better. You do what they tell you, what'cha think they want'cha to do, . . . what looks easy.

"I know lots of families," he continues, "where only one person can read. That one person'll have to read ever'thing to everybody . . . ever' thing the mailman brings.

"I won't be able to read it," Donald laughs, referring to this book. "Other people can."

Education nationally, no less than in eastern North Carolina (from where the large majority of the area's teachers come), has long cared more for the student and his acculturation than the subject itself; more for methodology than for immersion in an academic discipline. Progressivism valued "the whole child," laying seige on all fronts to the content-centered curriculum – a profound misdirection, but long-lived. Yet if the schools have no particular intellectual authority, neither do they have any other; if they equate the academic with everything else, the intellectual heritage thus available merely in fragments, regarded as an option and primarily just for some students, then the loss is irreparable. Competence alone isn't enough. Teachers without, also, a scholarly cast of mind stand before their students oddly bereft, as if they were clerks in stores and had no notion of the products they dispensed; they lack that theoretical and comprehensive understanding that is the mark of the true professional.

A teacher's authority isn't simply a matter of discipline but also of knowledge; ideally, he or she will command personal respect, but, as important, respect for the subject itself. Once this vital connection is severed, nobody assuming any particular relationship between teachers and the subject of which they are but the mediators, students may be hard-pressed to discover why either the teacher or the course any longer matters. Yet success in the classroom is typically rewarded by removal from it, and, in fact, schools neither require nor assume any special intimacy between teachers and their fields; the two are as separable as anything else only tangentially related. An assistant principalship is seen as a promotion, and driver's education, for example, is commonly regarded as preferable to classroom instruction.

Teachers whose education is in history or English may spend half-days taking attendance, monitoring school buses, or meting out punishment. Teenagers they're teaching how to drive chauffer them about the countryside. The notion that a teacher happy and effective in the classroom will also be happy doing these other things doesn't strike most school people as inherently illogical or as indicative of anything especially disturbing about education.

From such a perspective, academic classes cannot but seem incidental to the larger concerns of life; their immediate uses – stale, flat, and unprofitable. School is important for many students only insofar as they see it enabling them to arrive later, always later, at where they (presumably) want to be. What occurs in English class, in history and science and algebra, isn't commonly understood as significant for its own sake: the payoff isn't so much now, students are encouraged to think, as later.

That there is pleasure in coming to grips with a body of knowledge, and that such pleasure is, in fact, inherent in the experience of learning itself, isn't anything most people in eastern North Carolina, including school people, believe.

For courses not academic, curiously, such as typing, welding, home economics, small-engine repair, and many others, where the connection between the teacher and his discipline – between learning and employment, knowing and doing – is explicit and direct, the fact that students often like what they're taking doesn't surprise us. That a boy may sign up for auto mechanics merely because he likes tinkering with cars, nobody finds unusual. No one winces at the argument that the real worth of the course lies in this basic satisfaction it proves capable of providing: the mental solution of a problem, the mechanical expertise required for fixing it, even the grime. That a specific job may await those excelling at such work is secondary.

But to say, on the other hand, that a boy and girl like English because they enjoy tinkering with words, or history because they're fascinated by time is to invite quite another response, if not disbelief. Not everybody will grant that pleasure is not only desirable but also necessary for the serious engagement of geometry and chemistry, the Civil War and Shakespeare; that these subjects, too, a teacher finding them pleasurable herself, may be communicated such that they enliven and enlarge the mind, sharpen the intellectual capacity, and provide a realm other than the present, a knowledge broader than a child's own family and town and time – at whatever level they're taught, and for young people of widely varying academic abilities and interests.

Area teachers remark these misplaced emphases, of course; of professionalization that, for all the strides forward the schools may rightly claim, still centers more on appearance than substance. Statewide competency testing may still address but the bare surface of functional illiteracy (though at least now, the argument goes, every student must demonstrate some minimal ability to read and compute before being handed a diploma). Schools maintain watch over their students' scores on the national standardized tests as zealously as ever my father eyed his tobacco crop, knowing that in each year's published results they, too, are being weighed. Never have certification requirements for teachers been more rigid; never have local school boards paid them more mind. Raleigh and the central offices mandate more and more.

But eastern North Carolina schools don't yet confront the intellectual deficiency at the heart of the matter. Instead, there is this mechanical formalizing of requirements and criteria, these piecemeal attempts to define classroom learning as primarily that which lends itself to objective measurement; and there is the development within the system itself of such complaisance that smart and well-educated teachers are as likely to find themselves in as tiny a minority now as twenty and thirty years ago. Many more teachers and administrators now have master's degrees, though I met few who conducted themselves as if the life of the mind was crucial. The question begs asking whether the integrity of that over which school people have authority, which is not simply people and matériel, but learning itself, can be held intact by those for whom it's never especially mattered; who may be good people, but aren't readers, their mental lives as likely denuded of significance as anybody else's. Schools that have lost the capacity to symbolize learning will not easily be reclaimed.

Excellent teachers decry the inadequacies of poor ones; administrators, they take as they find them. Their career as teachers they likely find frustrating and demoralizing, and not always for the usual reasons having to do with recalcitrant or unprepared or uninterested students. So much is expected of school that has nothing to do with education; the tenor of American life, as of eastern North Carolina, seldom is conducive to the reflection necessary for scholarship. Little wonder is it that teachers, no better equipped than the rest of us to combat such an endemic passivity as they typically encounter, sometimes lose their way, the sense "that there's something fine about knowing things"[9] withering within them. If they had more time and fewer students, more support and less paperwork, less pressure and more money, fewer nonteaching responsibilities and . . . but the list is a long one.

"There's a peak time in a teacher's life . . . after a while she just doesn't have it anymore. . . . *My* education's outdated!" The woman telling me this, a retired teacher in Duplin County, had more in mind, I think, than just the need for teachers to keep up; nor did she mean just that age may undermine competence. Rather, she put her finger on something else, something particularly important to teaching. There's a fine balance between the sheer bravura required for commanding an audience, the *same* audience, day in and day out, the authority upon which this rests, and the inevitable feeling after a while of being ensnared within one's own repetitions. Even to themselves, teachers may begin to sound like teachers; they begin to experience the peculiar bafflement of people who are always working, yet who never fully know whether or not they're accomplishing anything much. Teaching young people, they never have a finished product (or, or course, a "product" at all). Theirs is the special anxiety befalling anybody whose traffic is in ideas, and that is the abstractness, the ineffability, of their true work; hence, the absurdity of comparing teachers with, for example, businessmen – or farmers.

A teacher's peak time is brief, transitory. Students are always young; teachers get old, and in more ways than one. But what's left once the peak time passes doesn't have to be simply a lazy vacuity, an unattachment of mind so profound that everything unlucky enough to fall under its gaze is heedlessly diminished. Dullness is always the occupational dragon, the Grendel to be subdued. For teachers, however, it's an affliction more devastating than practically any other; neither competence nor dedication can conceal or offset a fundamental drabness of mind – not in a classroom – and the accumulative effect upon a child who has two or three such teachers is stultifying. Teachers who don't read, whose careers have come to an emotional deadend, who have lost the capacity or the will for digging down within themselves in pursuit of some happier resolution: they may be middle-aged and tenured or fresh out of college, black or white, men or women; they may teach in reportedly good schools or poor, public or private, but they're not hard to find.

They were everywhere in the schools I visited. That the life of the mind requires for its sustenance a deep and abiding commitment; that close reading and critical analysis are perhaps the most crucial of all things to be taught, and hence to be demonstrated; that a self-satisfied parochialism is incommensurate with, indeed devastating to, learning: some few teachers may still hold these beliefs, but not many. What the teachers of my childhood took for granted, knew to be as absolute as the changing seasons, these teachers seem never to have known; most think *they,* if not the person down the hall, are doing a good job, and that the schools are in pretty good shape. If they aren't all as given to boosterism as superintendents are, neither are they usually very critical.

Local schools hire a good many teachers born and raised in the immediate area, many having gone to the nearest college and never having traveled much outside the region. They have the same fields to drive alongside of on their way to work in the mornings as perhaps their parents once tended. In spring, rows of tobacco plants just set out are as straight as lines on notebook paper, and in December the land is clean.

They think (perhaps) of the capaciousness of language, coming upon a country store calling itself the "Zackly-Rite"; of history, remembering that along here Sherman rampaged, and Cornwallis (though Yorktown awaited *him*), the Tuscarora and the Lumbee; of God, there being nothing finer among us than the churches built in the eighteenth and nineteenth centuries, white and plain. Or perhaps they see none of this, and think nothing, the fast-food places and shopping malls, the franchised Chinese restaurants, Holiday Inns, gas stations, mobile-home dealerships, and anywhere else a man can spend or make a dollar, interesting them more.

Not everything has changed. Students and their parents submit themselves still to the authority of school, and schools have still the central place in a community (or, where they don't, something's deeply wrong). Conversations fueled by local rivalries, as by school news generally, are likely to be as heated now as thirty years ago, teams and players as much debated. People in town think their schools better than those in the country, and for every rural school, there's always another one across the way that somebody thinks is worse. Still, one end of Duplin County considers itself superior to the other, Edgecombe County still plays catch-up with Nash, and Talton – for years now, people have just shaken their head over Talton County. In 1985, twenty percent of those responding to a state survey said their local schools were better than those elsewhere; only five percent rated their own schools as poor.[10] Men and women who have not stepped inside a school in years, their children long since out and on their own, still may hold forth with the greatest conviction, the pluses and minuses of such-and-such a school, such-and-such a teacher as clear to them as that the sun rose this morning. Nobody contradicts them.

More determinedly progressive than ever in our history; more fully engaged in bringing students of whatever race together under one system, the disbursement of public money for education thus being more equitable than ever before, and by far the most costly: public education in eastern North Carolina in the 1980s. The achievements of the last quarter-century have been real, and, in many particulars, they remain impressive. To have weathered the early years of integration, the system itself not just surviving but also stronger for the conflict; to have made the enormous effort of educating every person of school age; to have broadened the curriculum, strengthening, especially, the sciences and mathematics, and expanding offierings in vocational education: these are solid gains, and school people here take justifiable pride in them, as may we all.

But inherent in such progressivism is the betrayal of a generation.[11] Unable to fend for themselves, the academically weak are often enough, also, the poor. They are young people whose parents may be no better able to fathom school than they, and whose homes may be no comfort. The irony cuts hard: that in reform should lie this profound inequity; that in striving to provide a better education for all, we should have perpetuated the virtual entrapment of so many; and that failure should have become what too often even parent, child, teacher, and school now expect.

There is a final irony: that these should be the children and grandchildren of people themselves undone by progress, the new agriculture of the 1960s that forced their grandparents off the land, and the new industrialism of the 1970s and 1980s that, for their parents, is a long way still from making good on the promises seemingly inherent in it. Their parents have had to come to terms with just how grindingly hard it is for them even to keep up, much less earn their way into an appreciably better standard of living. In the 1980s, learning one's way "up and out" is, for all but the academically superior, increasingly problematic, too. Working people still believe an education is the best hope their children can have. Too few students, however, are sufficiently empowered by their classes to take such a lesson to heart; for most, this is just something else their parents and other old folks say.

Donald and Glenda, Corinne and Joanie and Larry, the boy trying to find Florida in Mr. Karl's class, others whose classes I observed and with whom I talked, at Coastal Plains and Edison, Timmons and Wexler and Henderson: what will happen to them? where will they end up? They are caught between two worlds—the farms from which eastern North Carolina has long drawn sustenance and definition, and the factories and plants now providing most of the best jobs around—and they lack the education to participate fully in, even if they could afford, whatever we mean by the good life. How will they endure, marrying and raising their own children in a world whose material rewards increasingly will go to the educated and assured? For them, too, as for the children of the affluent, school days may prove their happiest.

In house after house "Down East" there are no books. Poverty isn't always or necessarily the reason, either. "Plenty of people living in

[Brushwood]," a guidance counselor tells me, "didn't graduate from high school"; their hundred- or hundred-and-fifty-thousand-dollar house may be as bereft of books, if not of the local paper and *Southern Living,* as anybody else's. And in the country, except for the Bible, for the school books and papers and occasional notes a child brings home, the light bill and telephone bill and junk mail the mailman leaves, there may be nothing to read at all. Teachers approaching retirement may not yet have developed their own library. Public education more accessible than ever before, more insistently professional, hasn't yet changed the fact that most adults have still to work, and work hard, nearly all the time, many at more than one job; nor have the schools convinced many that learning is anything to be taken seriously.

Not, however, that even if people didn't have to work as hard as they do they would take the pains to seek out a bookstore, buy a book, and read. More likely they would go to the motorcycle races off a dirt road in the country near Pinetops (where on summer Saturday nights sometimes, in 1985 at least, a little blonde girl no more than seven or eight raced her three-wheeler, pigtail flying); supper over and the dishes washed, they'd sit on one another's porches, their words of no more moment than the smoke from a cigarette; they'd watch television and look through the *News-Argus* or the *Sampson Independent,* drive by the Tastee-Freeze or go to bed early. As for education, they would say that's what the schools are for, reading and writing and arithmetic.

As for school people, by whom they would mean their children's teachers and principal, they'd say they're pretty much like everybody else nowadays.

8. Little Black (Little White) Schoolhouse

Dominion High School, in Athens County, and Edison High School, in Talton County, reflect the impact on education of such white havens as the private academies and certain of the public schools. Both schools are still, in the 1980s, predominantly black, many white parents having pulled their children our deliberately, the pattern of their lives taking them more and more to the surrounding countrysides where, increasingly, they choose to live, where as the years pass the jobs tend increasingly to be. The effect is twofold. Some public schools, as well as all the private schools, are comprised overwhelmingly of white students; on the other hand, schools in Dominion, as within the Edison area of Talton County, tend to be just as pervasively black. The plain truth is that, where these racial separations figure, city schools tend to be black and county schools white, especially when, as here, a county has within it a dominant, larger city. For counties without a dominant town, however, Duplin County, for example, schools are more evenly balanced racially. This is to say, also, that where there is but one system of educational jurisdiction in a given geographic area, schools are apt to be more integrated than not.

The 1970 Census displayed for the first time the kind of profound demographic shifts which undergird these generalizations. In eastern North Carolina as throughout the South those hands and tenants leaving the farms since the 1960s, if they've not rented a house in the country, have relocated in neighboring towns and villages; black people in relatively large numbers have moved into housing projects. Middle-class whites, on the other hand, have moved to the country and into the suburbs. Area schools bear still the imprint of such patterns.

School systems, ever alert to the competition between public schools and private, proved considerably less alert to the growing competition, beginning in the late 1960s, between different interests within the system of public education itself. Most people had always assumed that "the schools" were a unified bureaucracy; that is, the dual systems existing under segregation were each seen singly, though of course as mutually exclusive. The pressures consequent upon integration, however, as well as the racially lopsided enrollments to be found where people live in and thus perpetuate segregated neighborhoods, have meant that public schools may no longer be perceived as one. In place after place, whether a school employee now works for a city system or a county, he likely has a harder job convincing us that schools as a whole are all part of the same endeavor; that they share a common social and philosophical ground.

To this extent, education in eastern North Carolina looks like that in the South generally and bears comparison as well with the kind of inner-city ghettoization that is often the case elsewhere. Yet the phenomenon is especially interesting here for several reasons. Because here there are not huge figures to comprehend, the population even in a city the size of Dominion or Rocky Mount being no more than forty-five thousand or so; because so much of this population is stable, thus providing a social continuum capable of reflection upon such a change; for these reasons, there is a clarity to the issue here that is not everywhere available. There is, this is to say, general public awareness of the split. The scene is not so crowded that its basic configuration is not apparent to those willing to see it.

To drive by Dominion High School early in the morning as its students are arriving can leave no one in doubt about the racial composition of the student body; a drive by the county schools makes the same point. If you were a long-time resident of the area, if you remembered the schools as they were prior to, say, 1970, then the difference would be all the more compelling. Dominion High School was once, in the 1940s and 1950s, even into the early 1960s, not just lily white, as of course was every "white" school, but as anti–poor white almost as it was anti-black; thus it seemed to me then. Class snobbishness then tended to be deliberate and conscious, whereas racial prejudice was so deeply ingrained in most of us that those slights and injuries stemming from it, cruel as they were, were often (usually?) neither personal nor purposeful. Not that Dominion High School had not always had some poor white students; it had, of course. Nonetheless, there was a mystique about Dominion, an aura of sophistication, and whether there was any factual basis for our feelings or not, those of us who lived in the country and attended a county school found even the building itself to be rather intimidating.

When, in the late 1950s, Peggy Tyndall left Adamsville, and the county high school she otherwise would have attended, in order that she might live with a relative in Dominion and take Latin at Dominion High School, people were properly impressed. Of the schools we then knew anything about, Dominion was, we had no doubt, the best. On a windy, icy day in November 1962, it had been Dominion High School, for example, where I had to go to take, together with perhaps as many as two hundred others, the SAT. (My father's pickup had no working heater, and I had ridden huddled in a quilt, memorizing for the last time my list of algebraic formulae.)

Now, on these mornings in the early fall of 1982, as again I made my way to Dominion High School, this time to observe classes and talk with students and school personnel, I thought of us test-takers that pilgrim-gray day twenty years ago. We were the pride of our small, consolidated high schools, many of us: white; middle class or upper or aspiring to be, treated by our schools as if we were; a serious lot. Now, this November, I had reason to compare not just my own former self but also the generation of which I was a part with these young people for whom Dominion was just the high school they happened to attend.

Nothing of course was more revealing of the catalysm the times had endured than the mere physical presence of black men and women, black boys and girls, now quite at home in a school that their parents could never have entered except as custodians. There was something perversely right, even in a strange way comforting, in the fact that obviously and unmistakably these students felt themselves under no compulsion to "be nice" especially, or other than their usual boisterous selves, in the presence of this new and unknown white woman suddenly in their midst. That they should react to my being there with such utter casualness spoke volumes (not, however, to be taken for any lack of awareness on their part, they knowing very well that I was *there.*).

Besides the teacher, I was the only white person present the day I sat in on a small class in Basic English, and I knew that I was as much observed as observer. Young as these students were, fifteen or sixteen, maybe one or two seventeen or eighteen, they were, at some inner core of their being, also and forever old. Never would the eyes of the girl across from me get any more worldly, nor the face of the boy next to

Above: A community school throughout the forties, fifties, and sixties. Now the site of a sewing plant. *Below:* "And the private schools that sprang up, . . . how appropriate that they should be established within the shells of the former segregated public schools: oiled floors, . . . gallery-width central halls, high ceilings, . . ." An area private academy housed in a former "white" public school. (Photos by Linda Flowers, 1989.)

A former community school, now abandoned. Note the Palladian windows. (Photo by Linda Flowers, 1989.)

"Nothing finer . . . than the plain white churches, . . . dating from the eighteenth and early nineteenth centuries." (Photo by Linda Flowers, 1989.)

After the logging crew has left. Forests in eastern North Carolina are fast disappearing, the lumber companies taking their toll. (Photo by Linda Flowers, 1989.)

her any more contemptuous. I looked at them: at their white, cloth tennis shoes, their clothes all the thinnest of materials, the cheapest polyester, but for their coats the same clothes thay had worn in August when school began. (I and most of my classmates used to wear our one set of "school clothes" the whole year, too.)

These, so their teacher told me, were the hard core, "students deemed almost sure to fail the Competency Test," some not for the first time. They were the ones who by every measure were most severely marked for lives of one failure after another, and every one of them knew that this was so: that this was not only the way it was, but the way it was going to be; and more even than this, they knew that they—that the fellow sitting next to them—knew the score, and that the teacher in the room, despite everything to the contrary she had told them or ever could tell them, knew it, too. This white interloper with her pad and pen, watching *them,* studying *them*—they had had no say-so about that, either.

"And the beat goes on, . . . and the beat goes on. . . ." Giggling, the student carrying on the song cuts her eyes at me, then grins, smirks, really. The class is General Math and the teacher is sixty, perhaps, fluttery, as alien to these young people as if she were of another species. The room is too small for the size of the class, and the students, gangling and half-grown, sit practically touching. Do they care at all that a lesson is being conducted? Will any of them ever have a Mastercard or Visa, their teacher telling them now how such cards work, and will they have mailboxes, too, these bills and all the others falling there? Isn't installment debt almost the *last* thing they need to be encouraged to think is all right?

A boy shows some snapshots to the fellows around him. Six or seven others huddled together at the side of the room suddenly break into song, not loud but not soft either, snapping their fingers to its rhythm. The teacher moves about among them, helping those who are doing the seat-work she assigned. The bell sounding, I and the students hurry away, Mrs. Patrick's parting words in my ear: "I warned you."

A guidance counselor, Mr. Gillette, tells me that this year for the first time since integration students are "fussing if they can't get academic classes"; that "before, they didn't want academic classes." The school, he says, is seventy-five to eighty percent black, and not many of its students come from middle- or upper-class homes. Most live in or within range of the five housing projects in Dominion. Yet, Mr. Gillette thinks, neither the college-preparatory, private school nor the Christian academy, both within a few miles of Dominion, hurts Dominion "that much": for one thing, "there just simply aren't that many white people in the city anymore"; for another, the majority of Dominion's black students have no thought of college. The private school, therefore, is no more a rival for these students than the fundamentalist academy. The Christian school, however, does draw off some white students, Mr. Gillette concludes, and would likely draw more if more parents could afford it. But "whites who used to come here," he points out, "now go to [Wexler]," a county school whose student body is largely white.

"A lot of people," Mr. Gillette adds, making an effort to distinguish between the public's perception of Dominion High School and what he thinks to be the truth, "see the riff-raff and judge the whole school by them." White people who think they know the school, he continues, often don't. Tales of Dominion's internal problems are exaggerated.

Dominion's tradition is one of distinguished performance and leadership. Fifty years ago its faculty and administrative staff were second to none, and not just in eastern North Carolina. There has always been in Dominion a cadre of teachers, black perhaps even more than white, the more impressive for the general tenor of its professionalism. Not many high schools in the state, much less "Down East" where most public-school teachers have typically been, as they still are, home-grown and locally educated, could have numbered among their faculty, as did Dominion in 1978, graduates of Columbia and Connecticut Wesleyan, Pennsylvania, Howard, Tulane and Indiana, Harvard, as well as the better colleges and universities in North Carolina. Why this should be the case bears consideration. When desegregation came, and the merger of the dual racial systems was accomplished (here, by 1970), both black teachers and white now for the first time working side by side in the same schools, teaching many of the same students, Dominion could at last draw fully and as an integrated unit upon the talent and experience of a superior black faculty.

Black teachers had historically held Franklin High, Dominion's "black" high school, in some esteem; accredited by the State Department of Public Instruction since 1926, Franklin had long been known for its reportedly excellent academic program. Because teaching positions even when times were good had always been relatively scarce, the best black teachers had tended to remain at the best "black" schools, as, given a choice, their white counterparts had likely gravitated toward the better "white" schools. In Dominion, where both the "white" and "black" high schools had been good, desegregation had the effect of bringing together two especially well-educated and sophisticated faculties. (Franklin, however, wasn't the only "black" school in Athens County thus recognized. Booker T. Washington High, south of Dominion, was for years the only school in the county system, black or white, to be regionally accredited by the Southern Association of Colleges and Schools.)

Pride of profession, this is to affirm, had long been the rule for both blacks and whites within the two systems from which the initial faculty of an integrated Dominion High School was eventually drawn; and, more than anything else, it is the education of its older teachers that sets the school apart still, in 1982, despite its many problems: overcrowding, the threatened decay of its once fine, old central building, the lack of interest and unruliness of some of its students, the drugs and occasional violence. Despite such tensions, Dominion both knows and honors its history. Are students affected by Dominion's past? Do they know or care where their teachers went to college? Does this matter to them, finally, they who so seldom think of the past as anything but what the old people are always talking about? I believe that for teenagers, too, and especially, the reputation of a place, of the school they attend, is crucial.

In Dominion desegregation, when it began in the early 1960s, was met with unusual foresight by both races. An early published study drew this conclusion:

> Community leaders became convinced by their own philosophy of the public interest, and got "hooked" into supporting the public schools rather than behaving as a special interest group, as did their neighbors who deserted the public schools for the [private school opening in 1969].

Plans were developed that dealt with the merger of the two school systems, one black and one white, as well as with "white flight," no single plan (of course) winning universal approval:

> Opposition to the plan [to reduce "white flight"] came primarily from fundamentalist churches under whose auspices private schools were spawned.

The fact that there *were* plans, however, and that community leaders of both races worked together cannot be overestimated.

Some three hours north of Dominion, in Edison, another story may be told. Though desegregation here, as in Dominion, has left Edison

High School "black" and the high school in the next town "white," never was there an enlightened white leadership that worked toward preserving the Edison public schools. From the beginning, integration was vigorously resisted. And although Edison High is less than one-third the size of Dominion (which ought to mean that life here is more easily managed than there), its problems loom at least as large. In Edison during the early years of desegregation, an internal study concludes, "community leaders placed their children in private schools and showed little interest in the public schools." Thus established, this pattern of neglect has apparently changed little in the twenty to twenty-five years since.[1]

Resources and community involvement are intimately related to a school's enrollment. Nor is it simply numbers alone that matter, or even their racial breakdown. More than this, the differing sectors of a community supporting a school are crucial to the school's sense of itself. Whether a school perceives itself as an integral part of its setting, neither an unwanted, barely mentionable offspring nor the heir, pampered and petted: either point of view will be engraved upon its students, whatever their race or background may be. Schools that are peripheral, irrelevant to the people who count in the community, lose after a while their souls: the buildings may remain, certain teachers still may fight the good fight, but "the school" no longer exists. What else was segregation, if not precisely this willful sidetracking of one race by the other? Yet there was black autonomy *within* the old Negro school system, and to the black community their own schools never were peripheral.

Nowadays in Edison, however, as elsewhere, the high school that is only nominally integrated lacks both the town's financial support and its pride. For the large part, only those whites having no other choice any longer enroll, though Edison still, in 1982, is governed by a self-perpetuating white school board and a white superintendent. Blacks, seeing that they have so little real influence anymore, have withdrawn a good measure of their support, too. Locked in mortal combat as such schools and towns are, what they are ultimately fighting for is the right to be a part of that definition a community forms of itself. Anybody listening knows that Edison's students are only too well aware of where they stand in Edison.

Three or four private academies, their enrollments hovering between 300 and 350, today flourish within commuting distance of Edison. Divided as they are racially from the public schools, these private schools are separated also along the lines of economic class, although they do enroll some white children of modest means (their parents working two jobs sometimes in order to send them, some on full or partial scholarship). As its own study makes clear, however, Edison High School can have but one view of the matter:

> . . . the poverty level of [our] high school population is much higher than that of the community as a whole, because many of the whites, who considered themselves to be "well off" financially, migrated to the private school community.

Inevitably, such "white flight" has resulted in "diminishing community support of the [Edison] schools," the study concludes.

Those Edison High School students with whom I talked and in whose classes I sat in October 1982 had a profound sense that their education was not as good as that offered elsewhere; their perception of inferiority, of the fact that other people regarded their school, and hence them, as inferior, was, I think, crippling to them. For one thing, they seemed very much affected by what they described as a lack of leadership in the school itself. Their principal was not a person they admired. "He just *here,* that's all," one of them said to me, his voice quiet and sad. "He like a firecracker with no fire." For many students and teachers, the principal no longer much mattered. Neither did the school as a whole see itself as any longer important within the larger community. The victim of continued "white flight," and of the neglect by the white power structure that is synonymous with it, Edison had, if not broken down entirely, at least lost its direction.

Edison High sits off to the side of a street around a bend. (A white country club is across the way, not itself visible from here, although the trees surrounding it and on its golf course are the forest that you see.) Morning sunlight hits it in front, the shades in some classrooms remaining drawn until late in the afternoon. Emerging from the building's darkened halls after much of the day spent inside is like walking from night into a light you had almost forgotten could exist. Something nearly indefinable marks the place as having once been a "Negro school." It isn't just that the small, frame houses surrounding Edison are inhabited by black people, that the women and old men you see on the porches and in the yards, hanging out wash and talking to each other in twos and threes, all are black. There is the drabness of the building, though it's clean enough; the cheapness of construction; the fact that money was spent only where it had to be spent—excepting just the new gymnasium behind the main building: but for the gym, all earmarks of a school once thought to be more appropriate for blacks than for whites. That the school is still eighty-five percent black is not, therefore, surprising.

"A lot of the parents," I was told, "live up North, their kids being raised by grandparents or somebody else." Some parents, white and black alike, live in Norfolk, Virginia, and work in the shipyards there, coming home to be with their families only on weekends. "There *is* no community anymore," a teacher said: "Integration has destroyed that, too." Not even many of the *black* teachers, white teachers were quick to point out, actually live *in* Edison. Of the twenty-five or so teachers then on the faculty, probably as many as fifteen or sixteen live somewhere else, a history teacher said. Nor do the principal, the guidance counselor, or the assistant principal – none of the school's officials, that is – live in Edison.

Some teachers just don't care, students told me. They spoke resignedly of not having a yearbook or a booster club, taking it for granted (if bitterly) that Edison had given them up. A teacher, however, said that with attendance as bad as it was, not many students would buy a yearbook even if there were one. These were juniors and seniors just come from an English class, and on the day we met at the back of the room and talked, the lesson had been on *Great Expectations*.

These are the children of welfare, and of the mills, and for them a factory job is the best deal going. If school or town has throwed them away, then school and Edison are no different from most other things in their lives. The median household income in Talton County in 1979 was $10,461, but 25 percent of the county's families had earnings that put them below the poverty line (which, for a family of four in 1981, was $9,287, whereas for North Carolina as a whole, median household income in 1979 was $14,481; 11.6 percent of the state's families then fell below the poverty level [13.8 percent of rural, farm families]).

For the United States in 1980, median family income (not household) was $21,023, although 6.2 percent of the nation's families earned less than five thousand dollars. Youth unemployment in Talton County in 1978 was 22.6 percent; unemployment generally, in January 1982, stood at 14.1 percent – the sixth highest among the state's one hundred counties.

Comparable figures for Athens County, to think again of Dominion High School, reveal that, in 1979, median household income was $12,931, with 14.6 percent of the area's families earning below the poverty line.

In 1978 youth unemployment here was 15 percent, whereas unemployment generally, in January 1982, was 9.8 percent.

More than 25 percent of Edison High's eleventh-graders who took the North Carolina Competency Test for the first time, in the fall of 1980, failed the reading section; 33.8 percent failed the math part. When this is set against the comparable figures for Judson River High, a predominantly white school in an adjacent city system, the difference is startling: just 2.8 percent failed reading, only 3.2 percent failed math. For 1979–80, the retention rate at Edison was 69.2 percent (and for Judson River, 74.3 percent). Edison City Schools as a whole then had a per pupil expenditure *from local funds* of just $290.83, which put the system 109th among the state's 144 school systems. Judson River City Schools, on the other hand, ranked 28th in this regard (and Dominion City Schools, 23rd). Of the two county systems that concern me here, Talton ranked 124th and Athens, 82nd.

Yet there are area citizens who believe there's no relationship between funding and academic performance; between community support and the overall quality of a school. There are white citizens here who, if they have not taken their own children out of the public schools, applaud others who have, and who, in the same breath, decry these same statistics, apparently not thinking the two may possibly be connected or that "white flight" may erode a school's academic confidence. There are white and black citizens alike who have never heard Edison's assistant principal say that "the hardest thing" he had to learn was "that you can't reach all of them"; that because the school was "gutted by the lack of community support," students were just that much more "unreachable."

In 1982 Mary Ann Fellows, an established reporter long familiar with the Talton County schools, as with the Edison and Judson River city systems within the county, asked readers of the *Chronicle* to "consider the tax . . . [they paid] toward perpetuating the county school system." She continues:

> Although [the county schools] do, occasionally, turn out a student with a smattering of education, I am convinced this phenomenon occurs in spite of—not because of—the system. Judging by the forms graduating seniors submit . . . every spring, these kids are entering a demanding world armed only with a high school diploma, a piece of paper that won't even keep off the rain.

When I asked this reporter why the county schools suffered in comparison with Judson River, she merely pointed me to a map showing the school-districting lines. Zones haven't been redrawn, she said, since nobody can remember when. A history teacher at Timmons High School made this same point, emphasizing that for Edison three sets of boundaries are important: Edison's city limits, "which [the town] expands at every chance" in order to reap the benefit of an enlarged tax base; the sanitation districts, which at last now "finally take in two black neighborhoods"; and the school districts, "not redrawn since 1907." Mr. Charles concluded, "Bet there aren't fifty black kids in the Judson River city schools." Though Edison High isn't a county school, its students are nonetheless victimized by these disparities, throwed away by them.

Driving back to Rocky Mount from Edison each day those late afternoons in 1982 I learned to watch for the patched house in the country, the one leaning backward, the cinder blocks, on which it sat precipitously, uneven and broken; the house whose only prideful thing was the bright orange school bus parked beside it, larger and more costly, more solid by far than the house now was or had ever been.

And I thought sometimes then of the secretary I had met at a local college who had told me of the many "Negroes" she knew in the area: men and women still living on the land she and her husband had inherited, people she said who were "just as happy living in those shacks" as she or I would have been "happy to be living in a new brick house."

Off the beaten roads in Warren and Halifax, Talton and Bertie and Nash, Northampton and Edgecombe counties, beyond what is called "Historic Halifax" with its antique shops (where you can buy postcards that say "Each Yankee tourist is worth a bale of cotton and is much easier to pick"), the renovated colonial buildings, the fine old home of William R. Davie, "Father of the University" (at Chapel Hill, or course), the houses more often than not are poor and ramshackly. Some seem held together more by fierce determination than by any significant carpentry, yards and curtains and porches revealing a sense of order on the part of families living there, a sharp desire that what can be made to look pretty be made so. Country houses here are fairly far apart; they may be set back some distance from the road. Some are just visible behind acres of corn or peanuts or milo. Not much looks prosperous. Driving for hours, it is possible even in the 1980s not to see a single factory where a man might go to ask for a job. In the few places for employment there are, there can be little turnover, little real chance for the young to get on. Houses, the occasional filling station and country store, are so worn and spindly-looking, so forlorn and throwed away as dwelling places or business establishments, that only a curtain in a window or a chair on a porch marks the reality that human lives are, in fact, being shaped within them.

For miles the most imposing public structure is not one of the restored buildings in "Historic Halifax," but the Department of Social Services out in the country north of town, which is housed rather spaciously in what appears to have once been an inn: the main building is dominated by the white columns evocative of the antebellum South, the two wings curving gracefully to embrace an attractive lawn and parking area. It is as if the primacy of social programs in the county, the deep need for help, was deliberately mirrored in and lent outward, visible shape through the building itself. Aside from an infrequent private home far more handsome and costly than the rest, and the public schools (unluxurious as they are), the places where most people actually live and work bear no comparison with the Department of Social Services; nor do the weathered barns and houses of the outlying farms seem to have any connection in this world with the splendid buildings and grounds, the moneyed-look, of the Federal Land Banks and the Production Credit Associations that are, for many of them, their own lifeblood.

The black people without jobs who cluster in the doorways of convenient marts and around gas stations in Gumberry and Brinkleyville and Garysburg presumably are not much concerned with the fact that it was along this same route, in 1781, that Cornwallis and his army heading for Virginia whipped the local militia gathered to confront them at Halifax. The black girl dressed up as a colonial serving girl sitting in a doorway of a renovated building, this day in May 1983, a day slack in tourists and seasonably warm, her long skirt and billowing sleeves catching the accent of a time we can hardly imagine, has, at least and for the time being, a job; the pride in our past that such employment embodies contrasts meaningfully, however, with so many other indications that for the people now, the present may not much matter and will have to keep on taking care of itself. Little seen elsewhere in the area, other than the character of the struggle that is everywhere revealed, gives us pause for any similar observance.

But of course the present matters, as it must. If the American Revolution is remembered here especially, at Edison High School itself, as at Timmons and Judson River, Dominion and Wexler and Coastal Plains, Henderson, it is the present that is inexorable. The poster above the blackboard admonishing students to "STAY IN SCHOOL" probably has as little impact upon those worn down and discouraged enough to be on the verge of dropping out as the English teacher's efforts to interest them in the term paper she has assigned. Neither past nor present can be as real as the jobless men leaning in the doorways, as this familiar tedium called school. A classroom drawing of a rainbow may indeed proclaim "The sky is the limit," but who among them can believe it? Or believe it enough?

Their school abandoned by the community, by the white citizenry providing the measure against which their lives in the larger world will increasingly be weighed, Edison's students may well confront a poster such as this one: "IALAC" at the top in large letters, the profile of a black face in the center, and across the bottom, "*I* a*m* *l*ovable *a*nd *c*apable." This in a history class in 1982 where at stake was another lesson than the threat by Cornwallis two hundred years ago.

Edison High School on the one hand; Dominion High School on the other. For all their differences, together they are representative of an extreme within the system of public education itself. Both are overwhelmingly black, both stand in some danger of reverting to an unacknowledged segregation almost as absolute as that taken for granted in the years before the Brown decision changed everything. Here, however, "almost" is an important qualifier. No one thinks that either school ever will be completely black; there will always be some white students, and faculties and staffs will continue to be integrated. Yet it is fair to say that, in general, white students at both schools are there primarily out of necessity. The vicitms both of racial prejudice (their own as well as that directed at them) and class, they seemed to me often waif-like, silent and withdrawn; or else insistent for attention, especially if the teacher also was white.

Black students, here the majority, were as different from their peers in predominantly white schools as if they were of another gradation of being altogether. Watching Edison's seniors march proudly and with some solemnity into the auditorium, the audience standing as they entered, I could not help but be moved by the way they carried themselves; at that moment, nobody was better than they felt themselves to be.

What, then, of the area's private schools, especially those coming into being in the mid-to-late 1960s, most of them a direct response to integration? Some have taken over the old public school buildings the state put up for sale or lease once the consolidation of community schools made such buildings redundant. Consolidation, whatever its rationale otherwise, often was coincident with the common sympathy of white people in the 1960s for racially separate schools; or, if integration *had* to be, for racially-mixed schools on neutral ground and without any history. (It is my suspicion that where desegregation was accompanied by the worst violence, the school at the center was far more likely to have been old than new.) But for the public schools then abandoned, it was as if the new order required almost its own architecture, as if the old buildings themselves looked wryly and askance upon what was happening. Would it have been anathema to both races, separated as they had always been, to have sat together in a classroom that never before had held but one color of people? And the private schools that sprang up, devoted as many of them are still to enshrining the past, how appropriate that they should be established within the shells of these old structures: oiled floors, iron-and-wood desks, gallery-width central halls, high ceilings, aged stairs.

Seated comfortably at the rear of such a classroom on a fall day in 1982, a visitor might have remembered another classroom, one but for the Apple II computer gathering dust in a corner, the blue-jeans and shirts the girls were wearing, had been identical. The school might have been Faison School; the year, easily 1950.

This illusion of another time is not one that the Christian academies, especially, or some of the other private schools, would find objectionable; headmasters, in fact, go to some length to cultivate this difference between private schools and public. It is what they and their teachers stressed most often when I talked with them (though they would not likely articulate the point exactly as I do here). Fiercely proud of these schools, as they almost invariably are, they are quick to single out for praise the fact that here every attempt is made to inculcate the values associated with traditional American education: the flag is saluted, prayer is observed, discipline is emphasized. Many teachers are retirees from the public schools. Some left deliberately in order to complete their careers in a private-school setting. They tend to be older, therefore, than their counterparts in public education, although this was not true for the two college-preparatory schools I visited, Yarrow and Dalton Academy. Teachers at the three fundamentalist academies I visited, however, were older: Springfield Academy, Butler Christian School, and Greenway School.

Headmasters included a retired county superintendent from the public system, a former college official, two retired military men, and a former private-school teacher. Whether it was the setting in which I found them or they themselves, as a group they struck me as being very different from public-school principals. The five, one a woman, had an intensity about them, an authority perhaps derived from the fact that they had more autonomy than principals; the bureaucratic structure of which they were a part being not nearly as massive as that choking the public schools, though, to be sure, their personal responsibility for keeping their schools financially afloat more than offset this. All chose to be not just in education, but in *private* education; they tended to be committed to education as an intellecutal endeavor. For the best of them, school wasn't just an enterprise like any other, but a calling. All expressed both envy of and disappointment in the public schools: envy for the resources public schools enjoy, disappointment that the near-insurmountable problems they face should prove so damaging. Time and again, headmasters and private-school teachers voiced their personal support for public education; time and again, they either said outright or implied that they had moved into the private arena in order to try to do what they could not do–or do as readily–in the public. If race still mattered to them, as clearly it did to some, nonetheless it was the *educational* turmoil accompanying integration they dwelt upon.

These private schools are small, 200 to 350 students this year. Dalton Academy and Yarrow may be in towns of some size, but not the others; they might as well be in the country, the villages they occupy being no more than a post office, gas station, and a few stores strung along a single street. Students look up from their lessons onto the fields, and though a town of thirty or forty-five thousand, Rocky Mount or Goldsboro, Greenville or Kinston, Clinton perhaps, may be within an easy drive, it is from the country that most of them come, the country they know.

"Farming is all the boys know, all they've ever been exposed to," a guidance counselor says. "Most who go on to college eventually come back," particularly if they drop out after a semester or two. They come back to work the land, if usually for someone else, or to pick up what jobs they can find; later on, in another year or so, they may–or may not–move away: to Greensboro or Raleigh, but more likely to Greenville, say, or Fayetteville, Wilmington, perhaps.

Only one of these five schools seemed not to be in obvious need of money; at only two, Yarrow and Dalton Acadamy, did students seem aware of being affluent, though not especially so. A good number, particularly of those attending the fundamentalist academies, in fact are no wealthier than anybody else. Teachers and guidance counselors alike stressed the number of families for whom private education required sacrifice. They resented and scorned the perception, which nonetheless is widespread, that private schools exist primarily in order to serve the rich; instead, teacher after teacher told me that it was concern for the kind of education their children were getting in the public schools—or not getting—that led their parents to send them to the private. Profoundly conservative, as most people here are, such private schools as these are seen as valid alternatives to public education—and to its entangling alliances with government, its affinity for the values of a secular age. And, yet, it was my impression, also, that all five schools were having a hard time sustaining enrollment, that the heyday for being able to count on a white, essentially reactionary public to send them its children may have passed.

Springfield Academy opened in 1970 with an enrollment of about 500; in the spring of 1982, fewer than 350 students attended. Such falling-off is typical. Public fury over integration tended to swell private-school enrollments in the 1960s and early 1970s, its abatement since then being accompanied by a general decline. But because Springfield is situated very near that section of an adjacent county where the population still is overwhelmingly black, it continues to draw a significant number of its students from the comparatively few white families there. The school is located within a few miles of the county line, and white students living in the other county, if they attended their own public schools, would find themselves as racially isolated as the white students at Edison and Dominion; many, therefore, enroll at Springfield. This pattern is, I think, fairly representative: private schools so advantageously located still have the capacity for draining off students from the public schools. Not infrequently, more than one public-school system is affected.

At the same time, however, even these students are proving more and more difficult for the private schools to attract, in part because the area as a whole remains economically depressed. Poverty cuts deep and wide, not least among people who continue to think of themselves as getting along more or less all right.

In some quarters, rivalries ran high between private schools and public. A common perception was that the two are in competition, which, if undeclared, nonetheless is real. "You can't teach in Edgecombe County public schools if your children are in private school," a counselor at Dalton Academy insisted. "The [official] told me this himself," she continued, even "if the door *was* closed." In Sampson County a private-school librarian told me that after working for ten years in a public school in neighboring Pender County, she had been "treated shabbily" when "they" had learned her two children were in private school; she had later resigned. Other instances could be cited. Yet public-school officials expressed surprisingly little concern that there are so many private schools spread throughout the region.

Principals of schools victimized by "white flight," in fact, tended to reserve their worry and anger for other public schools, especially those in the same county if their own school was urban. For principals of predominantly white schools, the term "private school" seemed to mean just the college-preparatory private schools that, they admitted, indeed probably did attract a number of the kind of white students they would especially like to have enrolled themselves: affluent young people whose parents were professional or business people, leaders in the community. Yet, the logical extension of such an admission, that the impact of the private schools upon the public weal may consist not simply (or even primarily) in the number of students they enroll, but in the *kind,* in the sectors of the community from which they come—and to which as adults they will likely aspire to return—was never drawn.

More outspoken than others with whom I raised this question, a former principal told me that the private schools in Lenoir County, those around La Grange and Kinston, while they may have been detrimental to the public schools "when integration first started," may now, in 1982, even be beneficial to them. "They're helping, in fact," because "most public schools couldn't really handle any extra students anyway." From the perspective of a principal's daily work, classrooms that not infrequently are overflowing, the need (in some schools) for improved and sometimes even basic materials and equipment, a teaching staff taxed to its utmost by those students already enrolled: the immediacy of such problems as these tends to make fewer students seem ideal. Numbers have a way of obscuring everything else. Enrollment and state funding are inextricably linked, however; students moving to the private schools take with them, in effect, certain revenues.

For their part, the college-preparatory private schools can perhaps more readily afford to go their own way than can either the fundamentalist academies or those public schools that, because of where they happen to be located, are especially hard hit by shrinking enrollment. "Enrollment here," said a guidance counselor at Yarrow School, in Athens County, "hasn't had anything to do with what" has gone on "in the public schools." The private schools, Yarrow no less than Springfield and Dalton, different as they otherwise are, go far to sustain the impression that enrollment isn't a problem; that all is well financially; that they are weathering the effects of social and demographic change without adverse result. Public schools, of course, do the same thing, and for the same reasons: in the business of education, as in whatever else depends on the public's support, success may be inseparable from that general sense of well-being a school has taken such pains to create. This being so, it is no wonder that even the people most intimately a part of a school's official family may sometimes succumb to the illusion. No institution is more vulnerable to common opinion than a school.

But I very much doubt that so delicate and precarious a thing as a school can long flourish where area schools, in general, be they public or private, go to such lengths affecting not to notice one another, and the truth is, I suspect, that in fact they notice each other all the time. Relationships would seem at best to be guarded where schools draw upon the same communities for support. Especially where the number of young people of school age is decreasing, and where racial imbalance in the general population is severe, a wary unease among the schools is more often to be encountered than not.

No black students then attended these five private schools. Both Yarrow School and Dalton Academy have in the past, however, had black students, though never more than two or three at once. In 1982 when I was there, Butler Christian School had never enrolled a black student, despite its announced policy that "students of any race, color [or] national and ethnic origin," might apply.

Not much more than a crossroads really, the community of Butler is in Sampson County, some one hundred miles or so southeast of Springfield, and southeast, too, of Edison and Dominion, where in 1980 black students outnumbered white by margins of more than three to one. Both at Butler Christian School and at Springfield Academy, teachers spoke fervently of freedom of choice; of a child having just one chance for an education; of schools having not just the right but the obligation to teach values and beliefs, to inculcate in a formal way the basic verities underlying both Christianity and the American way of life – as they were there defined.

"We are proud of our little school," the secretary at Springfield Academy told me. A teacher wrote at the bottom of my questionnaire, "Thank you for visiting our school. We are proud of what we are doing." Nothing distinguishes the private schools from the public as much as this compelling sense of mission; out of nothing more solid than dream and commitment, private-school people have seen their work endure. Some have taught in the same school since its founding. Public-school bureaucracy, on the other hand, leaves teachers little room or time for pride in the system. Although many expressed satisfaction at the progress of individual students, surprisingly few teachers in the public schools had anything beyond the perfunctory to say in praise of schools. Because private-school people tend to view private education as academically superior to public, and their own school as, if not the best, at least defensible, their sense of accomplishment is manifest and pervasive; and this is true whether or not their school is, in fact, very good.

Clearly, more than objective or educational criteria are at play here. Private-school people think they have single-handedly salvaged something of value, another way of life, perhaps, that of a time forever lost to the rest of us, and especially lost to the young. It is their own childhood they would protect, whose milieu they would transmit. If, as a teacher at Springfield Academy put it, "teaching in private school is like teaching in the 'old' public schools," then it is almost as if this alone is enough.

"If some public schools would get their act together," a teacher at Butler Christian School said heatedly, "perhaps there wouldn't be a need to go to the private schools." That, in fact, private schools "fill a void created by the public schools" few private-school people doubt. Competition between the two, public versus private, they see almost invariably as "good, not detrimental." At Yarrow School an English teacher argued, "Until our demands for quality education are met by the public systems, we must elect private education."

Yet integration, or rather the reluctance of most private schools in eastern North Carolina to admit black students, continues to haunt the private-schools. Especially do teachers at Yarrow School and Dalton Academy reject any implication of racism. Quick to draw the difference between themselves and other private schools in the area, Butler Christian School and Springfield Academy for example, they point to their record of having had enrolled at various times, some—no matter how few—black students; and while frankly admitting that probably they, too, have benefited from "white flight," they insist that segregation was not instrumental in their founding, or that *if* it was, if in the early 1970s segregationist sympathy contributed greatly to their survival, nowadays this isn't the case. Teachers and administrators here said that, indeed, they would welcome more black students, and black teachers, as well. "Integration is dead," Yarrow's headmaster said, no longer an issue to be fought over or even much discussed.

That no black students were then enrolled, or any black teachers or administrators employed, "is one of the main weaknesses" of Yarrow, the headmaster insisted. On the other hand, teachers and other personnel at Yarrow and Dalton evidently are as resigned as their counterparts in the fundamentalist academies to leaving the racial problems of the public schools to—the public schools. I know of no campaign they or any of the other private schools have put on to recruit blacks, either students or faculty.

There's "a lot of racial prejudice still," a teacher at Springfield Academy said, which was, in any case, plain. Members of the faculty there made no particular effort to conceal their racial feelings, either when talking with each other in my presence or when talking with me directly. More than one person spoke of having left public-school teaching after the first year or two of integration because of having to work with blacks: other teachers, administrative personnel, students, and parents. Just as "many students" enroll still at Springfield "in order to get away from blacks," a teacher confided, so, also, have some—not all—private school teachers sought a similar refuge.

White students enrolled in the private schools differ in important ways from students attending public schools.[2] If young people at Edison, as at Dominion though not to the same degree, see themselves as written off by their community, their school as abandoned and pitifully inferior, then private school students in the same locale, but especially at Yarrow and Dalton, see themselves very much at the center of things. Failure isn't anything these students have ever had to think much about. The chance that one day they may be on the outside, that the world may not be amenable to them personally, seems not to have occurred to them. The difference is that between a classroom poster imploring "STAY IN SCHOOL" and one that declares, "MATHEMATICS IS THE QUEEN OF THE SCIENCES"; between a senior wearing an oxford-cloth shirt, chinos, and

Adidas, and a boy dressed day after day in shirt, trousers, and tennis shoes made in Taiwan, synthetic and thin and cheap; between classes that are largely black and poor, the students almost entirely from working-class or welfare families, many of whom lack any formal education, and classes that are wholly white, who, if they are not affluent, at least do not think of themselves as poor. White students going to the private schools may come from working-class families or professional, but their parents stress formal education.

It is the difference between people nurtured on the expectation that a successful – by which they mean financially secure – life is something into which they will move with relative ease, and those who know past all questioning that for them there's not likely to be much out there besides a catch-as-catch-can job, perhaps a semester or two at a technical school or community college, a place at the factory or mill.

Yet for the student at Yarrow who bragged that "Right now there's two cars out there," in the student parking lot, "worth together forty thousand dollars," there were those among his friends who found such an attitude distasteful. Students everywhere, however, equated money with happiness.

Most private-school students did not impress me as seriously engaged in academic work, nor were the five private schools I visited all excellent; three I would have called academically inadequate. Neither were the most disadvantaged of the public schools bad in every area or in every class, their students uniformly disinterested. Whether private-school students, almost all of whom were college-bound, were any more caught up in their classes than many of the students I saw at Edison and Dominion, few of whom expected to enter a four-year college, is, at the very least, debatable. The caliber of instruction in the better private schools was considerably higher than that in the public, yet the private schools, too, have their poor teachers.

That insularity peculiar to eastern North Carolina is everywhere underscored in the area's schools. Teachers at Butler and Springfield, Yarrow and Dalton and Greenway tend overwhelmingly to have been born and raised here, though so, too, have most public-school people. At Springfield in 1982–83, eleven of the eighteen teachers, as well as the headmaster, had earned their degreees at the same college: East Carolina University, in Greenville, no more than an hour or so south of the small village of Springfield. Of the other seven only one had gone to college farther away than Greensboro. The point of course isn't East Carolina or the quality of teacher-education programs at local colleges, much less the integrity of life in the area, but the natural and inevitable sameness of these professional backgrounds, a sameness that, I think, is inherently detrimental. (A guidance counselor at Yarrow, which by every measure is academically superior to Springfield, complained that "Some teachers have a B.A. or B.S. from some little college thirty miles down the road . . . and that's it!")

The larger public schools have a tradition of being more capacious, more sophisticated, though few among them have faculties rivaling that at Dominion High School in the late 1970s. The difference, although difficult to measure, is nonetheless profound. Education, the development of a critical intelligence capable of analysis and judgment, is more the result of meaningful contrasts than homogeneity: teachers use themselves as well as their materials, and nothing that they know or have experienced, seen or been taught or read or done, is irrelevant. Self-evident as this may be for a single teacher, more important is it that a *faculty* be comprised of people who collectively have a range of backgrounds, personal as well as professional. Diversity, however, is not something that schools prize. If anything, the contrary is true. Whether public or private, school officials (and everybody else as well) stress as an advantage the fact that so many teachers are natives of the region and locally educated. If school people here think outsiders have anything important to contribute, they keep it to themselves.

Headmasters reminded me that private education has a long and distinguished history in North Carolina, as in the South. In many of the larger towns, private academies flourished well before there was any such thing as a public-school system, many having sprung up in the wake of the Civil War. Much can be made of the fact that these schools were never for the poor of either race, that they were for white people only, and at that seldom for white women. But this isn't the lesson the men talking with me meant to teach. On the contrary, they would legitimize the existence now of the fundamentalist academies. From this perspective, it is the public schools that may appear to be upstarts, Johnny-come-latelies; the notion that these academies must somehow justify themselves would thus be deflected. But history is sometimes diversionary.

Private schools springing up in the 1960s and 1970s came after a long hiatus during which private education was all but forgotten, if, except for a very few, it had ever been in mind. In the twelve years I was a public-school student, from 1951 through 1963, I wasn't aware of anybody in Faison who went to a private school. A boy in my sister's grade in the late 1940s *had* gone to a private high school, however; he wanted to be a doctor and his parents sent him away to prep school. There was a private military school in nearby Salemburg and some of the cadets must have come from the surrounding area, but I was a senior before I had heard of it. Local private schools were few and far between; nobody thought of them as an option. Present rivalries between private schools and public, insofar as they occur, are of recent vintage, dating only from the 1960s. For anybody to attempt to trace a continuous line from the private academies at the turn of the century to the small private schools spread now throughout the region is, I think, unfortunate.

If by their very existence certain private schools perpetuate racial imbalance, then they are detrimental. By attracting disproportionate numbers of certain kinds of students, they likely further the separation between people and accentuate class differences. Fairly or not, the inference is inescapable that of the dozens of private academies now in the area, some owe their continued support, as typically their origin, to segregationist feeling. Of the five I visited, perhaps three fit this description. It cannot be doubted that those public schools most directly affected by their proximity to these three schools, as of the public system generally, are the weaker for the relationship.

But the private schools I visited have a lesson the public schools will do well to heed: that the heart matters, too, and that there remain ideals worth cherishing. My quarrel with Springfield Academy and Butler Christian School is that they would bring back the 1950s if they could, as they may think they *have;* that they would subvert the pluralism of American life, deny the diversities among us. We disagree upon ideals. But the public schools . . . One may ask if most public-school people, and, of those I met, especially administrators, any longer have any real commitments; or whether, on the other hand, if the unremitting reality of their daily work doesn't erode all sense of the larger perspective. "White flight" has hurt us, both as a place and as a people; area schools bear still the burden, be they public or private.

9. Working and Living and Getting By

The changing face of the eastern North Carolina small town is, in part, attributable to the impact of industry. Plants and factories are built in the countryside because of the abundance of land (and to reduce municipal taxation), the agriculture they've usurped now providing them place and bearing: parking lots and pavements, steel fences and access roads, the physical plant itself, and more often than not, in the distance against the woods, a tobacco patch or corn field. But business is off on main street, and many of the interests formerly comprising our idea of town, the doctor's office, grocery stores and dry-good, the feed and grain, the hardware store, schools and banks and eating places, the insurance office and barber shop, have long since pulled out, relocating along the highways, on the outskirts, in the ubiquitous shopping malls: urban sprawl, yet without much of a sense of anything *urban*, these villages and towns and crossroads still small and countrylike. A town is no longer a central place. "Town" isn't any more thought of as a place of general employment, especially; not these towns, though for Raleigh and Durham and Greensboro, the thinking is different. Goldsboro and Rocky Mount, Wilson and Clinton, Dunn and Tarboro – they no longer loom very large in our imagination. Nor do they mean what they once did. If, for some, they remain places where independence can be achieved, where the promises are kept, they are so for fewer and fewer.

People looking for work nowadays follow the plants and factories. Some of these are in or near Goldsboro and Rocky Mount, of course – Dunn and Wilson and Clinton, Tarboro – but it isn't the town that people think of first. Firestone, Texfi, General Electric and Hevi-Duty, Black and Decker: it's these newer and more impressive companies that draw them. Increasingly, towns take their meaning from the industry they attract, and, like the rippling effect of a pebble thrown into a pond, concerns heretofore seemingly unrelated fall into place. In Nash County, Consolidated Diesel came into Whitakers in 1981, and directly across from it went up, as though another crop out of the ground, what is now, in 1989, the Whitakers campus of Nash Technical College. Firestone, in 1973, built a large plant beside Highway 301 north of Wilson, then expanded so that today its landscaped grounds cover acres and acres, stretching back along and off Firestone Parkway, where once was but raw earth and abandoned stubble.

Rumors of a new plant coming in, as of another shutting down, will be the stuff of conversation for months; lives in the silence of night before sleep are remade in the darkness, men and women thinking how when the time comes they will put in their applications.

In October and November 1982, when Perdue Farms advertised in local newspapers for some two hundred workers for its new chicken-processing plant going up in Robersonville in Martin County, between 1,200 and 1,400 people applied. This for a base pay of $4.60 an hour after thirty days of employment, as well as "free health, dental and vision coverage, eight paid holidays, free life insurance and a free pension plan"–good pay for the region and excellent benefits.

"We don't believe we'll have any problem filling the jobs we have at the Robersonville plant," a spokesman for Perdue said.[1]

Better paid are the state's manufacturing workers, who in November 1981 received an average wage of $6.16 an hour, yet this was still twenty-five percent below the national average.[2] By December 1986, this average had risen to $7.01 an hour. Only in Mississippi, however, is the average wage for manufacturing less.

The largest turkey-processing plant in the world, so we think, has recently opened in the Scott's Store area, and, at the other end of Duplin County, Cogentrix is putting up an electricity-generating facility that will, when operative, supply energy for a local textile firm, Guilford East. Since 1980, however, at least two poultry firms in the county, Watson's and Ramsey's, both in Rose Hill, have gone out of business; the rumors in 1985 that at J. P. Stevens in Wallace, "*something's* happening," have since been confirmed. Because the textile industry has been in such a tailspin the last several years, layoffs and shortened workweeks and closings threatening workers across the state, the merest suspicion of trouble at J. P. Stevens, at Burlington Industries, West Point Pepperell, DuPont, and the like, evokes fear and dread.

In the first ten months of 1984, for example, thirty-five textile or textile-related plants closed in North Carolina; 5,644 people lost their jobs.[3] Such closings came fast on the heels of one of the worst years for the industry in recent memory; with its recession and high interest rates, 1982 had been quite bad enough. In 1984, employment in textile plants in North Carolina and the other Southeastern states dropped by 34,000 people—17,900 of them in North Carolina.[4]

Yet textiles remain the state's largest employer, and still North Carolina leads the nation in textile employment: 220,000 workers in 1984, nearly thirty percent of the industry.[5] Headquartered in the Piedmont, as most of the major textile corporations are, in Greensboro and Gastonia, Kannapolis and High Point and Haw River, the industry is, in this one respect, characteristic of others having established plants in the eastern counties. Offshoots, rather than companies native to the area, are typical. Since the mid-1960s, when Northern and Midwestern companies first began setting up subsidiary operations here, eastern North Carolina has had more than its share of manufacturing firms whose homes, whose chief capital outlay and investment, were elsewhere; relative to the total number of companies here, the number fitting this description is high. Yet, in comparison with urban areas, North Carolina's "rural communities are simply not competitive in the attraction of branch plants for many expanding industries."[6] Branches or not, industries coming in have not usually been the ones paying top dollar or requiring the highest-skilled labor.

"Low taxes attracted declining Northern industries to [these] rural areas," a Raleigh newspaper concluded.[7] What is important here, however, is the word "declining." Too often, plants relocating "Down East" have done so as a last resort, hoping to recoup after prolonged and increasingly severe problems elsewhere. A question worth asking is whether the state's ability to attract such firms as have had relocation forced on them, and whose potential for staying afloat anywhere may be minimal, is not in the long run, more harmful than good.

And there is growing speculation that such industrialization as eastern North Carolina and the rural South itself have enjoyed, rather than continuing and becoming more competitive, stands perhaps a better chance of declining or, at best, of leveling off; the "Sun Belt outlook," as *The News and Observer* headline put it, "may turn cloudy."[8] Economists point to the increased difficulty rural areas are likely to face in attracting and retaining outside companies, largely because the attitudes and many of the policies historically conducive to this end now work somewhat against it: cheap, abundant labor aggressively advertised, low corporate taxes, right-to-work legislation, anti-unionism, governmental cooperation, and the like. Exploitations on which Southern manufacturing has always been dependent may now be coming home to roost. The same low taxes that traditionally have made us attractive to industry also keep us poor: our schools, especially, as well as, in some ways, our quality of life. Companies that can pick and choose will likely relocate where they can have the best of both worlds: cooperation from state and local governments, but, also, good schools and cultural enrichment. "Low taxes, used to lure industry, also have retarded the growth of needed services." Furthermore, "low wages—long an inducement for companies seeking to escape high labor costs in the unionized North," are now relatively less important "as more . . . companies leave the country altogether for low-wage nations."[9] It's not only New York's garment district that the North Carolina textile industry must now consider, but Japan and Taiwan and Korea. Few companies native to the state and few coming in can be said to thrive independently of international competition.

Defining the position in which the South now finds itself, economists frequently cite its loss of comparative advantage:[10] if everybody begins to offer the same economic (or other) incentives for attracting industry, then the area traditionally relying on such measures will lose any advantage it may once have had. Northeastern cities and states, partly in response to the Sun Belt phenomenon, have apparently taken a leaf from our own strategy: New York now advertises itself as having the "most comprehensive package of financial incentives of any city in America."[11] That economic edge the South has in the past been willing to advance means less now—although the South is still promoting it—when states and cities, some with considerably deeper resources than, for example, eastern North Carolina, choose to compete on the same terms. But North Carolina has done well to offset even this factor, notably in the Research Triangle area. The state's eastern counties, however, lack the Triangle's educational opportunities and its metropolitan-like living, and the gap between the two areas remains wide.[12]

In those rural areas where the South has tried to become "more like the rest of the country . . . [it] is losing certain magnets it has had for attracting industry."[13] Where it has resisted the influence of change, on the other hand, the South is often no more appealing to outsiders than it ever was. Between this frying pan and fire, many a small town reels.

To the extent that industrial expansion in eastern North Carolina (or in the Triangle area) has been the result of trends and events originating elsewhere, progress may be more a reflection of the larger world than the result of anything we have changed ourselves. Such readily apparent differences may be less than profound. The plant that relocated here in, say, the 1960s can as easily pull up and leave in the 1980s–and there's little that local chambers of commerce can do about it.

Mount Olive in Wayne County, its population about five thousand in 1980, had probably less than a dozen manufacturing firms in 1982. At least two, however, have since closed. Young Squire out of New York had set up a branch in Mount Olive in 1965. A maker of men's and boys' clothing, the company eventually employed some three hundred people before it shut down in 1983. Sonoco Products, a maker of paper tubing and recylced paper board, whose headquarters is in South Carolina, came into Mount Olive in 1975. Although it was always a small operation, the fifty or so people who for nearly ten years made their living from it had to look for something else when it pulled out late in 1984. (Mary Lynn Fashions came in and left in the same year, 1984.)

At least two other Mount Olive plants, as the 1980s got underway, were off and on resorting to reduced workweeks: Burlington, out of Greensboro, and The Boling Company (maker of fine desks and bookcases), out of Siler City, both of which opened in 1968. A young single woman with no dependents may say of the shortened schedule, the four or sometimes three days of work a week, "Yes, and I'm glad, too," but a mother with three children will almost certainly think, "It's tough . . . Yeah, it shore is. . . ."

It may be true, as Charles Liner (for one) argues, that in the South now, "the huge supply of labor from agriculture has been largely exhausted," and that though "the post-war baby boom has added to the labor supply, . . . in the near future this source will also decline."[14] Yet the kind of manufacturing jobs most likely to be available in rural areas will, for the time being at least, continue to draw heavily on men and women differing only in degree from the earlier displaced farmers and their children: people without advanced technical or highly-specialized skills, whose formal education outstrips that of their parents merely in the number of school-years attained. In North Carolina's eastern counties, there is no foreseeable shortage of such workers. More sophisticated jobs in manufacturing are sometimes available, notably in urban areas, but they're not typical. To be kept in mind, also, is the likelihood that in the future manufacturing will be less important, relatively, than it now is.

Job analysts who know eastern North Carolina well point to a growing shift in the region's economy "away from a manufacturing base," as a Fayetteville analyst describes it, "to a service base": the trend is away from industry *per se* and into sales and finance, banking and accounting, restaurants and real estate, hospitals and nursing homes, government.[15] For these fields, especially, educated people are needed; thus the urgency for college, for retraining. What this means is that area young people whose parents and grandparents were farmers in the 1960s, many of whom gave up farming and went into public work, are now often no better off in the job search than were their parents. They may even be in worse shape. The plants and factories otherwise open to them have themselves, many of them, fallen on hard times. No longer does industry hold out the hope and promise it once did. And neither young people nor their elders have a chance at a job requiring much specialized training and education unless they have gone to college or technical school, and sometimes not then.

Industrialization here, as in other places, has been a mixed blessing. Most people in 1989 may in fact be living better than they've ever lived before (not that they're living well), but in order for this to be true, if it is, more is required of them than they could have imagined when they first started. Public work changed a way of life: in just twenty years, from roughly 1960 to 1980, habits and attitudes bred of generations were transformed, and necessarily so. Yet if we but scratch the surface of contemporary life, we'll find much of the tenant and hand, the small landowner – of farmers dispossessed – from whom so many people nowadays in the factories trace their heritage. It's not the plantation any more that informs the relationship here between men and work, as W. J. Cash said of Southern labor at the turn of the century;[16] that's much too exalted an analogy.

The agricultural background still is central to the comparison, however, but tenantry is the compelling metaphor. Tenantry evokes the right alembic of pride and abjectness, hardheadedness and compliance, faith and resignation. For working people in their forties and fifties, at least, this is true; for their children, maybe not. Having raised themselves often enough, Mama and Daddy both on the job, both trying to make a living, younger people now themselves at the assembly line or running the sander, connecting circuitry or assembling parts – as those younger still, the ones in or just out of high school or maybe in a community college or technical school – they may lack all historical bearing, may be unmoored, may have no more feeling for time, for sequence and continuity, than that which they absorb from the week's television schedule.

Parents and grandparents are different. At the job by seven o'clock in the morning, they will remember that on the farm they may already have been in the field some days an hour before then, and without any assurance of when quitting time might come or any confidence they would have anything but sweat to show for their labor. They'll tell you they believe in giving a man an honest day's work; that when they hit that door, they're there to put in their time the best way then can; that when they knock off on Friday, they're through with it then until Monday morning (unlike farming, which couldn't be put out of mind). Asked what kind of day they've had, they'll say, "pretty steady . . . pretty steady," only the tone revealing whether good or bad or, more likely, only tolerable. The women–not so much the men–say they like what they do; seldom do they think "it's all that hard." Asked what the best thing about their job is, they'll say "that paycheck coming on Friday," but a woman will then more often than not mention the pleasure she takes in "being out among people."

Women will tell you they're treated fairly. If they can't name more than one or two women supervisors or foremen out of the dozen or more they know, they'll say it's because women don't "really want that type of responsibility or worriation." Asked about promotions for women, they'll say "They's not too far you *can* go, really . . . not really that much promotion that can be done." Blacks, they think, are treated the same as everybody else.[17] Men are more likely to say their present wages are a far cry from what they should be; women are quick to mention health and other benefits. Everybody can name the plants most frequently laying off workers ("without no notice whatsoever"); people speak highly of plants that, instead of using layoffs, go to a shortened workweek.

"I look at it this way," a woman who works at Boling, in Mount Olive, says. "I been there fourteen years and they put the groceries on my table. . . . I got one out of school and in college on it, and two more in school now on it. . . . It's hot and it gets boring sometimes . . . but I'm thankful for it."

A worker at Kemp Furniture in Goldsboro says, "You got to take a little bad along with the good. Yes, you sure have. Furniture pay *is* low in this state. . . . They tole us how come it is so low, but I forgot. I don't remember what all they said. . . . It's a family company. Our pay scale is low, but our benefits are just as good as other plants around. . . . He cut our hours, but ain't nobody been laid off."

Another says she left National Spinning in Warsaw in the mid-1970s, after being there eight years. She had run a machine that made thread into yarn. Asked why she left, she says, "When you go to bed and dread to get up in the morning, it's time for a change."

Now at a furniture plant, she told me, in 1985, that it's better there than "at any of the sewing plants," but that working at, for example, AP Parts in Goldsboro would likely be better still. "They start you between six and seven dollars an hour," she said, whereas after eleven years where she is now, she makes ". . . $5.10 an hour—top dollar!"

These three people, two of whom are sisters, were raised on tenant farms south of Mount Olive; their parents have since retired or died. The oldest, now in her late forties, still lives in the country, in a rented house not far from the land that as a child growing up she helped her family tend. Another, when she graduated from high school in 1962, went before the summer was out to Goldsboro and lived with an older sister while looking for a job. She was a waitress for a while, a stock clerk at Leder Brothers, a clerk in a children's clothing store, and a worker at Scott's Barbecue before landing her job at Kemp, which she has held now for nearly twenty years. (In 1964, her younger sister followed her lead. After graduation, she too went to Goldsboro and looked for work. Now she's employed at Hevi-Duty, and a member of one of the few unions in the area. The women are married, their children grown or nearly so. One has a son at Howard University studying to be an industrial engineer.)

The third graduated from Coastal Plains in 1965. Pretty and articulate, Shirley is single and lives with her parents in a house they have at last been able to buy and renovate. ("After all these years of living in somebody else's house," her mother says, "it's good to have something that's yours.") Shirley says, however, "I wish I had tried harder . . . had taken advantage of school . . . I wish I had gone and done something, . . . and I wouldn't be stuck in a factory job. It's too late now . . . or it doesn't have to be, I reckon, but . . . I am where I am."

Such workers have had to get used to more than just punching a clock. They've accommodated themselves to a more complicated world than the one into which they were born, a place and time that but little resembles that of their childhood; they've learned another vocabulary, and while it may be strange in their mouth and to their ear, it's not to be thrown off. Other people don't understand anything else, and they're the ones running things: income tax in April; the ins-and-outs of Workmen's Compensation, and the battles waged sometimes to force an employer to come through with it; insurance claims and medical coverage; credit cards; installment debt; the continual, nagging obligations that eat up the hundred-and-fifty-or-so dollars they bring home a week (*if* that, if they've not been laid off, if they have a job). Not many tenants in the early 1950s ever filed a tax return, the large majority having kept no such records – some landlords discouraging such presumption – and others seeing no need of declaring the fix they were in; few would have owed taxes anyway, and nobody much understood that they would likely have money due them. (The notion that debt could, at tax time, be profitable would have struck them as laughable.) Some never even had a Social Security card, and if they had insurance, it was with a burial association. They were a private people, these farmers and their wives, the men and women of forty and thirty and even twenty years ago: the less anybody knew about their business, especially "the gov'ment," the better off they felt themselves to be; the fewer pieces of paper they had to send anywhere or keep track of, the less name-signing, the less talk about money.

Debt itself, of course, working people are on long and intimate terms with, though not the particular kind of debt that now more than likely engulfs them. Tenant debt had been disposable once a year if it involved, as it always did, the landlord; local merchants would be paid twice or maybe three times a year, little except groceries and what it took for making a crop ever being charged in the first place. Getting hold of cash money was so largely a matter of chance then that nobody could risk being tied down to a fixed and rigid schedule of repayment. (Settling-up time was never any particular day or even month, just sometime after the last of the crop had been sold.) Nowadays, however, no matter how meager a worker's earnings, their mere predictability (as well as the fact of their meagerness) sets in motion another kind of thinking from that habitual with farming. A weekly paycheck where none has been before changes a man's relationship to money: little as it may be, it's apt to *seem* like a lot – and out of this illusion, much else follows.

Where wages are too low to permit paying for things all at once, debt is inevitable, yet, because now there is money coming in, because "more money's stirring," and because, little though it is, it's more than most workers ever imagined making, the fantasy for a while isn't so hard to sustain that you're no worse off than anybody else, really. And, indeed, this will be true enough; the average worker lives from day to day, his livelihood no more substantial than his credit and good name (which, however solid and prized, of course have their breaking point). People will say that everybody lives this way. That life need not be hounded by debt isn't something that occurs to them, or that they would much believe. The wearying repetitions of the assembly line, of whatever labor that requires the same movements enacted countless times over and over, are here corroborated in a kind of mental grinding-down: a perpetual and ingrained worry over money from which there's never any foreseeable relief.

Farmers always owed somebody, and yet debts, burdensome as they were, didn't usually fall unremittingly – as debts do now on their children and grandchildren – month after month. Existence wasn't piecemeal, a matter of clockwork as defined by billings reaching them through the mail. Except for the electric bill, and unless against all odds they *had* gone out and bought something on time, nobody twenty years ago dreaded the mailman. Life moved to the rhythm of another calendar than that of the coupon-book.

Most people today probably do have more money, yet what money they have may be relatively meaningless, given how much it takes simply to live. Wages their parents and grandparents would find inconceivable go no further than, if they cover, the necessities. Chronic indebtedness may run parallel even with steady work; for people laid off or out of work, the severity of their suffering may be but a deepening of that considered normal by people still with jobs. For untold numbers of families, who, if they were pushed, might admit to being poor, poverty still is something that overtakes other people, never them; for those calling themselves poor, any other job than their own, if they're working, looks good. For people generally, the likelihood is that debt is as essential for existence as air, as much taken for granted. When being poor is no longer temporary; when you know you're not going to be able to get out from under a debt that's never-ending, that, what with the interest alone, increases more than it subsides, the response is to let what's happening anyway go ahead and happen. You take the pleasure you can in what you can while you can; you pay off as far as your money lets you, leaving the rest for another and as inevitable a day.

For tenants, this is pretty much the way life always was. What is new now is that husbands and wives who are both working, even at reasonably good jobs, are as apt to be seriously behind and struggling as ahead and doing all right. For many, the real trial is not as much outright unemployment as it is pitifully low wages.[18] Public work has no more liberated workers from a debt-ridden, ill-rewarded life than did the fields of another era; not on the whole.

In a society gassed and oiled by indebtedness, the lack of cash money is no longer much of a barrier to buying things. People able to keep up the illusion of stability usually find they can buy more and more, their current indebtedness no obstacle; and if, in this respect, eastern North Carolina hardly differs from other parts of the country, the fact of its insularity aids and abets the subterfuge. Merchants, bankers, and businessmen know their customers as members of the community, if not also as friends. For a family they trust, credit will likely be available. Looked at coldly, such an easy familiarity, which has always been among the finest and most valued aspects of area life, insofar as it spawns an easy encumbrance, isn't without fault; the economic paternalism enjoyed by some (yet never by all) has exacted its toll.

The time was, of course, when poor people knew what not to want. Nowadays the poor want the same things as everybody else—a natural-enough result of the several influences here coming to a head. The children and grandchildren of eastern North Carolina's farms were the beneficiaries of a hopefulness that, for once, had a real possibility of fulfillment. More than any previous generation, young people graduating from area high schools in the 1960s and early 1970s came into their own at a time when the region was opening up; for blacks and the poor generally, as increasingly for women, people who had always before been shunted aside, opportunity may then have been more than just rhetorical. For all, television had made accessible another sensibility; this purveyor of dreams was to shape the aspirations of the age. If the affluent society exists first of all as a state of mind, its unspoken assumption that success is self-evident from the number and kind of things a person owns, and if this pseudo-reality proves sufficiently compelling, then the poor, too (probably they more than others), will likely be caught up in the lie.

It has made all the difference that the call to a better life, the clarion of the 1960s, has gone, as we know, not unheeded, but for the majority who rose to its implicit challenge, unfulfilled: that the legacy of the time is a thoroughgoing materialism, a hunger for goods, a child-like wishfulness manifesting itself in first one thing, then another. That there's a difference profoundly moral between a debt incurred to put a meal on the table or to make a living and that for a color television, a microwave, an ice-maker, a new pickup with somewhat more horsepower than the old – or, if the situation is severe enough, between buying potatoes or Tweakies; that to live well involves something more than having things, and ought not, in any case, to be grounded upon a perpetual urgency of acquisition; that peace of mind matters: if working people here any longer believe this, they don't show it. (The point bears emphasizing, however, that the poor and ill-paid, the children of poverty, are as deserving of pickup trucks and color televisions and Tweakies as anybody else, and have as much or more right to them, for it's their hardship that makes them possible.)

But this isn't all of it, either. Men and women who, if they didn't lose quite everything when they left the land, lost a good deal, may now be at the least understood for this insistence that they *will* have something: that they are, in some fashion, the same people as who once owned – or, if tenants, had the use of – infinitely more than they can now look around and claim as theirs. A hunger for goods may not be, despite so much else to the contrary, the hardest or most inexplicable appetite the poor and almost-poor have to feed; getting and spending may be, for all its waste, the one transaction still (momentarily) within their domain. Contracting a debt, as the buying of anything you want, isn't without its pleasures; the few minutes it takes you, other people weigh you seriously.[19]

If such attitudes toward money suggest more the decadence of contemporary life than the heritage of the farms, and thus say no more about eastern North Carolina than anywhere else, the specific agricultural background is nonetheless readily discoverable in, namely, the assumptions older workers still bring to their jobs in the plants and factories. Theirs is a respect for the integrity of work that has long been characteristic of people raised in close connection with the land. Farm people may have preferred one task over another, but seldom could they have thought that any could be passed by – not without risk to a year's labor. Work was, literally, the most significant thing in their lives. It consumed the most hours, required the most mental effort, took precedence over everything else. More than one farmer of my father's generation spoke bitterly of his children growing up and leaving home, "at jest about the damn time they git big enough to be some use," and school typically took a back seat when a child's labor was needed on the farm.

Each routine or chore, every aspect of making a crop or raising livestock for sale or slaughter, was important and necessary because it eventually contributed to a family's livelihood. Urban people may think in terms of particular employment, but rural sensibility is here more holistic: the affinity is for the work itself; the job of the moment is meaningful both at the time and in the long run. Farmers, men and women who stereotypically evince little capacity for abstract thinking, know well enough that their labor may never come to any profitable fruition; that, in any case, cause and effect—their labor and the crop flowering from it—are separated by weeks and sometimes months. Satisfaction inheres in, if not the work exactly (and yet in the work too), then in the next thing to it: that on which the exertion of work is focused. There's pleasure in the awakening land in spring; in all the arduous processes, laying in a plant-bed in winter from which in July and August tobacco in a field is harvested; there's the point of a continuing, deepening investment. As the skilled craftsman, a farmer is proud of what he's made; the sheer looks of it count for much with him, as much almost, though on another level, as the money he will get from it.

Farmers commonly refer to a good crop, as to an animal they admire, as "pretty"; a sorry one they scorn as something that's "plumb throwed away." The sense here is economic, ultimately; yet appreciation is, also, aesthetic and unself-conscious; sensuous. I know of no other people who as matter-of-factly respond to beauty, whose intuition that the physical world is sometimes capable of sustaining them is more natural and honest. A woman who has pushed herself all day at a plant may still come home and be addressed by hens she's named Henrietta and Lucille, a rooster called Simon. Countless families born of the farms now live in crowded public housing in towns, in apartments not much more than boxes, in neighborhoods and on streets abandoned by the white middle class, the houses decaying now—to their actual owners, nothing but cash-producing rentals. But people still living in the country, no matter that the land may have changed hands since they were children, have before them at least a cleanly spaciousness of scene. Emotion in such a setting will seldom be much beneath the surface: the better to get up in the morning and compose one's self again, the mechanical and ugly awaiting you, uglier still for your need of it, for your having to have it.

On the job, then, work is taken for granted. Nor are people being insincere or speaking merely for the record when they tell you they like what they do. The same young Smithfield woman who described "most of these plants around here" as like "the sweatshops you read about in history books," spoke, also, of the compassion individuals in authority sometimes show toward the workers under them; though hardened to factory work, and viewing it as exploitative, she nonetheless says she *likes* her present job assembling computer boards. Work is frequently important at a level of people's lives deeper and more personal than that arising out of just their necessity for an income. Though I have said earlier that, unlike farming, a factory job can be forgotten on the weekend, it's true, too, that the plant, "that place," is very often the subject of casual conversation; that everybody close to a worker soon learns the names and positions of the people with whom he works, because he talks about them so much; their significance in his emotional life may rival that of his family. Yet there's never a sense here of the kind of thinking necessary for politicalization; grievance and assertion are both doggedly personal, and a group isn't a meaningful unit.

Nothing could be more tenant-like. Whatever else a tenant may have believed, he knew nobody outside himself had his best interest at heart; not the people he regarded monolithically—landlords, politicians, blacks (or, if a black himself, then white people), "the laws"—and not other tenants, men who had all they could do just looking after themselves. A good landlord was an exception that in no way invalidated the general antipathy for landlords; a Franklin Roosevelt didn't make politicians in general any more palatable. Enjoyment of a present good was seldom delayed or held in abeyance on the assumption that if you waited long enough, or wished for something else, a greater good might come along. "Wait's [weight's] what broke the camel's back," children joked, their parents laughing, too. "Shit in one hand and wish in the other," they said, "and see which one gets full the quickest."

The notion that people might unite in their own self-interest was as antithetical to them, went as much against their grain, as confrontation or lawlessness did. Knowing their powerlessness as individuals, nothing was more unimaginable than that together they would be any different. If a tenant by himself had no say-so, wouldn't ten tenants have had ten times *less*? So the thinking. It wasn't by any means that tenants were so naive, or cowed, or that they thought might made right; simply, they knew that people in charge generally got their way. More than this, however, the farm people of my childhood never really conceived, any more than they do now, of society as divided along economic or class lines. Such knowledge as they permitted themselves to have, they turned inward and around so that they themselves became the butt of it. The fact that they seldom admired anybody else didn't mean (on the other hand) that they thought well of their own kind, even if the phrase "their own kind" had meant anything to them; such a finely-honed sense of the ridiculous as they possessed was incompatible, finally, with the tendency to generalize. It was the detail, the particular, the exception, on which they were likely to seize; anything that happened to *them*, no matter how trivial or atypical, became forever afterward nothing but the truth.

North Carolina—for long the least unionized state in the nation.[20] Can anybody really wonder why? Especially do people "Down East" look at unions and their leadership pretty much as they would Gadarene swine; insular as the region is, any encroachment invites a hard time. Workers have an attitude appreciably no different from that of owners and bosses, and if this suits the powers-that-be especially, so, too, do most employees claim to be satisfied. What else could be the effect of an individualism as rampant as it is cussed? Working people believe no less fervently than the rich that a company or business, a public school or college, has the right to deal with its employees more or less as it sees fit. Political-mindedness being probably the least developed faculty they have, workers no more than a generation off the land haven't yet acquired the means for seeing themselves in opposition to management; that such an antagonism may be natural, even inherent, still is alien to them. Victims of the business ethic, subscribing fully and enthusiastically to the claims of progress (even when they've had but its crumbs), the victims all their lives of a palliative and inadequate education that's left them unequipped for probing much beyond the clichés of the status quo: how can they, therefore, not be happy? Especially when they consider how far they've come, how can they not look upon industrialization just as state government does? Just as local chambers of commerce do? As public work itself does? The answer is plain: they *can't*. Whatever should threaten them now, after they've worked so long and hard to get where they are, is to be resented and held at bay. Understandably.

Though I doubt that many contemporary workers "Down East" recall the push in the 1920s and 1930s to unionize the Southern textile industry, the 1929 strike in Gastonia, which soon spread to mills in other Piedmont towns, and then the General Strike of 1934 had been bloody; at that time, too, some workers "simply feared and distrusted the union" or for fear of losing their jobs, we need not doubt, "sided with the company." Millhands paid a high price for striking; "the lesson for many was a deep distrust of . . . trade unions. . . . Better the familiar securities of job and home," Jacquelyn Hall and her collaborators conclude in a recent study, "than 'air and promises,' followed by exile, suffering, and defeat."

Eastern North Carolinians would agree. But insofar as these "mill folk [saw] themselves as a people apart, exploited by men with interests opposed to their own and denied opportunities for progress that had seemed within their grasp,"[21] they differ fundamentally from the vast majority of workers now trying to make a living in the small plants and factories. These are people apt to look bitterly, though with bemusement, at television footage of striking union members in the North, their demands for seventeen or twenty or more dollars an hour as unreal to them as, say, minimum wage was when it first came in. Perversely, their sympathy is more than likely to be with the company; outrageous union demands, they'll tell you, have been the ruination of American manufacturing. They don't quarrel with the benefits organized labor has won for working people, though union paternalism they likely regard as arrogance. That unions are having their own troubles nationally (in 1982, winning just 43 percent of their elections, an all-time low), such that they comprised, in 1983, but twenty percent of the work force:[22] such an erosion of power and influence they take as indicative of general union impotence.

Intensely loyal to their employer, as most older, not so much the younger, workers are, not many people nowadays think unions are essential to their employment. Such people still are defined by their "inbred humility and low expectations." For many, "fundamentalist religious training, which stresse[s] acceptance of one's lot in life," together "with regional mores that stigmatiz[e] ambition or any attempt to 'get above' one's raising, . . . militat[e] against the kind of collective action" underlying unions.[23] The fact that unions seldom have any real effect on the one thing that workers here dread the most—their own plant shutting down—doesn't help their cause; nor do the heavy-handed tactics some organizers employ.

"It was the people in charge that got to me the most," a non-union worker recalls, describing union activists at her plant. "They thought they *were* somethin'. One of 'em told me if he passed me on the road and I had a flat tire, he'd just keep on goin' . . . that if I didn't watch my tires at work . . . Boy! Did my husband go through the roof when I told him about *that*!"

As in the 1920s and 1930s, women comprise a major part of the labor force, which, as then, likely impedes unionization. Though women stood side by side with men at Gastonia and in the General Strike, the fact remains that not until the 1920s did women have even the right to vote. Just as "nothing in the experience of mill village women encouraged political participation,"[24] neither is the background of these rural women conducive to such thought. Women in the factories nowadays are bound and determined to keep what's theirs; little enough it may be, but nobody gave it to them, and they aren't quite ready yet to risk its loss. For eastern North Carolina, public work is still so recent, economic hardship still so pervasive, that life's anchor isn't the state, but the family; especially for women is this true. Political interest, however, is of course antithetical to that of the family, the larger more abstract group taking precedence over particular persons joined by blood. For these reasons, I think, unions have held little appeal for farm women or for farm people. While some plants in the eastern counties are unionized, the state's overall low rate of unionization – 6.5 to 7.0 percent in 1982 – is here lower still.

No plant coming into the area in the 1960s held out more promise for its workers than GTE Sylvania (General Telephone and Electronics), in Smithfield, or, in the 1980s, proved more disappointing. Setting up operations in 1966 in this small town of some six thousand, Sylvania was for more than fifteen years – or until the summer of 1982 when it, too, closed its doors – the largest industrial employer in Johnston County. People spoke of it even in 1985 as having provided the best jobs around, the best pay and benefits, about five dollars an hour for an assembler, in 1980. At one time, in the mid-1970s, more than two thousand people worked there; but production and employment fell off sharply in the years thereafter, largely as a result of the declining market in consumer electronics. In Janaury 1981, GTE sold out to North American Phillips (NAP), and from that day on, the handwriting was plain for anybody wanting to read it.[25]

"It was a shock, I tell you," Carol says now, her layoff from Sylvania coming as early as 1979. "We kept hearing rumors that somethin' was goin' on" even then, she recalls. "We'd heard 'em from several places, but not from Sylvania . . . not at that time . . . not then."

"Yeah," Marilyn agrees. "Seems like they didn't tell us 'til they absolute *had* to."

Rocky Mount Mills. Est. 1818. On the banks of the Tar River. (Photo by Linda Flowers, 1989.)

Townhouses and abandoned tobacco barns: the changing face of eastern North Carolina. (Photo by Linda Flowers, 1989. Courtesy of Richard Lane.)

A test engineer with the plant, Tom Johnson was one of about forty-five salaried employees North American Phillips transferred to Tennessee where it relocated. Having been with Sylvania in Smithfield until practically the end, he remembers the meeting at which a company official broke the news. "'They wouldn't have bought us,'" he quotes the official as having said of NAP, "'if they hadn't a wanted us'"; the point being, Johnson insists, that Sylvania workers were at first reassured that NAP meant to keep the Smithfield plant going. But from where he is now, and as he looks back upon the transition, he's convinced that "the man didn't believe it when he said it. . . . He said it to keep everybody calmed down," to keep Sylvania's employees from leaving all at once, the company still having work for at least some of them to do.

(I should make clear that what interests me here isn't Sylvania *per se*, but the way people remember the closing; how they think of it now; what it meant to them then. That NAP and Sylvania would have a somewhat different story to tell, I take for granted – as ought the reader.)

"A lot of people did leave," Carol remembers, "once the rumors picked up."

"It was somethin'," Marilyn adds, "to be working along and all of a sudden realize that the person next to you . . . your friends . . . won't there any more, that they'd looked them somethin' else and gone to a job that paid *less*, . . . and here you were, still working away like nothin' was goin' on. You didn't know *what* to do."

But Carol and Marilyn both came through the ordeal in better shape (finally) than a good many others, though for Carol, especially, divorced and with two children, the experience is one she doesn't want to have repeated.

"Jack Kelly, poor fellow," she grimaces, "when he got laid off at Sylvania, after . . . I don't know how long it took him . . . but he got on at Burlington, and then he got laid off there! Burlington closed, too! . . . Now he's just like me . . . works second-shift in Raleigh."

They smile indulgently when I wonder aloud if Sylvania had helped them find another job. "The ESC [Employment Security Commission] did. . . . They set up interviews and sent us places," Marilyn recalls, "but not Sylvania. It didn't." Carol nods in agreement.

I think of the altogether different treatment of those more highly-skilled and educated workers accepting transfer to Greeneville, Tennessee. For Tom Johnson, not only did the company pay all his and his family's moving expenses, "they did more than that. They gave us what you might call incidental money . . . [that] paid for new drapes. They paid for hooking up our ice-maker. . . . Moving didn't cost us a cent."

Carol and Marilyn stress the fact that not everybody lost their job at the same time; that the actual closing had taken most of a year to complete, workers being let go at intervals, and that, reasonable as this was, it had had its dark side, too.

"The people there at the end . . . as it got nearer the shutdown . . . had the hardest time," Marilyn believes. "What jobs there might have been, had already been grabbed up. . . . They weren't anything left."

Listening to them, I am reminded of the effort the local *Smithfield Herald* devoted to making Sylvania's leaving explicable to the community. Through its editorials, especially, the paper was instrumental in shaping public feeling about the move. Early in its coverage, for example, the *Herald* confronted the rumor (which persisted, nonetheless) that it was the union, Communication Workers of America (CWA), driving Sylvania out. "The truth of the matter is," an October 1981 editorial concluded, "that a very large corporation made a purely business decision. . . . In a soft and highly-competitive TV market, the industry is cutting losses through consolidation."[26]

An article appearing a little more than a week before had taken pains to point out that Sylvania had recognized Local 3677 of CWA as early as 1970; that there had never been a strike at the plant (and just one incidence of workers picketing, in 1979); that a new three-year contract had been ratified in 1979; and that the Greeneville plant in Tennessee, "as the Smithfield plant, has union-represented employees."[27] The *Herald* thus took a firm stand in trying to dispel what anti-union sentiment there was.

Yet, as the months passed and still no buyer for the Smithfield facility came forth, "local officials both inside and outside of Sylvania's management," the paper reported, began expressing their opinion that "any transaction" with potential buyers "that may be in the making won't be culminated until the Smithfield plant is officially closed." And why not? "Apparently, a key reason for that thinking is the presence of union representation for a goodly portion of Sylvania's work force."[28] On the one hand, CWA had nothing to do with Sylvania's decision to close the plant; on the other hand, Sylvania seemed to be saying that until CWA was out of the picture, no other buyer wanted to commit. Employees, former employees, and the public alike could be forgiven their confusion.

The Greeneville plant is larger and more sophisticated than the one in Smithfield had been, Tom Johnson says; also, Greeneville is just eighty miles or so from NAP's regional headquarters in Knoxville, and "that makes things easier all the way around." He has heard, too, although he doesn't know it for a fact, that "the work force here is willing to work cheaper" than the people in Smithfield.

Closer to home, however, people had more immediate worries to contend with than the intricacies of industrial wheeling-and-dealing. Carol and Marilyn and Jack Kelly (as undoubtedly the thousand or so others out of a job) found their own situation of more pressing concern; whereas still today Jack holds CWA responsible for the whole state of affairs, neither of the women appears ever to have spent much time puzzling it out (perhaps because both were laid off early-on, Carol in 1979 and Marilyn in 1981). Then a member of CWA himself, Jack was working at Sylvania in June 1982, when it finally closed.

"Ever' time they was any kind of question," he remembers now, "the union'd file a grievance. They was all the time doin' that . . . acted like anythin' that hap'ned . . . didn't make no difference what . . . it was always Sylvania's fault. . . . The comp'ny just got tarred of it, what I believe, got tarred . . . and that's how come they left. . . . We didn't know how good we *did* have it . . . dental plan, free insurance . . . the best pay you could get. . . ."

"If Smithfield won't so close to Raleigh and Clayton," Carol muses, "we'd have had it worse than we did."

"I tell you where it hit the hardest," Marilyn offers, "was where the husband and the wife both worked at Sylvania. They, seem like, were the scaredest."

"When I first got laid off," Carol says, "people still at Sylvania'd ask me where I was at now, and I'd tell 'em maybe I was a waitress (which I was, when I could get it, part-time), . . . and they'd look at me like I don't know what. But then toward the end, when jobs got harder to find, and everybody was lookin', these same people . . . some of 'em, they'd laugh and ask me if they had any more openings where I was at."

Marilyn's situation, she readily acknowledges, was easier. "My husband had a good job, and so I was a lot better off than most people. But I'll tell you what I did do, though. I picked up bottles by the side of the road to pay my first tuition at Johnston Tech. That's how tight it was!

"A lot of people wound up right at Johnston Tech," she concludes. "For retraining. Some of 'em are out now and have good jobs."

Marilyn is in her mid-thirties, white, brought up in the country between Selma and Clayton. Her parents were tenants, she says, "just regular tobacco farmers." She had been at Sylvania "off and on, it was thirteen years. . . . I had my children then, and I'd stopped work, but if you add it all up, I was there about thirteen years."

Asked to summarize how she feels now about Sylvania's closing, her layoff, the decision to take up a program in computers at the local technical school, Marilyn is adamant. "It was the best thing that ever happened to me. . . . I didn't think so at the time, . . . I sure didn't . . . but it was. I made up my mind from it that I'd learn something so I'd never have to work in a plant again!"

Carol is more subdued. Raised in the Brogden area (her father's people, farmers), she has lived, also, in Virginia and, after marrying just out of high school, in Ohio. White, in her thirties, the sole support of her girls, she had been with Sylvania going on four years when she was laid off. "It was a whole lot more convenient for me to work in Smithfield," she says, "than to have to drive back and forth to Raleigh. Then, too, I worked in the daytime, whereas now I go in at three and get off at twelve. . . . That makes it hard, sometimes."

She had a rough year following her layoff; getting by then was largely a matter of the availability of restaurant work at area truckstops. Her unemployment ran out, but about when it did, she managed to get on at Telex, in Raleigh (Terminal Communications, out of Tulsa, the plant in Raleigh opeing in 1969); she likes the job, and the pay is good–between six and seven dollars an hour–but she would rather have been able to stay at Sylvania. "This second-shift can get with you," she says.

"I hope they go broke," Carol now says of Sylvania. "The devil'll probably get me, but I hope they lose everything. . . . That last year I was there, I worked on a lot of stuff shipped back from Mexico, that hadn't been done right. They sent it down there in the first place because those people worked even cheaper than us, and then we had to straighten it out. . . . That's why they come here, too. These plants, they . . . a lot of 'em . . . they just go where help's the cheapest. They don't *care*."

(A poem published in the *Herald* upon Sylvania's closing, the author having worked on a production-line there for sixteen years, emphasizes this lack of feeling: "This company that we're working for,/They don't even care;/They're tearing down all the lines;/It's more than I can bear./You got your slip and I'll get mine–/It's just a matter of time./But all I'm getting lately/Is leaving on my mind."[29])

Neither Carol nor Marilyn received any of Sylvania's much-publicized severance pay. The formula for determining eligibility excluded Carol, she'd been there such a short time, and, apparently, Marilyn's thirteen years somehow didn't count, their not being consecutive; thus—it's fair to say—they fell through the cracks. But Jack Kelly got $1,700 for his twelve years, and his wife May got proportionately less for her ten.

"But it didn't go nowhere," Jack scoffs. "It was gone in a month . . . a month and a half, two months." Black, thirty-six in 1985 when he talked with me, Jack has lived all his life in the Smithfield area. He and May have three children.

"We had a mobile home out in the country, out from Selma," Jack says, "out there in no man's land . . . and when I got the check, we moved it to town. . . . That took a lot of money. . . . I had my car payment, that was two thirty-five a month . . . my mobile home was about paid for, didn't like but three more years, that was a hundred and forty-six a month, and then the lot was fifty. They was insurance. I had to pay seven hundred dollars tax on the trailer when I had it moved.

"May got laid off about six months before I did," Jack recalls. "She stayed out of work . . . six, seven months, I reckon. . . . Then she went to Telex, in Raleigh, at five dollars an hour. That helped.

"But I laid out near 'bout a year. Won't no jobs. I looked ever'where . . . Goldsboro, Clayton, right here in Smithfield . . . Selma. . . . I got my unemployment. That come ever' two weeks.

"We eat fatback meat and pinto beans . . . mackerels in the can . . . stuff like that . . . neckbones . . . cheap stuff, you know.

"It scarred me right on up to the year 1985, really. I felt disgusted and mad and down and out, but I just kept strivin'. . . . It messed with your mind a lot. . . . I didn't do nothin' bad, you know, didn't go off or nothin', but I can understand somebody that would.

"It worried me so bad at times, I didn't even show it to my wife. . . . I'd get a six-pack, and she'd say 'Jack, what you do that for?' and I wouldn't say nothin'.

"I couldn't buy clothes like I wanted. I always wanted to look good, you know. Now, seems like, I just had my work clothes. They was clean and neat, had a crease in 'em, but I missed my cowboy boots and stuff."

Late in 1983, Jack at last got on at Burlington in Smithfield, but he had no more settled in, really, when this plant, too, announced plans for shutting down. Yet he has fared better than after his layoff from Sylvania; working now in Raleigh for a food distributor, he makes $6.33 an hour.

Tom Johnson and his wife Lorraine "like it here" in Greeneville, Tom says, "we really do." The offer Sylvania made him "was very lucrative," Tom continues. "We had the opportunity to buy another house again, something we didn't think we'd ever be able to do. . . . My job gives me the chance to assume more responsibility . . . to work with robotics, which they didn't have in Smithfield."

Some of the other transferred employees, however – Tom guesses as many as a third – didn't like Tennessee and have since moved back home around Smithfield. "They'd never lived anywhere else before," Tom explains, "and they got out here and were just devastated, it was so different to them. A lot of 'em's working in Raleigh now, or in Clayton at Data General. They all found something, the ones I know anything about, anyway." Tom attributes his own capacity for adapting to having been raised in a military family, as well as to his experience in the Navy.

Smithfield as a town, however, has suffered less from Sylvania's departure than might be expected. The same pressures pulling resources away from the heart of a small town and into the surrounding shopping malls and countryside, once a plant comes in, work to keep the town itself pretty much on an even keel even if the plant closes. Like a magnet, a factory draws employees from dozens of villages and crossroads, not simply from the town in or near which it's located. The effect of a pullout is, therefore, dispersed. The regional impact is cumulative; the area as a whole suffers. Of the 670 Sylvania workers scheduled to be let go at the plant's actual closing, 82 were from Wayne County (61 from the Goldsboro area), 27 from Harnett County, 30 from Sampson County, 143 from Smithfield itself, 123 from Selma, 58 from Four Oaks, and so forth. About one-fourth of Sylvania's hourly work force at the end were from outside Johnston County;[30] still, of course, the impact of 143 people out of work in a town the size of Smithfield isn't to be taken lightly – this on top of hundreds of others laid off in the months prior to closure.

There's a rather generalized malaise to be reckoned with, an endemic resignation, as if no matter what the day brings, that's just the way life is. The kind of security other people take for granted (at least as an idea) here falls outside the thinking, much less the experience, of the average working person. People have for so long scraped by, lived from hand to mouth, that anything else would be – *unusual* – maybe not quite right. Farmers felt this way, too, yet with an important difference: what befell a man back then was more circumscribed than that overtaking him nowadays; ruination of the kind involving money (*other* kinds, not having changed much) came in but one form – bad or profitless crops. People had less to lose, I suppose, though "everything" isn't comparative; aspirations hadn't been fanned to as high a flame. The land, at least, didn't pull up and move to Tennessee; *it* wasn't competitive.

Industry is something else again. Plants are here today – but in ten years? tomorrow? They are courted assiduously by local business people,[31] their way into a community paved by good will and financial advantage; the lifeblood of local workers. Yet, for most people, living and working and getting by are, finally, about as problematic as for their parents and grandparents, often more so. Some *have* gotten ahead, of course; most, however, think themselves well-off if this year they're no further behind than last.

Good Country People

An Epilogue

You don't see them much anymore. Not in Rocky Mount and Goldsboro, Wilson, Smithfield and Clinton; in Faison, yes, in little towns like that, sometimes. Especially if on Saturday you buy your groceries at one of the less-than-grand supermarkets, your clothes, when you have to have them, at the dry-goods store. They stay out of the shopping malls, away from the stores dazzling as operating rooms. At Christmas time, everybody sees them (but tries not to); they stumble along, slower than other people, more uncertain, as if they're not quite sure where they are. As for the men, you can spot them without too much trouble. At the tractor places, the filling stations where they go to pass the time of day, the run-down ones; they're driving battered pickup trucks and looking out across the land, poking along at forty and forty-five. But they're not as common as they used to be, these old farmers in faded overalls, in khaki shirts washed thin and almost white, brogans, hats usually: dusty as a March field. And the women, the country women of my childhood are as scarce now almost as hen's teeth.

Oh, but they were something! The beauty they'd had as girls wrung out of them, and in its place another: faces composed, purposeful as iron. A look that went right through you, bottomless and sad. People my mother's age, the blacks who had known her all her life, would stop me on the street sometimes and after getting it right ("Ain'cha Miss Geneva's girl? Ain'cha now? Ain'cha?"), they'd tell me what a fine-looking woman my mama had been; how in the fields chopping, picking cotton maybe, she could outwork anybody, them too, and *did.* They said she hadn't the need for conversation ("all sech as that"), and suffered no fools, gladly or otherwise, that she was all business, as good as her word and meant what she said. They'd tell me they knew my people. "Sho' do! Mist' Jim . . . Miss Annie, all of 'em!" And they did.

To have stood there on the sidewalk with these people, six or seven or eight years old, the year 1950, 1951, 1952, on a Saturday more than likely, and Faison full to beat the band, old black women congregated in the doorways, come to town. And you pulling away even as they told you, yet not wanting to offend, and their high cackle, the start on something else if you weren't quick, backing away: you knew that you were *known,* and exactly who you *were.*

This was a generation the like of which will never be seen again; they were the last of that breed of farmer and hand who had started out during the Great Depression. Their sons and daughters were the first taking up public work, and their grandchildren, the first in an entire lineage never to have known the land at all. Housewives in the 1960s wore pedalpushers and went to the beauty shop. If they didn't yet work at the sewing plant or Hamilton-Beach, they kept up with "As the World Turns" and "The Edge of Night," and they'd put supper on the table some nights out of a can. The men would wear overall pants and low-cut shoes, wide white belts and slacks when they dressed up, Mennen Skin Bracer maybe, or Old Spice; they'd go when they could to Topsail fishing (calling it "Topsl"), or they'd take the family to the drive-in at Mount Olive where, in the 1950s, it had cost a dollar a car, but a dollar a head in the 1960s.

Farm people still, and they'd seldom had much schooling, but the plants and factories then springing up wanted them anyway, and as surely as the sun was going to rise tomorrow, women and men both did need *them.* Tenantry going to hell like it was, and small landowners having a time of it, too, the 1960s and early 1970s saw the virtual disappearance of one way of life, the birth of another: the dying out of good country people and the emergence of a semi-skilled class of laborers, their roots in the land but their future, as that of their children, in—why, whatever job they could pick up; they weren't particular, and they knew how to work.

Of course it was getting to the place where you had to know a little something extra to get on at some plants, education and training coming to matter more and more in the 1970s and 1980s, but nobody had asked them, and they couldn't help it; and if their children hadn't got what they ought to out of school, they couldn't help that, either. They'd done all right so far, and they reckoned the young people just starting out would, too—soon as they settled down some. They were making more than they ever had before, even if they couldn't begin to tell you where it all went, and if the plant where they worked would just stay open, if their hours weren't cut any more, if they didn't get layed off, why they thought they'd fare right well.

For their children a community college or technical school has sometimes made the difference, taking up the slack after high school, bridging the gap between the training they need for certain kinds of employment and the skills they, in fact, have; associate-degree programs provide entry into some of the technical fields, and for those not finishing high school or unable to read, courses in basic education are available. People thrown out of work by changes in the job market, as by layoffs and closings, can sometimes take advantage of the chance to try something else, computers, maybe, or data processing. But not everybody has found retraining to be the answer, or, for that matter, a two-year program. Jobs of any kind, but especially if they hold much long-range promise, still don't grow on trees; wages still are among the lowest in the nation, and the gap between these eastern counties and the Piedmont cities, as between rich and poor, gets wider and wider. Manufacturing is not what it used to be, and, yet, most people looking for work aren't prepared for anything else.

But these are proud people. Throwed away they may be, but it won't do to count them out. Men and women who have seen how, in the 1960s, machines pushed up the demand for land, even as they made farm laborers increasingly obsolescent, who have experienced the breakup of smalltime agriculture, yet who have kept going nonetheless, kept looking ahead—they know they're up against a hard time, but they know, too, they'll make it somehow: they always have. Business is business, and if people still matter less than profits, why they've always known *that*.

It's a hard lesson for the young: the realization that they're not likely to do even as well as their parents; that as many plants are closing as are coming in; that by itself a high-school diploma, as increasingly a college degree, means little to the man doing the hiring. Having sat for twelve years in more modern, more costly schools than any in history, they aren't happier for the experience or scarcely any more prepared for meeting the world head-on; nor are their parents any happier or more financially secure for having taken up public work. Neither schools nor factories have fulfilled the promises inherent in them. The one too often seems irrelevant; the other, willfully capricious if not worse. Fairness is something only little children any longer much expect.

But blood is thicker than water, and in these youngsters as often different from us as night from day, there may yet survive a farmer's cussedness, his equable and solid understanding of what counts and of who really matters. Others have come into less, surely.

Notes and Commentary

No one writing anything set in the South can help but be touched by those books about the place she loves the best. Especially if she's a Southerner, her story historical, she will have needed the perspective of other people, knowing of course that none of them have told it all nor—but for luminous bits and pieces—told it right; and that she won't either: but she'll try, and her efforts will be the better for her reading. They may not suffice, they won't likely be memorable, but without James Agee and W. J. Cash, Eudora Welty and Flannery O'Connor, Faulkner and Katherine Anne Porter, C. Vann Woodward and Louis Rubin and Arthur Raper and, yes, even the twelve angry men of *I'll Take My Stand,* her own words might never come forth at all. "Mute, inglorious," she likely would stay. Faulkner said of *The Sound and the Fury* that of all his works it was the one in which he failed the least; that he nonetheless thought himself to have failed bespeaks his integrity, and the proper humility of an artist. Others will probably have less of both, and failure incomparably greater than his.

I owe as much to books not cited as to many I have named; to reading having nothing to do with "research" and that is apt to appear irrelevant to those whose work in education, in regional development or agriculture, in commerce and industry, is more specialized than my own. Mary Ellen Chase's *A Goodly Heritage,* for example; Ellen Glasgow's *The Sheltered Life;* Clarence Cason's *90° in the Shade,* I dug out and enjoyed, and Jonathan Daniels's *A Southerner Discovers the South.* People who have thought about such matters as style and content, however, will discern something of the true relationship here; the writing voice is neither formed nor sustained in a vacuum. I discovered early-on that the voice of reflection and memory doesn't permit much of other modes; the rhythms of eastern North Carolina speech, as the habits of expression common to the area, seldom lent themselves to the conventions of more scholarly prose. Because so much of this book is personal (even where the subjectivity is only implicit), this autobiographical apprehension proved difficult to leave off; or, rather, as I moved into material that was, in fact, objective, it seemed possible to forge the links necessary between what I knew firsthand and the larger history of my home, without much altering the familiar note struck at the outset. Not always successfully, however; not always with as firm a hand as I would have liked.

I was sometimes amused to discover how arcane much of the professional literature is. Strange it was to read learned treatises on – farming! – and, particularly, on the revolution having overtaken agriculture since the Depression. What my father knew with his sweat, what I knew at six and seven, those whose study of the land is done from within the shade and sinecure of universities and government agencies have now analyzed out of all but the most passing recognition. Real fields are as remote from such technical disquisitions as real boys and girls from the ponderous vacuity – the jargon-ridden mindlessness – typical of so much of the writing in education. I read what I could bear of such studies, yet I've been neither very thorough nor very systematic; so much the worse, perhaps. Richard Hofstadter (his brief survey in *Anti-Intellectualism in America*), Jonathan Kozol, Richard Hoggart, Richard Mitchell (irreverent, but right): them I learned from, and with pleasure. For the educationists themselves, however – but for Lawrence Cremin, Diane Ravitch, Sara Lightfoot, James Coleman, maybe one or two others – a reader may be, I think, forgiven his despair.

How much of my research truly informs my writing is, however, another matter. Statistics culled from the usual sources shore up my thesis from time to time, yet, for me at least, such figures confirm rather than newly illumine. They amplify and lend another kind of credence, but the theme I already had in mind before I came into possession of the documentation for it. I have thought it necessary neither to cite each statistical reference individually nor to say here anything more about either the people I interviewed or certain in-house or other publications, the naming of which in a bibliography or note would likely violate a promised confidentiality. Thus for a number of the passages quoted in the text, the source obviously a pamphlet or accreditation study, a local newspaper column or (in one instance) a book, no further mention is made.

Unless otherwise noted, all statistics and figures come from the following standard reference works:

U.S. Bureau of the Census, *Census of Population:* [1960, 1970, and 1980] *General Social and Economic Characteristics, North Carolina* (Washington, D.C.: U.S. Department of Commerce, 1961, 1972, and 1983).

U.S. Bureau of the Census, *Statistical Abstract of the United States: 1982–83,* 103rd ed. (Washington, D.C.: U.S. Department of Commerce, 1982).

North Carolina Public Schools Statistical Profile [1980, 1981, 1982, 1983, 1984, and 1985] (Raleigh, N.C.: State Board of Education, 1980–85).

[1983–84 and 1985–86] *Directory of North Carolina Manufacturing Firms* (Raleigh, N.C.: North Carolina Department of Commerce, 1982 and 1984).

Readers familiar with these works will know in which one a particular kind of figure appears; others will follow my argument more generally.

References cited that are fully documented under "Further Reading" are identified in the notes by author, short title, and date only. I have fully documented in the notes those works that are not included subsequently under "Further Reading."

Preface

1. Polls reveal just how satisfied most North Carolinians are with the state's institutions. See "Most residents of N.C. happy, survey indicates," *The News and Observer* [Raleigh, N.C.], September 29, 1982. The article summarizes the results of the *1981 N.C. Citizen Survey.* See, also, *Public Education in North Carolina: A Review of Public Opinion from 1978 to 1983.* (Raleigh, N.C.: Office of State Budget and Management, *n. d.*); and John Shelton Reed, *Southerners* (1983), a study based on the "Survey of North Carolina," conducted in 1971.

Home: An Introduction

1. *Annual Report: July 1, 1979/June 30, 1980 North Carolina Department of Human Resources* (Raleigh, N.C.: Department of Human Resources, *n. d.),* p. 1. For a family of four in 1980, the poverty level was $6,990.
2. Five years later, in 1985, North Carolina ranked thirty-seventh among the fifty states in per capita personal income.
3. I am indebted to Ken Auletta for the term. See Ken Auletta, *The Underclass* (New York: Random House, 1982).

4. Here and throughout the book, public work just means non-agricultural, non-professional employment, that is any work involving interaction with the public, except teaching, medicine, law, and the like.

1. Old Model T

1. The shoofly was the passenger train on Saturday night that went through Faison at nine o'clock.
2. In fact not Jews, but Syrians, I have since learned. The difference was lost to us then. According to a history of the town written by Miss Winifred Faison and excerpted in the *Duplin Record* [Warsaw, N.C.], February 18, 1928, the first store in Faison "was operated by Bloomingdale, who was a pedler [*sic*] and is now represented in the New York firm." This connection has, of course, long since been severed. Faison takes its name from the Faison family, the most prominent son being Samson Lane Faison, the brigadier general "commanding the 30th Division, who broke the Hindenburg Line."

   Around 1920, Miss Faison reports, "Faison had more students in college than any town between Goldsboro and Wilmington." The Faison family papers are held in the Southern Historical Collection at the Louis Round Wilson Library of the University of North Carolina, Chapel Hill. Letters from various of the Faison sons away at college to their parents at home date from the 1870s.
3. Legislative approval for a twelfth grade had, however, come through in 1942.
4. See *The Mount Olive Tribune* [Mount Olive, N.C.], August 26, 1983, which features the town's response to the upcoming flight.

2. School Days

That schools and teachers may indeed remain with us is amply confirmed in the many, and often poignant, testimonials of their former students. I like Eudora Welty's description of Miss Duling and Davis School, in *One Writer's Beginnings* (1984); the exchange between Louis Rubin, Eudora Welty, and Shelby Foote, in *The American South* (1980), ed. Louis Rubin; *An Apple for My Teacher* (1987), ed. Louis Rubin, especially the chapters by Fred Chappell and Alfred Kazin; "Primer Class," by Elizabeth Bishop, in *The Collected Prose,* ed. Robert Giroux (New York: Farrar, Straus, and Giroux, 1984), pp. 3–12. See, also, *Masters: Portraits of Great Teachers,* ed. Joseph Epstein (New York: Basic Books, Inc., 1981); and *Going to School: An Anthology of Prose about Teachers and Students,* ed. Abraham H. Lass and Norma L. Tasman, "A Mentor Book" (New York: New American Library, 1981).

Christopher Jencks argues "that differences between schools have rather trivial long-term effects, and that eliminating [such] differences . . . would do almost nothing to make adults more equal"; at a level other than Jencks intends here, however, a child's particular experience at school, not just of school in general but of his own school, is far from trivial. See Jencks et al., *Inequality: A Reassessment* (1972), p. 16, et pass.

1. *Educational Directory of North Carolina, 1954–1955* (Raleigh, N.C.: State Department of Public Instruction, *n. d.),* p. 57.
2. Teacher salaries are taken from *Southern Schools: Progress and Problems,* ed. Patrick McCauley and Edward D. Ball (Nashville, Tenn.: Southern Educational Reporting Service, 1959), pp. 141–43. In 1965, North Carolina ranked fortieth among the states in the salaries paid teachers; in 1974, twenty-seventh, and in 1984, twenty-ninth. See *How North Carolina Ranks Educationally among the Fifty States* (Raleigh, N.C.: State Department of Public Instruction), an annual publication. A Study conducted by the American Federation of Teachers, for 1987–88, put North Carolina twenty-ninth in the salary paid teachers. See "Average starting teacher pay tops $18,000," *The News and Observer* [Raleigh, N.C.], July 3, 1988.
3. North Carolina schools in the 1950s, despite my fond recall, generally came up short in national surveys and other assessments. The Comprehensive School Improvement Project begun in 1964, and funded over three years by the Ford Foundation for $2 million was sorely needed. See *CSIP: The Means to a Beginning. A Summary Report of the North Carolina Comprehensive School Improvement Project: 1967–1971* (Raleigh, N.C.: State Department of Public Instruction, 1971).
4. Much has been written about this generation, though no study is as true for every area of the country as it is for some. Our class had nothing in common with that so vividly evoked by Michael Medved and David Wallechinsky, in *What Really Happened to the Class of "65"?* (1977). We had far less money, were less sophisticated, and had less exalted notions of ourselves in the world. Probably we were more akin to the group Landon Y. Jones defines as "immediately older than the boom babies." Although we were born at the end of World War II, we were like that "in-between generation" born but a few years earlier. We "were teenagers when teenagers were still an emotionally deprived class." See Jones, *Great Expectations* (1981), p. 129. See, also, Bob Greene, *Be True to Your School* (1987).

3. The Hands and Us

Southern tenantry has often been the subject of inquiry. See, for example, Howard Odum's pioneering studies published in the 1930s and 1940s, especially *An American Epoch* (1930) and *The Way of the South* (1947); Arthur F. Raper and Ira Reid, *Sharecroppers All* (1941); Arthur F. Raper, *Tenants of the Almighty* (1943); James Agee (and Walker Evans), *Let Us Now Praise Famous Men* (1939); Margaret Jarman Hagood, *Mothers of the South* (1939); Tom E. Terrill and Jerrold Hirsch, eds., *Such As Us: Voices of the Thirties* (1979); "Federal Writers' Project," *These Are Our Lives* (1939); David E. Conrad, *The Forgotten Farmers: The Story of Sharecroppers in the New Deal* (1965); Pete Daniel, *Breaking the Land* (1985); Robert L. Hall and Carol B. Stack, eds., *Holding on to the Land and the Lord* (1982); J. Wayne Flynt, *Dixie's Forgotten People* (1979); and Roy G. Taylor, *Sharecroppers* (1984).

Taylor's is "a happy story," as he tells us in his foreword, "for it is viewed from the eyes of youth, with the tragic events and hardships forgotten." Less sanguine and, I think, much closer to the truth is, however, Harry Crews's *A Childhood* (1978). "The world that circumscribed the people I come from," Crews writes, "had so little margin for error, for bad luck, that when something went wrong, it almost always brought something else down with it. It was a world in which survival depended on raw courage, a courage born out of desperation and sustained by a lack of alternatives" (p. 40).

1. Prices cited for produce, as for cotton and corn, are those a local farmer of the time remembers; reasonable variation from the available record might, therefore, be expected.
2. Thus my own earnings in tobacco during the summers of 1960, 1961, and 1962.
3. Pat Watters, *The South and the Nation* (1969), p. 104. Watters cites Thomas D. Clark, *The Emerging South* (New York: Oxford University Press, 1961). For the other side of the story, the plight of native Southerners in the North once they left the South, see Robert Coles, *The South Goes North,* Vol. 3 of *Children of Crisis* (Boston: Little, Brown and Co., 1967).

4. Poor Grassy Farmer

For a professional study of agricultural change in the region, see, for example, John Fraser Hart and Ennis L. Chestang, "Rural Revolution in East Carolina," *Geographical Review* 68 (1978): 435–58, and for a study of the pattern generally, see, for example, Wayne C. Rohrer and Louis H. Douglas, *The Agrarian Transition in America: Dualism and Change* (Indianapolis, Ind.: The Bobbs-Merrill Co., 1969). Still relevant for its pungent criticism of the sociologist's belief in progress and quantification, when applied to tenantry, is the essay by Richard Croom Beatty and George Marion O'Donnell, "The Tenant Farmer in the South," *The American Review* 5 (April 1935): 75–96. "The chief dangers menacing the agrarian way of life in the South," they write, "are high taxes, high tariff, the gospel of Progress, and industrialist methods in agriculture" (p. 94). For an excellent study of how New Deal legislation affecting farmers was written, the controversy then over the subsidy programs and their likely impact on tenants and owners, see Jack T. Kirby, *Rural Worlds Lost* (1987), Chapter 2, "The South on the Federal Road," pp. 51–79; and for a more comprehensive study of the theme, see "Federal and Technological Intrusion into Traditional Cultures, 1933–1941," Book Two of Pete Daniel's *Breaking the Land,* pp. 63–298.

1. Jack T. Kirby, *Rural Worlds Lost,* p. 345.
2. *1978 Census of Agriculture: Preliminary Report: North Carolina* (Washington, D.C.: Department of Commerce, 1978). In 1920, 43.5 percent of the state's farmers were tenants. See Pete Daniel, *Breaking the Land,* p. 34.
3. Tenantry had always had the capacity to provide social value. Pete Daniel, in *Breaking the Land,* is sensitive to this point. "Despite the numbing aspects of

the old tenure system," he writes, "it existed in the context of a community life and culture that rural people built to protect and sustain themselves" (p. 296).

4. But the heyday of tobacco is, in 1989, well past. The number of the state's tobacco farms "dropped from 52,000 in 1977 to 46,000 in 1978–a 12 percent decline in one year." See Pete Daniel, *Breaking the Land,* p. 267. The ever-diminishing number of available hands, rising labor costs, federal restrictions, the relationship between cigarettes and cancer–all have eroded confidence in the long-range prospect of tobacco-farming. For an idea of what one area farmer in the early 1970s (clearly a landlord) thought of his harvester, however, consider his remark that "It is ready on Monday or Saturday. It don't get drunk. It don't have to be bailed out of jail. It don't borrow money all year to gripe when the work is to be done. . . . You can sleep at night because you can get the tobacco." Cited by Jack T. Kirby, *Rural Worlds Lost,* p. 334.
5. The 1959 and 1964 figures derive from my calculation, as based on the *1978 Census of Agriculture;* other figures are as given there. The trend away from farming has, of course, continued. From 1940 to 1978, the number of Negro farms (not necessarily tenant) dropped from 60,268 to 9,289. See "Black-run farms dwindling, study says," *The News and Observer* [Raleigh, N.C.], February 10, 1982. From 1973 to 1983, 45,000 farmers in North Carolina went out of business–more than in any other state. See "Small Tar Heel farmers losing ground, study says," *The News and Observer* [Raleigh, N.C.], December 12, 1984. These two studies were conducted by, respectively, the U.S. Civil Rights Commission and the Rural Advancement Fund in Pittsboro.
6. Jack T. Kirby, *Rural Worlds Lost,* p. 61.
7. For a penetrating study of the effect federal legislation and mechanization have had on tenants and small farmers, see, in addition to the studies cited above, Frances Fox Piven and Richard A. Cloward, "Agricultural Modernization and Mass Unemployment," in *Regulating the Poor* (1971), pp. 200–21. Pete Daniel, in *Breaking the Land,* posits that the "abrupt decline" in tobacco farms between 1954 and 1959 (a decline that nobody I knew then noticed) was caused "partly" by "landowners putting their land in the Soil Bank Program," just established in 1956. In these five years alone, Daniel says, "North Carolina lost 37,440 flue-cured tobacco farms, planted 218,311 fewer acres, and harvested 141.6 million fewer pounds" (p. 262). Legislation arising out of the New Deal had not, on the whole, proved beneficial to "bottom-rung farmers," Daniel argues (p. 187). "Instead of reviving the old system, as it promised, the New Deal in many areas destroyed that system's remnants more thoroughly than Sherman's troops had wrecked antebellum dreams" (p. 66). As for mechanization, Daniel acknowledges that it "emancipated millions of field workers," but it was also "a dubious freedom for people anchored in the soil and neither prepared nor eager for urban life." (p. 91).
8. Jack T. Kirby, in *Rural Worlds Lost,* is especially interesting on this point; see pp. 61–65.

9. Pete Daniel, in *Breaking the Land,* makes this same point. "The federal government supplanted landlords and merchants with relief," he writes. "Changes . . . altered the relationship between landlord and tenant and created a different attitude toward relief. . . . landlords . . . abdicated their paternalistic role" (p. 66). For a brief history of the Production Credit Association, that by Earl Butz is as useful as any. See Earl Butz, *The Production Credit System for Farmers* (Washington, D.C.: The Brookings Institution, 1944). See, also, W. N. Stokes, Jr., *Credit to Farmers: The Story of Federal Intermediate Credit Banks and Production Credit Associations* (Washington, D.C.: Farm Credit Administration, 1973).

10. For an eloquent discussion of the South's rejection of the idea of progress, and the argument that herein lies the region's distinctiveness, see C. Vann Woodward, *The Burden of Southern History* (1960), Chapter 9. Carl N. Degler, in *Place Over Time* (1977), says much the same thing. For local chambers of commerce, however, the thesis won't wash; progress is their stock in trade. It is rather the poor, the throwed away for whom the argument rings true. It is they who have never been able to subscribe uncritically to the tenets of progress.

But what I speak of here is not so much a southern attitude as the victimization that inevitably occurs when a place or people push ahead leaving others behind. Compare, for example, Michael Harrington's description of this phenomenon in *The Other America* (1962). "The other Americans," Harrington writes, "are the victims of the very inventions and machines that have provided a higher standard for the rest of society. They are upside-down in the economy, and for them greater productivity often means worse jobs" (p. 13). See, also, Jonathan Daniels, "The Ever-Ever Land," in *The South Today,* ed. Willie Morris (1965), pp. 115–25. Daniels observed that "Certainly industry had done little for these agriculturally dispossessed" (p. 120), which, I argue, remains true today. Wendell Berry has written tellingly of "the enraptured booster" of progress, of farmers forced off the land in the name of modernization, and of the "crisis of culture" arising out of such agricultural crisis. See Berry, *The Unsettling of America* (1977).

5. "Nothing to Do . . ."

For a brief description of North Carolina's industrial expansion in the 1960s, see, for example, Doris Mahaffey and Mercer Doty, "Which Way Now? Economic Development and Industrialization in N.C.," in *North Carolina Focus,* comp. Eric B. Herzik and Sallye Branch Teater (Raleigh: The North Carolina Center for Public Policy Research, Inc., 1981), pp. 227–41. Luther Hodges's autobiography, *Businessman in the State House: Six Years as Governor of North Carolina* (Chapel Hill: University of North Carolina Press, 1962), is still useful for its evocation of the period. See also, however, Jack Bass and Walter DeVries, "North Carolina: The Progressive Myth," in *The Transformation of Southern Politics: Social Change and Political Consequence Since 1945* (New York: Basic Books, Inc., 1976), pp. 218–47; James G. Maddox, et al., *The Advancing South: Manpower Prospects and Problems* (New York: The Twentieth Century Fund, 1967); and, especially, James C. Cobb, *The Selling of the South* (1982). For a study of the young unable to make their way, see, for example, Oscar Handlin and Mary F. Handlin, *Facing Life: Youth and the Family in American History* (Boston: Little, Brown and Company, 1971), esp. pp. 211–89.

1. James C. Cobb, in *The Selling of the South,* movingly describes the South's attempts at wooing outside industry and the consequent price of such progress. Analyzing industrial ads, and the kind of cooperation thus implied between state and local governments and companies relocating, Cobb remarks that "Southern governors seemed ready to don work clothes and help build the new plant if necessary" (p. 94).
2. *Manufacturing Employment in North Carolina: 1969 to 1979* (Raleigh, N.C.: Employment Security Commission, *n. d.*), p. 1.
3. *1978 Census of Agriculture.*
4. "In the heart of the North Carolina tobacco belt–Edgecombe, Green, Lenoir, Pitt, Nash, Wayne, and Wilson counties," Pete Daniel writes in *Breaking the Land,* "the number of workers employed in manufacturing rose from 24,700 in 1963 to 59,606 in 1976, while agricultural workers declined from 45,020 to 22,950, an almost perfect exchange." Daniel argues that "the *lateness* [my emphasis] of mechanization thus eased the transition of these farm workers to factory life"; that is, had the big machines been available earlier, before the factories came in, there would have been far fewer places to work once farmers left the land. See Daniel, p. 266.
5. Dennis Rogers, "They grew up 'on' Runnymede; are 'neighborhood proud,'" *The News and Observer* [Raleigh, N.C.], June 6, 1988. Rogers quotes a woman born and raised here: "It was a poor neighborhood, no doubt about it . . . I was born in the front room of my grandmother's house . . . in 1927 and lived there until I left home in 1947. Times were hard, but I never thought of myself as having a poor childhood. . . . No one went hungry on Runnymede. If your neighbor had something, you had it. . . . The neighborhood we had was special. Everybody knew everybody and took care of each other. . . ." Nostalgia aside, the fact that such neighborhoods were so clearly defined had, of course, important implications; the difference now is stark.

   But for the definitive study of the Southern mill village, see Jacquelyn Dowd Hall, et al., *Like a Family: The Making of a Southern Cotton Mill World* (1987). For the closeness of such communities, the pivotal role of women therein, see, esp., pp. 146–80.
6. *Manufacturing Employment in North Carolina: 1969 to 1979,* p. 53.
7. Statistics on farm foreclosures are derived from information supplied to me by James L. Olson, Statistician in Charge, North Carolina Crop and Livestock Reporting Service [Raleigh, N.C.], July 1983.
8. "Educational programs backed to help blacks keep farmland," *The News*

and Observer [Raleigh, N.C.], January 26, 1983; and see, also, "N.C. farmers feel money squeeze," *The News and Observer* [Raleigh, N.C.], March 24, 1985; and related articles et pass. But according to a recent study in *The New York Times,* "North Carolina Bustles with People and Money" (January 6, 1985). Like the elephant the blind men described, North Carolina can be very different, depending where you look.

9. *North Carolina Youth: Labor Market Statistics* (Raleigh, N.C.: Bureau of Employment Security Research, 1981), pp. 3–4, 5.

6. ". . . But Go to School"

Ivar Berg, in *Education and Jobs* (1970), has defined America's "education craze" as that cycle wherein employers insist on a level of formal education incommensurate with the level of the work they, in fact, have to offer, the employee thus having to acquire more and more years of schooling in order to be competitive on the job market. Everybody goes to college, and thus the degree is worth comparatively less and less. Actual work, however, especially that outside the professions, has seldom necessitated any but a modest level of education. See, also, Christopher Lasch, *The Culture of Narcissism* (1979), who says that "Schools in modern society serve largely to train people for work, but most of the available jobs, . . . no longer require a high level of technical or intellectual competence" (p. 223); "advanced industrial society," Lasch argues, "no longer rests on a population primed for achievement" (p. 224). But Lasch's formulation doesn't (yet?) apply in eastern North Carolina, where a disproportionately large number of job seekers lack even the low level of competence that area jobs require.

For an argument that community colleges and technical schools exist primarily in order to serve the political and social interests of the status quo, see L. Steven Zwerling, *Second Best: The Crisis of the Community College* (1976). Zwerling's thesis is that the real function of such schools is to control the distribution of B.A.s; that by providing access to large numbers of the poor and racially disadvantaged, they free up a state's four-year colleges for precisely the same group as has always attended them – white and largely middle and upper class. Zwerling argues that community colleges are, therefore, but another and more callous way of tracking the young, limiting a student's eventual choice of career far more than expanding it.

The traditional view that community colleges and technical schools are gateways of opportunity, thus liberating such groups as have never before had the chance to go to college, is assumed in, for example, K. Patricia Cross's *Beyond the Open Door: New Students in Higher Education* (San Francisco: Jossey-Bass, Inc., 1972).

For a discussion of the early community college movement in North Carolina, see, for example, former governor Terry Sanford, *But What About the People?* (New York: Harper & Row, 1966); and, also, *Planning For Higher Education in North Carolina: Special Report 2–68* (Raleigh: North Carolina Board of Higher Education, 1968).

1. The Woman's College of The University of North Carolina; since 1963–64, The University of North Carolina at Greensboro.
2. "What Becomes of Our High School Graduates" (Raleigh, N.C.: State Department of Public Instruction, 1955), pp. 3, 9, and 10.
3. See, for example, Eric. F. Goldman, *The Crucial Decade* (1956), pp. 56 and 95.
4. For an account of "Basic Education versus National Defense Education," see Lasch, *The Culture of Narcissism*, pp. 242–46.
5. *Annual Enrollment Report: Student Enrollment and Full-Time Equivalents: 1982–1983*, Vol. 18 (Raleigh: North Carolina Department of Community Colleges, *n. d.*), p. 37.
6. Gerald M. Bolik, *Socio-Economic Profile of Credit Students in the North Carolina Community College System* (Raleigh: North Carolina Department of Community Colleges, 1969), pp. 16–34, et pass.
7. On the place of education in "an age of diminishing expectations," see Lasch, *The Culture of Narcissism*, esp. pp. 221–65. Much to the point here is his assertion that even though "modern society has achieved unprecedented rates of formal literacy, . . . at the same time it has produced new forms of illiteracy (p. 225). On "Why Johnny Can't Earn," see Landon Y. Jones, *Great Expectations*, pp. 176–90. "The boom generation saw its future," Jones concludes, "and for the first time realized that it did not work. The older generation had opened the door but the younger generation could not squeeze in. The conviction of the sixties—that youth would *prevail*—was looking more and more like the boom generation's grand illusion. The human metaphor for its situation was no longer the phalanx but the queue. This was the generation doomed to wait in line . . . " (p. 190).
8. For the kind of students Governor Terry Sanford envisioned the state's community colleges attracting, consider his statement that they should "reach everybody who didn't want to go to college, who shouldn't go to college, who had already been to college, who had 'aged out' without finishing high school, who need retraining, those in need of technical and specialized training, illiterates, those who wanted college studies but couldn't afford a residence school, and any other groups which time might develop." See Sanford, *But What About the People?*, p. 99.
9. Ronald W. Shearon, Robert G. Templin, Jr., et al., *Putting Learning to Work: A Profile of Students in North Carolina Community Colleges, Technical Institutes, and Technical Colleges. A Summary of Research Findings* (Raleigh: North Carolina Department of Community Colleges, 1980).
10. *HRD: Yesterday and Today: A Statistical and Descriptive Study of the Human Resources Development Program Operated under the North Carolina Department of Community Colleges from 1973–1982. Final Report* (Chapel Hill, N.C.: MDC, Inc., 1982), pp. 2, 95. Governor Terry Sanford established the North Carolina Fund (financed in part by the Ford Foundation) in the early 1960s, under which a number of anti-poverty experimental programs were sponsored. But the economic plight of some groups still is staggering; see, for example, "Northeast ponders the face of poverty," *The News and Observer* [Raleigh, N.C.], May 16, 1982, et seq. Falling through the cracks is nothing new for poor people.

11. See, for example, Paul T. O'Connor, "Half of state's story is missing," *The Evening-Telegram* [Rocky Mount, N.C.], June 13, 1988, and, also, "N.C.'s record low jobless rate has a down side," *The Evening-Telegram* [Rocky Mount, N.C.], August 17, 1988.
12. I take my examples from an actual 1984 follow-up study of the graduates of an area technical college.
13. Compare Stuart Chase's observation twenty-five years ago that "While Americans universally favor education, the goal is primarily to improve earning power. Education for a better understanding of the world and of themselves is not often mentioned in the surveys." See Chase, *American Credos* (1962), p. 137.
14. I likely err on the side of optimism. Manufacturing in the 1980s is having the fight of its life; especially is the textile industry hard hit.
15. The costs in 1984–85 according to the respective college catalogues.

7. School Days

The best presentation I know of the tradition public education has carried forward in this country is that by Richard Hofstadter, in *Anti-Intellectualism in American Life* (1962), esp. pp. 197–229, 299–390; but see, also, Lawrence Cremin, *The Genius of American Education* (1965), *The Transformation of the School* (1961), and *Traditions of American Education* (1977); Christopher Jencks, et al., *Inequality: A Reassessment;* Sara Lightfoot, *The Good High School* (1983); Ernest Boyer, *High School* (1983); James S. Coleman, *The Adolescent Society* (1962) and James S. Coleman, Thomas Hoffer, and Sally Kilgore, *High School Achievement* (1982); Diane Ravitch, *The Schools We Deserve* (1984); Lasch, *The Culture of Narcissism;* Kenneth Keniston, *The Uncommitted* (1964); Pat Conroy, *The Water Is Wide* (1972); Jonathan Kozol, *Death at an Early Age* (1967) and *Illiterate America* (1985).

The New York Times Education Fall Survey [for 1983] provides a convenient summary of the four "Major Programs for Change" in the nation's public schools recently put forward: *A Nation at Risk, Action for Excellence, America's Competitive Challenge,* and *Educating Americans for the 21st Century;* see *The New York Times* for November 13, 1983. More recently still, two books especially have been bellwethers for criticism of American education: Allan Bloom's *The Closing of the American Mind* (1987) and E. D. Hirsch, Jr.'s, *Cultural Literacy* (1987); readers shouldn't overlook the intense scrutiny both books have received, however. Essays taking Bloom and Hirsch to task appear in both the professional and popular literature. Critics rarely claim that schools are as good as they should be. Rather the argument centers on the question of whether there's a canon of so-called "Great Books" in danger of being lost to the curriculum entirely, a body of knowledge that educated persons should know, which must be preserved and taught if we are not to forfeit a significant heritage. As my arguments suggest, I agree with Bloom (less so with Hirsch) that there is such a heritage, or rather, that there are heritages that the schools must seek to define and transmit; but the debate is complex.

For an idea of what North Carolinians think of public-school teachers and schools, see *Public Education in North Carolina: A Review of Public Opinion from 1978 to 1983* (Raleigh, N.C.: Office of State Budget and Management, *n. d.).* Fifty-five percent of the respondents, in the "Fall, 1983, Citizen Survey," rated the state's public schools as either "good" or "excellent." For comparison, only about a third of the respondents in the 1983 Gallup Poll rated the nation's schools as "above average." In the Fall 1985 "North Carolina Citizen Survey," sixty-one percent gave the schools an "excellent" or "good" rating. See, also, *Status of the American Public-School Teacher, 1970–71,* "Research Report 1972–R3" (Washington, D.C.: National Education Association, 1973).

1. Curricula have been expanded largely through the addition of vocational programs, not, however, that they have met with universal acceptance. See, for example, T. H. Fitzgerald, "Career Education: An Error Whose Time Has Come," *School Review* (November 1973): pp. 82, 91–105.
2. For a recent argument against tracking see, for example, Diane Ravitch, *The Schools We Deserve,* and for a case against grouping and tracking based on standardized tests see, for example, *Testing . . . Grouping: The New Segregation in Southern Schools?* (Atlanta: Southern Regional Council, 1976). See, also, *Report of the Task Force on Compulsory Education* (Washington, D.C.: National Education Association, 1972). Jencks argues, however – to me, inconceivably – that "if tracking affects test scores at all, the effect is too small to be pedagogically significant"; see Jencks et al., *Inequality: A Reassessment,* p. 107.
3. As of June 1, 1985, of the first-time takers of the Armed Services Vocational Aptitude Battery, 78.3 percent passed statewide (according to figures supplied to me by a local Marine recruiter). For a sense of how the South has fared historically on such tests, see James G. Maddox, et al., *The Advancing South,* p. 86.
4. See, for example, the report issued in June 1985 by the Southern Regional Education Board reviewing the curricula undertaken by students in Education at 127 Southern colleges and universities. The emphasis teacher education programs place on methodology has, of course, been long-lamented; news articles on the SREB's 1985 study raise the issue anew. See *The News and Observer* [Raleigh, N.C.], June 18, June 26, July 7, 1985. "How-to-teach" courses, however, have their defenders – not least among educationists; for one such argument put forth by a dean of education in the state, see *The News and Observer* [Raleigh, N.C.], June 19, 1985. See, as well, James D. Koerner, *The Miseducation of American Teachers* (1963). Richard Mitchell cuts to the heart of the matter: "Our schools are full of supposed teachers of mathematics who have studied 'education' when they should have studied mathematics," he writes in *The Graves of Academe* (1981), p. 14.

   For the background of the sweeping changes in public education as would come to define the 1960s, see Cremin, esp. *The Transformation of the School.*
5. Hofstadter makes this point; see *Anti-Intellectualism in American Life,* pp.

309, 310, et pass., and compare Richard Mitchell, *The Graves of Academe,* pp. 45, 141, et pass.

6. *Highlights from the 1983 Survey of Earned Doctorates* (Washington, D.C.: National Research Council, *n. d.).* For comparison, just 701 doctorates were granted in mathematics in 1983, 504 in a foreign language, 616 in history, and 714 in English. On the evidence of the doctorate as a symbol of the professional educationist, see Richard Mitchell, *The Graves of Academe,* pp. 23, 50, et pass.
7. For 1970 figures, see "The dropout: Whose failure?," *The News and Observer* [Raleigh, N.C.], June 13, 1982. Figures for 1985–86 are reported by the Southern Regional Education Board; see "Dropout rate in South is still grim," *The Evening-Telegram* [Rocky Mount, N.C.], July 9, 1987. In 1987, 44.7 percent of North Carolinians over twenty-five were without a high-school diploma, which put us forty-sixth nationally. See Emily Herring Wilson, *For the People of North Carolina: The Z. Smith Reynolds Foundation at Half-Century 1936–1986* (Chapel Hill, N.C.: University of North Carolina Press, 1988). Wilson says that "North Carolina has the tenth highest percentage of adults without an eighth grade education"; she finds the state to "have a sizeable (and growing) underclass" (p. 129). See, also, *School Dropouts: A Waste We Cannot Afford* (Raleigh, N.C.: State Department of Public Instruction, 1963). "Lack of ability," even this early study concludes, "is not the primary cause for dropping out." Moreover, "in 1960 67.8 percent of North Carolinians twenty-five years of age and over did not have a high school education," which is to say, over one-third of the state's total population (p. 2). North Carolina then ranked forty-fifth in median school years completed by persons twenty-five and older (p. 10).
8. Ernest Boyer is quoted in "The dropout: Whose failure?," *The News and Observer* [Raleigh, N.C.], June 13, 1982.
9. Louis Rubin talking with Eudora Welty and Shelby Foote; see *The American South,* ed. Louis Rubin, p. 66.
10. *Highlights 1985 North Carolina Citizen Survey* (Raleigh, N.C.: Office of State Budget and Management, *n. d.*).
11. Not a startling conclusion in view of such recent national assessments as *A Nation at Risk, Action for Excellence,* and the like.

8. Little Black (Little White) Schoolhouse

How Southern schools responded to integration is a compelling topic; from the professional history to the personal memoir, writing reflective of the experience is prolific and moving. See, among many such works, Sarah Patton Boyle, *The Desegregated Heart* (1962); Pat Watters, *Down to Now* (1971); Numan V. Bartley, *The Rise of Massive Resistance* (1969); Robert Coles, *The Desegregation of Southern Schools* (1963); Robert G. Wegmann, "White Flight and School Resegregation: Some Hypotheses," *Phi Delta Kappan* (January 1977): pp. 389–93; Robert Mayer, et al. *The Impact of School Desegregation in a Southern City: A Case Study in the Analysis of Educational Policy* (Lexington,

Mass.: D.C. Heath and Co., 1974); Howell Raines, *My Soul is Rested* (1978); Jack Bass, *Unlikely Heroes* (1981); William H. Chafe, *Civilities and Civil Rights* (1980); Bernard Schwartz, *Swann's Way* (1986); Melton A. McLaurin, *Separate Pasts* (1987); Daisy Bates, *The Long Shadow of Little Rock* (1962); Margaret Anderson, *The Children of The South* (1966); James Meredith, *Three Years in Mississippi* (1966); Carl T. Rowan, *Go South to Sorrow* (1957); and for an eloquent preamble to the period, see Lillian Smith, *Killers of the Dream* (1949).

1. The *1979–1980 Level II Accreditation Report* at one high school in Talton County asserts that "Racial imbalance in [the] County brought about an exodus of white students to the non-public schools, totaling 392 in the county school district in 1977–78."
2. For a generalized psychiatric study of the effects of school segregation on children, see Coles, *The Desegregation of Southern Schools.*

9. Working and Living and Getting By

On Southern labor see, for example, *Working Lives: The "Southern Exposure" History of Labor in the South,* ed. Marc S. Miller (1974); Mimi Conway, *Rise Gonna Rise* (1979); Jacquelyn Dowd Hall, et al. *Like a Family;* J. Wayne Flynt, *Dixie's Forgotten People;* and James C. Cobb, *The Selling of The South.* Of related interest, see Nancy Seifer, *Nobody Speaks for Me!* (1976); Studs Terkel, *Working* (1972) and *American Dreams* (1980); and Melvin Kranzberg and Joseph Gies, *By the Sweat of Thy Brow* (1975).

The widening gap between eastern North Carolina's economy (as that of the state's other disadvantaged areas) and that of the metropolitan Piedmont is well documented in the recent series of reports published by the Southern Growth Policies Board and the 1986 Commission on the Future of the South; see, esp., reports 1–5, which address such themes as "rural flight" versus "urban might," the difficulties of financing economic development in rural areas, and international trends affecting the same.

1. "Chicken firm has posts to fill at Martin plant," *The News and Observer* [Raleigh, N.C.], November 19, 1982.
2. *Industrial Recruitment and the Path of North Carolina's Economic Development to the Year 2000,* "A Public Discussion Paper for North Carolina's Project 2000" (Raleigh, N.C.: Department of Labor, 1982), p. 17; hereafter cited as *TY 2000.* This is an excellent review of how North Carolina, as other Southern states, has wooed outside industry even to the extent of selling out its people; the problems we now face as a result of this, and as a consequence of economic trends seemingly beyond local control, are here defined. I am indebted to the pamphlet for much of my argument, as my notes suggest, as well as for the paraphrase I have made of its thesis.
3. "N.C. textile workers fear plant closings, loss of jobs," *The News and Observer* [Raleigh, N.C.], November 26, 1984.
4. "Southern Textile jobs down 34,400 in 12 months," *The News and Observer* [Raleigh, N.C.], May 31, 1985.

5. "Southeast textile employment dips for 8th consecutive year," *The News and Observer* [Raleigh, N.C.], July 2, 1985. Figures cited throughout are from the Bureau of Labor Statistics.
6. *TY 2000*, p. 15; cited from the *Report of the Governor's Blue Ribbon Commission on the Possibility of a Rural Development Corporation for the State of North Carolina, vol. 1: Findings and Recommendations* (Raleigh, N.C.: Department of Natural Resources and Community Development, 1981), p. 6.
7. "Sun Belt outlook may turn cloudy," *The News and Observer* [Raleigh, N.C.], July 7, 1985.
8. For a detailed assessment of the dilemma, see, for example, *Rural Flight/Urban Might: Economic Development Challenges for the 1990s*, "1986 Commission on the Future of the South" (Research Triangle Park, N.C.: Southern Growth Policies Board, *n. d.*).
9. "Sun Belt outlook may turn cloudy," *The News and Observer* [Raleigh, N.C.], July 7, 1985.
10. *TY 2000*, pp. 7–8.
11. *TY 2000*, p. 7; cited from Jerry Jacobs, "Corporate Subsidies from the Fifty States," *Business and Society Review* 33 (Spring 1980): 47.
12. See, esp., Edward Bergman, "Urban and Rural Considerations in Southern Development," and Kenny Johnson, "The Southern Stake in Rural Development," in *Rural Flight/Urban Might*, pp. 7–12 and 13–19.
13. *TY 2000*, p. 8; cited from the *1980 Commission on the Future of the South: Executive Summary* (Research Triangle Park, N.C.: Southern Growth Policies Board, 1981), p. 11.
14. Charles D. Liner, "The Sun Belt Phenomenon–A Second War Between the States?," *Popular Government* 43 (Summer 1977): 23.
15. Mary Fisher, Employment Security Commission interview, September 16, 1982.
16. W. J. Cash, *The Mind of the South* (1941); see, esp., pp. 202–27.
17. Such attitudes are lodged in misconceptions. See, for example, *Equity: The Critical Link in Southern Economic Development*, "1986 Commission on the Future of the South" (Research Triangle Park, N.C.: Southern Growth Policies Board, *n. d.*), pp. 11–16 and pp. 25–36.
18. Especially in the 1980s are low wages the real issue. As the 1990s approach, the rate of employment appears better and better. See, for example, "N.C. unemployment at 15-year low," *The News-Argus* [Goldsboro, N.C.], July 10, 1988. But it's the other side of the story, that of wages trailing far behind the national averages, that local media are now beginning to address. See, for example, Paul T. O'Connor, "Half of state's story is missing," *The Evening-Telegram* [Rocky Mount, N.C.], June 13, 1988, and, also, "N.C.'s record low jobless rate has a down side," *The Evening-Telegram* [Rocky Mount, N.C.], August 17, 1988.
19. A University of North Carolina 1971 "Survey of North Carolina," based on responses from more than a thousand citizens statewide, revealed that "Far and away the most frequent complaint . . . was economic. . . . Many respondents mentioned low wages as the worst thing about the South, and a few brought it up as the 'most important difference' between South and

North." Others said that "the worst thing about the South is the absence of a tax base necessary for better public service . . . or the effects of poverty on the poor."

Most people surveyed, however, did *not* think "that the South's economy was lagging," and more than half (54 percent) "saw no difference" between recent economic progress in the North and that in the South. It wasn't until the 1983 "Survey of North Carolina" that for the first time a majority reported themselves "better off" that year than "last." The survey is given in John Shelton Reed, *Southerners,* pp. 40–41, 74, 81, et pass. Since 1976, annual *North Carolina Citizen Surveys,* conducted by the Office of State Budget and Management, have, in general, been corroborative.

20. Little has occurred since to alter Cash's assessment, in 1941, of the poor-white attitude toward labor unions; see Cash, *The Mind of the South,* esp. pp. 249–50, 398–404, et pass. Reed M. Wolcott, in *Rose Hill* (1976), prints a monologue by a leader in this Duplin County community that may still stand as typical of the local feeling:

> I think anybody can have honor enough to do what he says he'll do without havin' a contract with somebody that works with him. If you wanna work for me an' you are satisfied, whadda I care 'bout some man in New York bein' satisfied. If I can't be close to the people I'm workin' with, who can? I can do more for the people workin' for me than any union you can find.
>
> . . . The way my thinkin' is, the way to protect yourself, if I don't treat you decent, go to somebody that will. But don't you go out an' pay some outsiders, some union, to make me decent. Who made the union people as rich as they are? The poor people that need the money. That's made 'em rich, filthy rich. When you tell a man to give you justice an' he's gettin' rich an' you poor, where you startin'? Are you gettin' anywhere?

21. Jacquelyn Dowd Hall, et al., *Like a Family,* pp. 353, 354; et pass.
22. Figures cited are from "NBC Reports": "Labor in the Promised Land," March 5, 1983.
23. James C. Cobb, *The Selling of the South,* p. 108.
24. Jacquelyn Dowd Hall, et al., *Like a Family,* p. 309.
25. For the specific information here and below on GTE Sylvania's pull-out of Smithfield, I am indebted to the coverage provided in *The Smithfield Herald,* and, esp., the editorials and articles cited below.
26. Untitled editorial, *The Smithfield Herald* [Smithfield, N.C.], October 20, 1981.
27. "Sylvania Moving to Greeneville, Tenn.," *The Smithfield Herald* [Smithfield, N.C.], October 9, 1981.
28. "After 6,704,000 Television Sets, Sylvania Plant Stops Production," *The Smithfield Herald* [Smithfield, N.C.], October 25, 1982.
29. Barbara Bizzell, "Leaving On My Mind," *The Smithfield Herald* [Smithfield, N.C.], June 25, 1982.

30. "Smithfield to be an Industrial 'Ghostown'?" and "Sylvania Announces Shutdown Schedule," *The Smithfield Herald* [Smithfield, N.C.], November 10, 1981.
31. Not invariably, perhaps. Rumors persist that some established plants and businesses maneuver against a new firm coming in, thus keeping wages down, competition stable.

Further Reading

The books listed below bear directly, though not always explicitly, on the themes addressed herein. Works already documented in the notes, usually of a specialized or technical nature, are not again cited.

Agee, James (and Walker Evans). *Let Us Now Praise Famous Men.* Boston, Mass.: Houghton Mifflin Co., 1939.

Anderson, Margaret. *The Children of The South.* Foreword by Ralph McGill. New York: Farrar, Straus and Giroux, 1966.

Bartley, Numan V. *The Rise of Massive Resistance.* Baton Rouge: Louisiana State Univ. Press, 1969.

Bass, Jack. *Unlikely Heroes.* New York: Simon and Shuster, 1982.

Bates, Daisy. *The Long Shadow of Little Rock: A Memoir.* Foreword by Eleanor Roosevelt. New York: David McKay Company, Inc., 1962.

Berg, Ivar. *Education and Jobs: The Great Training Robbery.* With the Assistance of Sherry Gorelick. Foreword by Eli Ginzberg. New York: Praeger Publishers, 1970.

Berry, Wendell. *The Unsettling of America: Culture & Agriculture.* New York: Avon Books, 1977.

Bloom, Allan. *The Closing of the American Mind: How Higher Education Has Failed Democracy and Impoverished the Souls of Today's Students.* New York: Simon and Shuster, 1987.

Boyer, Ernest L. *High School: A Report on Secondary Education in America.* "The Carnegie Foundation for the Advancement of Teaching." New York: Harper & Row, Pub., 1983.

Boyle, Sarah Patton. *The Desegregated Heart: A Virginian's Stand in Time of Transition.* New York: William Morrow & Co., 1962.

Breen, T. H. *Tobacco Culture: The Mentality of the Great Tidewater Planters on the Eve of Revolution.* Princeton, N.J.: Princeton Univ. Press, 1985.

Brownell, Blaine A. *The Urban Ethos in the South: 1920–1930.* Baton Rouge: Louisiana State Univ. Press, 1975.

Cash, W. J. *The Mind of The South.* New York: Alfred A. Knopf, Inc., 1941; Reprint. New York: Random House, "Vintage Books," 1969.

Cason, Clarence. *90° in the Shade.* Illus. by J. Edward Rice. Chapel Hill: Univ. of North Carolina Press, 1935.
Caudill, Harry M. *Night Comes to the Cumberlands: A Biography of a Depressed Area.* Foreword by Stewart L. Udall. Boston, Mass.: Little, Brown and Co., 1962.
Chafe, William. *Civilities and Civil Rights: Greensboro, North Carolina, and the Black Struggle for Freedom.* New York: Oxford Univ. Press, 1980.
Chase, Stewart. *American Credos.* New York: Harper, 1962.
Cobb, James C. *The Selling of the South: The Southern Crusade for Industrial Development, 1936–1980.* Baton Rouge: Louisiana State Univ. Press, 1982.
Coleman, James S. *The Adolescent Society: The Social Life of the Teenager and Its Impact on Education.* Glencoe, Ill.: Free Press, 1962.
———, Thomas Hoffer, and Sally Kilgore. *High School Achievement: Public, Catholic, and Private Schools Compared.* New York: Basic Books, Inc., 1982.
Coles, Robert. *The Desegregation of Southern Schools: A Psychiatric Study.* Atlanta: Southern Regional Council, 1963.
———. *Migrants, Sharecroppers, Mountaineers.* Vol. 2 of *Children of Crisis.* Boston, Mass.: Little, Brown and Co., 1967.
Conrad, David E. *The Forgotten Farmers: The Story of Sharecroppers in the New Deal.* Urbana: Univ. of Illinois Press, 1965.
Conroy, Pat. *The Water is Wide.* New York: Avon, 1972.
Conway, Mimi. *Rise Gonna Rise: A Portrait of Southern Textile Workers.* Photographs by Earl Dotter. Garden City, N.Y.: Anchor Press, 1979.
Cremin, Lawrence. *The Genius of American Education.* Pittsburgh: Univ. of Pittsburgh Press, 1965.
———. *Traditions of American Education.* New York: Basic Books, Inc., 1977.
———. *The Transformation of the School: Progressivism in American Education, 1876–1957.* New York: Alfred A. Knopf, 1961.
Crews, Harry. *A Childhood: The Biography of a Place.* New York: Harper & Row, 1978.
Daniel, Pete. *Breaking the Land: The Transformation of Cotton, Tobacco, and Rice Cultures since 1880.* Urbana and Chicago: Univ. of Illinois Press, 1985.
Daniels, Jonathan. *A Southerner Discovers the South.* New York: The Macmillan Co., 1938.
Davis, Paxton. *Being a Boy.* Winston-Salem, N.C.: John E. Blair, Pub., 1988.
Degler, Carl N. *Place over Time: The Continuity of Southern Distinctiveness.* Baton Rouge, La.: Louisiana State Univ. Press, 1977.
Dollard, John. *Caste and Class in a Southern Town.* New York: Harper & Brothers, 1937.
Durr, Virginia. *Outside the Magic Circle: The Autobiography of Virginia Foster Durr.* Ed. Hollinger F. Barnard. Foreword by Studs Terkel. New York: Simon & Shuster, Inc., 1987.
Federal Writers' Project. *These Are Our Lives.* New York: W. W. Norton & Co., 1975.
Flynt, J. Wayne. *Dixie's Forgotten People: The South's Poor Whites.* Bloomington and London: Indiana Univ. Press, 1979.

Goldman, Eric. *The Crucial Decade: America, 1945–1955.* New York: Alfred A. Knopf, 1956.

Grantham, Dewey W. *Southern Progressivism: The Reconciliation of Progress and Tradition.* Knoxville: Univ. of Tennessee Press, 1983.

Greene, Bob. *Be True to Your School: A Diary of 1964.* New York: Atheneum, 1987.

Hagood, Margaret Jarman. *Mothers of the South: Portraiture of the White Tenant Farm Woman.* New York: W. W. Norton & Co., 1977.

Hall, Jacquelyn Dowd, James Leloudis, Robert Korstad, Mary Murphy, Lu Ann Jones, and Christopher B. Daly. *Like a Family: The Making of a Southern Cotton Mill World.* Chapel Hill and London: Univ. of North Carolina Press, 1987.

Hall, Robert L., and Carol B. Stack, eds. *Holding on to the Land and the Lord: Kinship, Ritual, Land Tenure, and Social Policy in the Rural South.* "Southern Anthropological Society Proceedings" No. 15. Robert L. Blakeley, Ser. Ed. Athens: Univ. of Georgia Press, 1982.

Harrington, Michael. *The Other America: Poverty in the United States.* New York: Penguin Books, 1962.

Harris, Alex, ed. and introd. *A World Unsuspected: Portraits of Southern Childhood.* The Lyndhurst Series on the South. Chapel Hill: Univ. of North Carolina Press, 1987.

Hirsch. E. D., Jr. *Cultural Literacy: What Every American Needs to Know.* Boston: Houghton Mifflin Co., 1987.

Hofstadter, Richard. *Anti-Intellectualism in American Life.* New York: Vintage Books, 1962.

Hoggart, Richard. *An English Temper: Essays on Education, Culture and Communications.* New York: Oxford Univ. Press, 1982.

Holt, John. *How Children Fail.* New York: Dell Publishing Co., 1964.

Jencks, Christopher, et al. *Inequality: A Reassessment of the Effect of Family and Schooling in America.* New York: Basic Books, Inc., 1972.

Jones, Landon Y. *Great Expectations: America and the Baby Boom Generation.* New York: Ballantine Books, 1981.

Keniston, Kenneth. *The Uncommitted: Alienated Youth in American Society.* New York: Harcourt, Brace & World, Inc., 1964.

Kirby, Jack T. *Rural Worlds Lost: The American South 1920–1960.* Baton Rouge: Louisiana State Univ. Press, 1987.

Koerner, James D. *The Miseducation of American Teachers.* Boston: Houghton Mifflin Co., 1963.

Kozol, Jonathan. *Death at an Early Age.* Boston: Houghton Mifflin Co., 1967.

———. *Illiterate America.* Garden City, N.Y.: Anchor Press, 1985.

Kranzberg, Melvin, and Joseph Gies. *By the Sweat of Thy Brow: Work in the Western World.* New York: G. P. Putnam's Sons, 1975.

Lasch, Christopher. *The Culture of Narcissism: American Life in an Age of Diminishing Expectations.* New York: Warner Books, 1979.

Lightfoot, Sara Lawrence. *The Good High School: Portraits of Character and Culture.* New York: Basic Books, Inc., 1983.

McLaurin, Melton A. *Separate Pasts: Growing Up White in the Segregated South.* Athens: Univ. of Georgia Press, 1987.

Medved, Michael, and David Wallechinsky. *What Really Happened to the Class of "65"?.* New York: Ballantine Books, 1977.

Meredith, James. *Three Years in Mississippi.* Bloomington: Indiana Univ. Press, 1966.

Miller, Marc S., ed. *Working Lives: The "Southern Exposure" History of Labor in the South.* New York: Pantheon Books, 1974.

Mitchell, Richard. *The Graves of Academe.* Boston: Houghton Mifflin Co., 1981.

Morris, Willie. *North toward Home.* Boston: Houghton Mifflin Co., 1967.

———, ed. *The South Today: 100 Years After Appomattox.* New York: Harper & Row, 1965.

Murray, Pauli. *Proud Shoes: The Story of an American Family.* New York: Harper & Row, 1978.

Myerson, Michael. *Nothing Could Be Finer.* New York: International Publishers, 1978.

Odum, Howard. *An American Epoch: Southern Portraiture in the National Picture.* New York: Henry Holt and Co., 1930.

———. *The Way of the South: Toward the Regional Balance of America.* New York: The Macmillan Co., 1947.

Piven, Frances Fox, and Richard A. Cloward. *Regulating the Poor: The Function of Public Welfare.* New York: Vintage Books, 1971.

Raines, Howell. *My Soul Is Rested: Movement Days in the Deep South Remembered.* New York: Penguin Books, 1983.

Raper, Arthur F. *Tenants of the Almighty.* New York: The Macmillan Co., 1943.

———, and Ira Reid. *Sharecroppers All.* Chapel Hill: Univ. of North Carolina Press, 1941.

Ravitch, Diane. *The Schools We Deserve: Reflections on the Educational Crises of Our Time.* New York: Basic Books, Inc., 1984.

Reed, John Shelton. *Southerners: The Social Psychology of Sectionalism.* Chapel Hill: Univ. of North Carolina Press, 1983.

Rowan, Carl T. *Go South to Sorrow.* New York: Random House, 1957.

Rubin, Louis, ed. *An Apple for My Teacher: Twelve Authors Tell about Teachers Who Made the Difference.* Chapel Hill, N.C.: Algonquin Books, 1987.

———, ed. *The American South: Portrait of a Culture.* Baton Rouge: Louisiana State Univ. Press, 1980.

Schwartz, Bernard. *Swann's Way: The School Busing Case and the Supreme Court.* New York: Oxford Univ. Press, 1986.

Seifer, Nancy. *Nobody Speaks for Me! Self-Portraits of American Working Class Women.* New York: Simon and Shuster, 1976.

Sennett, Richard, and Jonathan Cobb. *The Hidden Injuries of Class.* New York: Alfred A. Knopf, 1973.

Smith, Lillian. *Killers of the Dream.* 1949. Reprint. New York: W. W. Norton & Co., 1978.

Taylor, Roy, *Sharecroppers: The Way We Really Were.* Wilson, N.C.: J-Mark, 1984.

Terkel, Studs. *American Dreams: Lost and Found.* New York: Ballantine Books, 1981.

———. *Working.* New York: Avon, 1975.

Terrill, Tom E., and Jerrold Hirsch, eds. *Such As Us: Southern Voices of the Thirties.* New York: W. W. Norton & Co., 1979.

Twelve Southerners. *I'll Take My Stand: The South and the Agrarian Tradition.* Introd. Louis Rubin. Baton Rouge: Louisiana State Univ. Press, 1980.

Watters, Pat. *Down to Now: Reflections on the Southern Civil Rights Movement.* New York: Pantheon Books, 1971.

———. *The South and the Nation.* New York: Pantheon Books, 1969.

Welty, Eudora. *One Writer's Beginnings.* Cambridge, Mass.: Harvard Univ. Press, 1984.

Wolcott, Reed M. *Rose Hill.* New York: G. P. Putnam's Sons, 1976.

Woodward, C. Vann. *The Burden of Southern History.* Baton Rouge: Louisiana State Univ. Press, 1960.

Zwerling, L. Steven. *Second Best: The Crisis of the Community College.* New York: McGraw-Hill Book Co., 1976.

Index

Throwed Away was designed by Dariel Mayer, composed by Lithocraft, Inc., and printed and bound by BookCrafters, Inc. The book is set in Plantin and printed on 50-lb Glatfelter Natural.